THE BRUMBACK LIBRARY
OF VAN WERT COUNTY
VAN WERT, OHIO

GAYLORD

FIGHTING

CONFEDERATES

FIGHTING

☆ ☆ ☆ ☆ ☆

Books by CURT ANDERS

The Price of Courage (a novel)

Fighting Generals

Fighting Airmen

Fighting Confederates

CONFEDERATES

by CURT ANDERS

Dorset Press
New York

This edition published by Dorset Press,
a division of Marboro Books Corporation.
1990 Dorset Press

ISBN 0-88029-581-3

Printed in the United States of America
M 9 8 7 6 5 4 3 2

7.98

Contents

Introduction

The American Civil War has often been called the first modern conflict because so many of the weapons systems, tactics, and communications techniques that were developed and used in the 1861–65 period were to characterize warfare for the next century. The Crater at Petersburg was a crude ancestor of the nuclear device; and observation balloons established a reputation for military utility that was to give the airplane its start.

Edward Gibbon, writing in *The Decline and Fall of the Roman Empire*, noted an interesting aspect of the trend toward mechanization of warfare. The use of advanced weapons systems, he observed, proliferated as "personal valour and military skill declined with the Roman Empire. When men were no longer found, their place was supplied by machines."

We do not as yet have Gibbon's historical perspective, and we would prefer to believe that it was not a decline in valor but the flourishing of American ingenuity that accelerated the development of the weapons systems we have designed to win the wars we have been obliged to fight. If this thesis has validity, the Civil War surely affords a rich fund of data that can be cited in its defense.

Modern though the Civil War unquestionably was, the element of valor displayed on both sides during the struggle continues to fascinate us. It was a highly personal war—literally, as some have called it, the "Brothers' War." Commanders on both sides had attended West Point, fought side by side in Mexico,

7

and campaigned against the Indians together. James Longstreet was best man at Ulysses Grant's wedding; Union General Philip St. George Cooke was "Jeb" Stuart's father-in-law.

Moreover, the mere fact of one side's superiority in matériel required the leaders of the other to find resources that could withstand the enormous pressure modern technology brought to bear against them. In countless instances, the character of individual commanders made all the difference to the Confederates: "Stonewall" Jackson's flank march at Chancellorsville; Lee's stands at Cold Harbor and during the months of agony in the trenches at Petersburg; Nathan Bedford Forrest's aggressive raids that put Union General William T. Sherman in rage bordering on panic.

Without believing, with Edward Gibbon, that men find machines to replace eroded valor, it is possible for us to wonder how long the Confederacy might have endured if the magnificent military leadership the South enjoyed had not been available. And yet the Confederacy had its share of politically appointed officers and fools, and even Lee was not always brilliant. My own feeling is that it is the status of heroes that has declined, not their number or the extent of their valor.

A writer's duty, William Faulkner said in accepting the Nobel Prize at Stockholm in 1951, is to "help man endure by lifting his heart, by reminding him of the courage and honor and hope and pride and compassion and pity and sacrifice which have been the glory of his past." The lives of Jefferson Davis, Joseph E. Johnston, Nathan Bedford Forrest, James Ewell Brown Stuart, Thomas J. "Stonewall" Jackson, and Robert E. Lee, imperfect as they were, tell the kind of story Faulkner had in mind. For this reason, I consider it a high privilege to have this opportunity to show that men who won fame in war have much to teach us today, regardless of how much those of us who have known the subject at first hand deplore it and long for lasting peace.

C. A.

BRIEF CHRONOLOGY OF THE CIVIL WAR

1861

January	Southern states begin secession movement.
February	Confederate States of America established with Jefferson Davis as first President.
April	After failure of diplomatic moves, Confederate bombardment and capture of Fort Sumter in the harbor of Charleston, South Carolina, brings on general mobilization. Virginia secedes.
July	First major battle of the war is fought near Manassas, Virginia, and results in Confederate victory.

1862

February	Union forces open thrust into western Tennessee by capturing Forts Henry and Donelson.
April	Ulysses S. Grant wins important Union victory at Shiloh, Tennessee, and moves southward into Mississippi.
	George B. McClellan opens Union campaign on peninsula east of Richmond.
May	Thomas J. "Stonewall" Jackson opens campaign in the Shenandoah Valley of Virginia to divert Union troops from the Peninsular Campaign.
	Joseph E. Johnston fights the Battle of Seven Pines east of Richmond and is wounded.
June	Robert E. Lee replaces Johnston in command of the Army of Northern Virginia, which he will lead to the end of the war, and fights the Seven Days Battles east of Richmond, driving McClellan away from the Confederate capital.
July	Lee and Jackson defeat Union forces a second time at Manassas.
August	Lee mounts an offensive into Maryland but is obliged to withdraw into northern Virginia after a bitter battle near Sharpsburg (Antietam).
	Nathan Bedford Forrest raids Union forces in central Tennessee and establishes a reputation as a resourceful warrior.
December	Lee defeats Ambrose Burnside's forces at Fredericksburg.

1863

April–May	Lee and Jackson win stunning victory at Chancellorsville. Jackson is wounded and dies.

Forrest conducts brilliant campaign in Alabama.

June–July Lee invades Maryland and Pennsylvania, but is defeated at Gettysburg.

Vicksburg, Mississippi, falls to Grant.

September Braxton Bragg, aided by Forrest and James Longstreet, wins the Battle of Chickamauga, southeast of Chattanooga, Tennessee.

1864

January Forrest beats back a Union invasion of Mississippi.

March Union forces holding Fort Pillow, north of Memphis, are defeated by Forrest.

May Grant assumes command of all Union forces and launches drives by George Meade against Lee in Virginia and by William T. Sherman against Johnston in northwestern Georgia.

Lee inflicts heavy losses in the Battle of the Wilderness but is obliged to fight other bloody delaying actions at Spotsylvania and at the North Anna River as he retreats from northern Virginia toward Richmond.

Johnston gives ground slowly in Georgia as Sherman presses him toward Atlanta.

June Lee defeats Grant at Cold Harbor, east of Richmond, but must continue to block Union forces as they slide southward toward Petersburg. Both armies dig in south of Petersburg for siege operations that will last until March, 1865.

Forrest defeats Union force at Brice's Crossroads, Mississippi.

August Forrest leads a bold raid into Memphis.

Atlanta falls to Sherman after Johnston is replaced by John B. Hood.

November– Sherman marches from Atlanta to Savannah and then turns
December northward into the Carolinas.

Forrest attempts to assist Hood in saving the Army of Tennessee after defeat near Nashville.

1865

March Final battles south of Petersburg begin.

April Lee surrenders the Army of Northern Virginia to Grant a Appomattox, Virginia, on April 9.

Johnston surrenders the Army of Tennessee on April 14.

May Forrest dismisses his men, urging them to obey the laws.

Jefferson Davis is captured by Union forces and imprisoned at Fortress Monroe, Virginia, for two years, awaiting a trial that is never held.

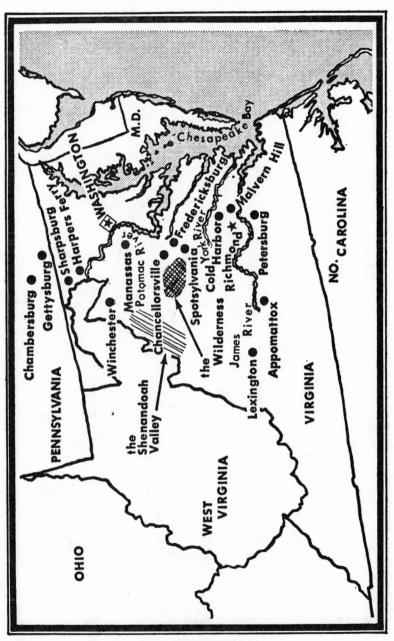

Eastern Battle Areas
Thomas Scheuerman

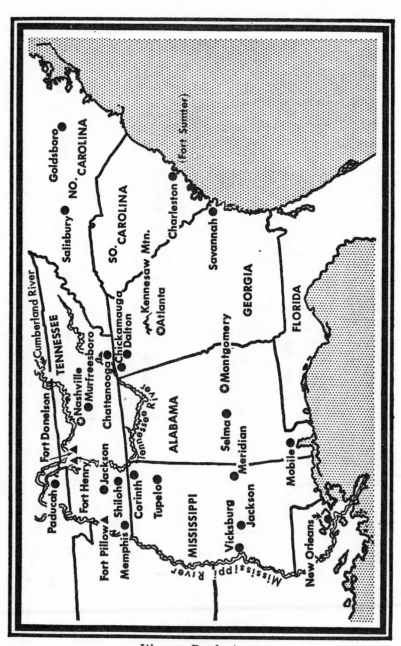

Western Battle Areas
Thomas Scheuerman

1

Jefferson Davis

The Splendid Failure

1808–1889

F OR some, the end began quietly.

In Richmond, on a Sunday morning in early April, 1865, a man walked down the aisle of St. Paul's Church to the pew in which the President of the Confederate States of America, Jefferson Davis, was sitting. The man handed the President a message. Davis read it. A moment later, he left.

Not many hours later, another President—Abraham Lincoln—entered the Confederate White House and sat down in the chair behind Jefferson Davis' desk. Later that evening, he walked the streets of Richmond, alone and unrecognized.

The Civil War was ending, but it was not over. It would be another week before General Robert E. Lee would meet General Ulysses S. Grant at Appomattox, and small pockets of Confederate soldiers scattered throughout the Southern states would still be unwilling to believe the incredible news that Yankee troops shouted across the lines to them a month or so later.

Hope was slow to die for Jefferson Davis, too.

When Davis left Richmond on that April Sunday, he went to Danville. Much had been lost, but some strength remained: Lee's army, which had been committed to the defense of Richmond and Petersburg, was now free to strike at Grant's lines of communication—or so Davis seemed to believe when he issued a proclamation to his nation which concluded: "Animated by that confidence in your spirit and fortitude which has never yet failed me, I announce to you, fellow countrymen, that it is my purpose to maintain your cause with my whole heart and soul."

News of Lee's surrender reached Danville the day after the Army of Northern Virginia ceased firing. Davis moved on to Greensboro, North Carolina, where he was met by Generals Joseph E. Johnston and Pierre G. T. Beauregard. "I think we can whip the enemy yet," Davis said, "if our people will turn out." The generals disagreed. The President listened as they described the situation. With reluctance, Davis gave Johnston authority to ask Union General William T. Sherman for terms. That decision made, Davis climbed into an ambulance which took him southward to Charlotte.

At Charlotte, Davis learned that Abraham Lincoln had been shot. "There are a great many men of whose end I would rather have learned than his," he said. Davis did not know it, but Lincoln's successor—Andrew Johnson—had linked Davis with the assassination plot and had put a price of $100,000 on his head.

One by one, the men who had served with Davis now began to leave him. He went to Yorkville, South Carolina, and then to Abbeville, and then to Washington, Georgia. There would be no more proclamations, no more attempts to rally men who were through with war. Davis thought now of the safety of his wife and children. When he found them, he tried to take them through southern Georgia to Florida.

Federal troops were under orders to make every effort to capture or kill the fugitive Confederate President. One morning in the early part of May, a Union patrol rode into Davis' camp. Davis grabbed a cloak, which happened to be his wife's, and dashed out of a tent just as the Yankees closed in. Pistols, Davis knew, were in the holsters on the saddle of a horse that was standing a few yards away, and he ran to get them.

"Halt!" a soldier shouted. Davis turned and came toward the man. "Halt!" the soldier repeated, aiming his carbine at Davis. Suddenly, Mrs. Davis ran over and threw her arms around her husband.

"Well, old Jeff," the colonel who commanded the cavalry detachment said, "we've got you at last."

The captive was moved under heavy guard to Fortress Monroe, Virginia, where he was placed in a dungeon cell. Not long after his arrival, a young lieutenant, some guards, and a black-smith came in. After the steel door had clanged shut behind them, the officer informed Davis that he was to be put into irons. The gaunt man protested against this vicious and un-necessary indignity. "Mr. Davis," the lieutenant said, "you are an old soldier and know what orders are."

"I *am* an old soldier," Davis replied, "and I know how to die. Let your men shoot me at once."

"Smith," the officer commanded, "do your work."

As the blacksmith leaned over to place the leg irons around the prisoner's ankles, Davis threw a punch which knocked the man to the floor. The soldiers rushed forward, and Davis lunged toward a rifle a guard was holding. The struggle was brief. While four men held Davis down on his cot, the smith did his work.

Beaten and shackled though Jefferson Davis now was, the ordeal still was not over. He would endure his captivity for two more years. During that time he would be watched night and day. In his cell a lamp would burn incessantly. He would be permitted to learn only that his countrymen damned him as a coward who had been caught while dressed in petticoats and a hoop skirt and that many Americans believed that he had conspired to have Abraham Lincoln murdered.

Ironically, a few powerful men in the North set aside the bit-terness they had once felt for the proud prisoner in Fortress Monroe's dungeon and applied pressure on President Andrew Johnson to bring Davis to trial. In an effort to avoid the em-barrassment a defeat in court might cause, officials of the John-son administration tried to persuade Davis to apply for a par-don. Davis angrily refused; he had not committed any crime, he insisted, and he would do nothing which implied a feeling of guilt he had no cause to admit.

Finally, in May, 1867, Davis was brought to Richmond—to the same building in which he had once served as the President of the Confederate States of America—to appear in Federal Court. The Attorney General of the United States advised the bench that the government did not intend to try the prisoner during that term, and Davis was released on $100,000 bond until such time as the prosecution might be prepared to pro-ceed. That time never came.

— 2 —

Jefferson Davis was a complex man caught in the vortex of complicated events, a wraithlike figure whose intellect and personal courage were admirable but whose mistakes were appalling. Ironically, he served with distinction in many of the positions to which he was called—and in a sense he was a man trapped by his own early success, doomed only to fail when the great tests came. Davis' tragedy was that he never learned to recognize his own limitations. Courage alone was not enough.

If Jefferson Davis had assumed the Presidency of the Confederacy with arrogance, it would be easy to dismiss him as nothing more than an overly ambitious politician who was obliged to learn, to his own sorrow and to the debilitating grief of the nation he took into defeat with him, that he had reached too far. But that was not the case. Jefferson Davis saw the end even as it was beginning.

In February, 1861, Davis came home to his Mississippi plantation, Brierfield, from Washington where he had been serving his state as a United States Senator. He was sick, exhausted, deeply depressed. A time of severe troubles, he knew, was immediately ahead for his beloved Southland. His own role—commanding general of Mississippi's forces—had been pressed upon him at Jackson as he was on his way home. He was content with it, trained and experienced as he was in both the art and the reality of war.

One afternoon during his convalescence at Brierfield, Mrs. Davis invited him to help her put out some rose cuttings. The sun that day was warm, and she knew that it would do him good to work at a constructive task in the fresh and comfortable air; the problems over which he had been brooding indoors would still be there after they finished.

While they were working in their garden, a man rode up and handed Davis a telegram. All warmth and pleasure vanished as he read the message. Mrs. Davis, suspecting that he would need time in which to get over the shock of whatever it was he had learned, wisely remained silent. After some moments, he told her—in the voice of a man condemned—that he had been elected President of the Confederate States of America.

Jefferson Davis had not sought that honor, and indeed he had played no significant role in the formation of the new government. Delegates of states which had seceded from the Union had met at Montgomery, Alabama, in order to frame a constitution and to establish a confederation. It was their will that Davis lead them.

There were many sound reasons Davis might have cited in declining that hard duty. He was not well. He had no idea of what resources would be available to him. Many of his fellow Southerners' actions of late had been rash ones, and he must have wondered if emotion had not triumphed over reason once again at Montgomery. War with the Union was not out of the question, and he had already accepted the responsibility for taking Mississippi's soldiers into action if it came to that.

Nearly fifty years before that February day in 1861 when fate closed in on Jefferson Davis, he had met a large buck in the woods one morning as he and his sister were on their way to a nearby log cabin school. The sight of the huge animal's antlers had frightened the little girl, but her brother said, "We will not run away." While young Jeff Davis stood his ground, the deer came over and sniffed him up and down. Defiance was in the boy's eyes, and the buck backed away.

That interlude was to become the pattern of Jefferson Davis' life. Given challenge, no matter what form it might take, he would not run away. Accordingly, he notified the honorable gentlemen in Montgomery that he would accept the charge they had laid upon him.

For a man to assume such risks while he is ignorant or beguiled by foolish illusion is one thing, but for a thoroughly seasoned and highly intelligent person to set aside every hard truth he has ever acquired and to plunge into the unknown and unknowable regardless of the possible consequences requires a special kind of courage. This, Jefferson Davis had. For the next four years it would be his greatest contribution to the cause he was to serve. At the end, it would be all that he had left.

— 3 —

There is nothing about Jeff Davis' early life which explains how it was that his courage became such a significant part of his personality. He was the last-born of ten children, and although he began his life on June 3, 1808, in a log cabin in Kentucky it does not appear that his early life was marked by undue hardship. His father, Samuel Davis, was an educated man who had served in the Revolutionary War and had once been a county clerk in Georgia—and the home he had made for his family in Kentucky was (by frontier standards) far more impressive than the one a hundred miles or so away in which the Lincolns a year later christened a son named Abraham. Sam Davis had wisely raised a string of fine-blooded horses, and when he felt the urge to move southward to more attractive territory he had no difficulty in selling them to raise the money with which he could reestablish a comfortable homestead in Mississippi.

One of Sam Davis' older sons, Joseph, established a law practice in Natchez which soon enabled him to acquire a substantial amount of acreage in the richest part of the cotton-growing region. Clearly, the Davis family was off to a good start in the new state.

After young Jeff had plodded through a year or so at the log cabin school near his home, his father decided to send him to a private institution in Kentucky that was conducted by Dominican Friars. On the boy's first trip northward, he traveled in the company of the family of a man who had served in the War of 1812 under General Andrew Jackson—and the welcome they received when they reached the Hermitage, the home of "Old Hickory," was an impressive one. War stories, especially when they are fresh—like those young Jeff heard—have a way of turning a boy's mind to what may yet be accomplished, and it is entirely possible that the figure of the seasoned general and the tales of valor he told had enduring value in the youngster's thinking.

Saint Thomas School, in Kentucky, provided Jeff Davis with Latin and enough religious instruction to persuade him—for a time—that he should become a Roman Catholic (he was the institution's only Protestant and youngest pupil), but it also sharpened his aptitude for getting into trouble. When a group of boys decided to bombard the sleeping monks with cabbages and squashes one evening, Jeff was detailed to protect the culprits from identification by snuffing the candle which illuminated the scene of the proposed crime. Jeff extinguished the flame, and the cabbages and squashes flew. At the inevitable inquiry, he promised to reveal the name of the boy who had pinched out the candle provided the guilty party would be granted immunity from punishment. The monks accepted Jeff's terms, only to learn that he was the culprit.

Davis' mother expressed a desire to have her child closer to home, and he returned to Mississippi on a river boat which seemed to be the ultimate in speed and luxury. After a year in a boarding school near Natchez, he entered an academy that had been established near his family's home. Young Jeff dropped out, and his father put him to work picking cotton. After a few weeks of dragging the long sack along the furrows, Jeff decided that there was something to be said for education, after all. He returned to the academy, and later—at the age of thirteen—he entered Transylvania University at Lexington, Kentucky.

Sam Davis died before he could launch his youngest son in a career, but his hopes were shared by the boy's older brother, Joseph. An appointment to West Point for young Jeff was arranged, and he entered the United States Military Academy in 1824. The understanding was that if Jeff did not wish to continue at West Point after his first year there, Joseph Davis would make it possible for him to complete his education at the University of Virginia.

Cadet Davis' record at West Point was remarkable in that he was not expelled. Conduct was his poorest subject, and he had to defend himself against court-martial charges after he had been caught at Benny Havens' tavern in nearby Highland Falls. Davis argued that the liquors he had consumed had not been "spiritous," but the court was not impressed. In view of the fact that Cadet Davis had admitted his presence at the forbidden tavern, his sentence of dismissal was set aside by the Secretary of War, and he was permitted to remain at the Military Academy. One close shave led to another, however, and Davis took a tumble over a forty-foot cliff in order to evade capture at Benny Havens' tavern a second time.

Even so, Davis may have gained much more from his years at West Point than he put into them. He did not relish the harsh discipline, but the curriculum broadened his interests and sharpened his powers of analysis. Moreover, he was drawn closer to one of his Transylvania classmates, Albert Sidney Johnston, and he met other young men of high promise—including Robert E. Lee.

The young Mississippian's manner, though, infuriated some of his instructors. One day, when a fuse of a grenade was ignited accidentally during an ordnance class, Davis calmly asked, "What shall we do, sir? This fireball is ignited."

"Run for your lives!" the astonished officer commanded as he dashed toward the door.

Cadet Davis picked the grenade up and tossed it out the window.

An old Southern custom, the consumption of eggnog at Christmastime, inspired Jeff Davis to his consummate breach of the Military Academy's peace. Just as a Yuletide party was reaching its peak, someone brought word that Captain Ethan Hitchcock—who had caught Davis at Benny Havens' tavern—was drawing nigh. "Put away the grog, boys, Old Hitch is coming!" Davis shouted. As it turned out, "Old Hitch" was standing directly behind him. He put Cadet Davis under arrest and consigned him to his quarters. While Jeff Davis slept, one of the greatest riots in the history of West Point raged: "Old Hitch" and his reinforcements were beaten back with pieces of stovewood, and one officer fled before a drawn saber while Hitchcock was ducking a ball fired from a pistol. Davis, thanks to his early arrest, was merely confined to his room in punishment; his guests were tried by court-martial and dismissed.

In June, 1828, Jefferson Davis stood twenty-third in his class of 33—mathematics as well as conduct had given him trouble—and he was commissioned as a second lieutenant in an army which seemed to have little to do.

Fort Crawford, a forlorn outpost on the Wisconsin River, was Davis' first station after a brief stay at Jefferson Barracks, Missouri. The stockade needed timber, and Davis was sent into Indian country to procure it. The natives were not always friendly, and on one occasion the young West Pointer rode into a war party, grabbed a brave by the scalp lock, and pulled him to the ground while the soldiers behind him headed for cover.

Later, after Davis had established a sawmill deep in Indian territory, he developed pneumonia and almost died. Although he recovered, the illness left him vulnerable to the respiratory ailments which were to plague him for the rest of his life.

Back at Fort Crawford, Lieutenant Davis had to prove himself before his men one day when a soldier under his command refused to obey an order he had given. The man reached for a plank, but Davis struck him down. After the soldier cried for mercy, Davis said: "This has been a fight between man and man, and I shall not notice it officially."

When Davis was ordered to drive squatters from lands claimed by Indians, he elected to try reason rather than force. After he had explained the facts of the situation to the people he was supposed to displace, he went away for a time so that they could think about his arguments. When he returned, he insured his success by entering the local saloon and offering to buy drinks for all present. After many refills, the squatters saw unusual merit in the United States Army's point of view and agreed to vacate their land while negotiations which would protect their claims were concluded with the Indians.

Lieutenant Davis' standing around Fort Crawford was such that he was the natural choice for aide to Colonel Zachary Taylor, the post commander. The professional rapport which "Old Rough and Ready" and the rather stiff young West Pointer established was strengthened by the conduct of the younger man during the later stages of the Black Hawk War of 1832 when he escorted the captured warrior chieftain to Jefferson Barracks with dignity and courtesy, but it was strained not long afterward when Davis became interested in the colonel's daughter, Sarah Knox Taylor.

Zachary Taylor had seen one daughter marry into the army, and for him one was enough—or so he indicated to Lieutenant Davis. Despite a frown that was doubly disturbing because it was official as well as parental, Jeff and Sarah Knox found ways of meeting often enough to learn that they were in love and that they wanted to be married.

As they might have expected, Colonel Taylor opposed their

plans. The irate father sent Davis to a post in Arkansas, but banishment merely stimulated the romance. An altercation with his new commanding officer resulted in Davis' having to defend himself against the charge of "conduct subversive of good order and military discipline," but once the young lieutenant had won acquittal he went home to Mississippi, where his brother Joseph encouraged him to resign from the army and to become a planter.

On June 17, 1835, Jefferson Davis and Sarah Knox Taylor were married in the home of her aunt near Louisville, Kentucky. They honeymooned on a river boat which took them down the Mississippi to Hurricane, Joseph Davis' plantation. After they arrived, Jeff Davis started clearing the land his brother had set aside for him—but before long, he contracted malaria. Soon, Sarah Knox Davis was also brought down by the "fevers." Within three months of her wedding day, she was dead.

Jefferson Davis' youth was buried with Sarah Knox. He took a long trip to Havana, New York, and Washington—but it did him no good. After he returned to Hurricane, he set himself apart from the world. His life, as far as he was concerned, had ended.

— 4 —

Jefferson Davis and his older brother Joseph were unusual Southerners. Joseph Davis' great wealth set them apart from their peers: he had selected his land carefully, and the cotton crops he had reaped had been abundant. Released as the two brothers were from the necessity of working for a living, they turned their attention to statecraft—and it was in the study of political philosophy that they were to spend the next seven years.

Joseph Davis was old enough to have been Jefferson's father, and he seems to have adopted the role even before Samuel Davis died. Young Jeff had been appointed to West Point through Joseph's influence, and Joseph had encouraged his brother to marry Sarah Knox Taylor whose ancestors, he knew, included the illustrious Lees of Virginia. Limited as Joseph Davis' own horizons may have been, he saw no limitations to the future his younger brother might have. He may even have dreamed of establishing—through Jefferson—a political and social dynasty which would rival in quality and accomplishment the ones which had produced the founding fathers of the Republic.

Accordingly, Joseph Davis saw to it that his grief-stricken brother had ample opportunity to study everything that had ever been written about the establishment of the United States. Jefferson Davis' reading during his seven years as a virtual recluse was not confined to political documents, but his curiosity tended to center on the development and content of the Constitution. Joseph stimulated that interest by having long discussions with the man who was quickly becoming his apt pupil.

The primary concern of the Davis brothers, however, was federal. They were poorly equipped to involve themselves with the problems of state or even local government: Joseph had established himself in an enclave of prosperity and culture which was hardly typical of most Mississippi plantations in that era, and his brother had spent most of his life in other states—and neither of them could really comprehend local conditions or concepts. Moreover, Joseph seems to have felt that the grand scale of thinking was an obligation of learned gentlemen. The Virginians of the Revolutionary War days had not been men of narrow, parochial turns of mind; and if the tradition of greatness which the founding fathers of the nation had established was to be maintained, the widest possible scope of intellect would be needed.

During this seven-year hermitage, then, Jefferson Davis became something of a statesman. He would know no allegiance to Kentucky, where he had been born, or to Mississippi, from whose soil his leisure had been procured, or to New York, in which West Point happens to be located. For him, the abstract idea of a union of sovereign states was a concrete reality, and he saw nothing seriously wrong with that scheme of organization. The problem, as he then saw it, was to preserve the United States government as it had been designed.

Even slavery failed to make much of an impression on Jefferson Davis' thinking. Slaves were considered property by the founding fathers, and the Constitution they produced was (to

Davis, at least) perfectly clear on the subject of property even though it did not make use of the term *slave*. The Negroes on the Davis plantations, however, enjoyed a standard of living which was much higher than that which prevailed on neighboring, less prosperous farms. James Pemberton, a Negro and technically a slave, was one of Jefferson Davis' closest friends on a man-to-man basis. Slavery, to Jeff Davis, was a fact in the law, and he left it at that—feeling as he did that the law, until it might be changed through due legislative process, should prevail.

Still, there was a wide gulf which separated the scholarly and benign Davis brothers from the aristocratic traditions to which they aspired. In the eyes of many other Southerners, they were parvenus, upstarts. Their wealth won them the envy rather than the respect of many of their neighbors; and old families elsewhere in the South hardly took notice of men who were not able to trace the antecedents of even one grandfather.

Ultimately, Jefferson Davis was to become the South's most prominent political leader, but the men who were to serve with him when the time of severe trial came would be men of similar background who had little in common with the guiding geniuses who were the founders of this country. The Confederate States of America's revolution was not destined to have Thomas Jeffersons, James Madisons, or George Washingtons to power it: most of the men it did involve, particularly in positions of civil authority, would not match Jefferson Davis in fervor, conviction, or intellect.

As the supply of eminent Virginians began to run thin in the 1830's and 1840's, the positions of political leadership they had occupied were taken over by men such as Daniel Webster of Massachusetts, John C. Calhoun of South Carolina, and Henry Clay of Kentucky—but even these would be gone by the early 1850's. Moreover, migrations of families westward through the Southern states tended to create sectional rather than national loyalties.

Similarly, the people who were to be led were vastly different from the Americans of Revolutionary War days. In the early decades of the nineteenth century they pushed the frontier westward beyond the Mississippi River. Many of them established themselves in occupations such as farming or merchandising which obliged them to look to other states for markets or supplies. Accordingly, sectional patterns developed: cotton growers from Mississippi to Georgia had the interests of their industry in common, and merchants were linked not only with the distribution centers of the nation but with its manufacturing complexes as well.

In the South, however, geography and migratory patterns produced a curious result. While planters were accumulating land and slaves in the rich and fertile valleys and were stretching the cotton belt westward, men and women in the mountainous regions of east Tennessee, western Virginia, and the northern portions of Alabama, Georgia, and North Carolina were having little success in improving the material quality of their lives. The highlanders owned small farms and had no slaves. They took pride in their ability to provide for themselves, and this attitude carried over into their political ideas. Having nothing much in common with the cotton planters in the lowlands, they tended to oppose the extension of slavery into new territories—and when abolition movements were started, they supported them.

The nation Jefferson Davis had prepared himself to serve during his long period of seclusion and study, then, was a complex agglomeration of peoples and sectional interests which he could comprehend only in part. On the laws which covered the land and its inhabitants, however, he was an expert. This dichotomy between the ideal of how society ought to be governed and the reality of the task of coping with actual needs and aspirations of those he was to serve would trouble him again and again in the years to come.

— 5 —

Jefferson Davis' first opportunity to stand for public office came in 1843 only one week before Election Day. The Democrats of his county had withdrawn their candidate for the state legislature, and Whig Party supremacy in the region virtually insured the defeat of any substitute: even so, Davis let his name be entered. He lost, but not without the kind of fight men respected.

During the campaign, Davis stopped off at his niece's home one day in December to perform a family errand. Miss Varina Howell, who was visiting the McCalebs, had been invited to spend the Christmas season of 1843 at Joseph Davis' plantation, Hurricane—and Jefferson reminded her that she was expected and would be most welcome.

Though the encounter between the girl of seventeen and the man of twice her years was brief, Varina was able to render an uncommonly accurate word picture of Jefferson Davis in the letter she sent her mother that night:

> He impresses me as a remarkable kind of man, but of uncertain temper, and has a way of taking for granted that everybody agrees with him when he expresses an opinion, which offends me; yet he is most agreeable and has a particularly sweet voice and a winning manner of asserting himself. The fact is, he is the kind of person I should expect to rescue me from a mad dog at any risk, but to insist upon a stoical indifference to the fright afterward. I do not think I shall ever like him as I do his brother Joe. Would you believe it, he is refined and cultivated and yet he is a democrat!

For Miss Howell to be alarmed by Jefferson Davis' political persuasion was not surprising, for she had been raised in Natchez where Whigs were numerous and Democrats were merely tolerated. Her father had come to Mississippi from New Jersey, where his father had capped his service in the Revolutionary War with eight terms as that state's governor, and he had established a law practice which was successful from the start. Joseph Davis had been best man at his wedding, and the Howell and Davis families remained close as time went by. Varina Howell's education was enhanced by her association with an old family friend, Judge George Winchester, who saw to it that the girl read the classics and grew up with an understanding of politics —with some bias, perhaps, toward Whig ideas.

"Uncle Joe" Davis, as Varina Howell referred to him, may have been doing some grand-scale thinking when he invited the young lady to Hurricane for the Christmas festivities of 1843, just at the time Jefferson was coming out of his seclusion. In any event, the weeks Varina spent at Hurricane turned out to be important ones for her. Before long, she was engaged to marry Jefferson Davis.

Politics intruded during 1844, for Jefferson Davis was busy working for the election of James K. Polk as President on the Democratic ticket—to the horror of his fiancée. Despite his unpopular political beliefs, however, he won the blessing of Varina's parents.

On his way to Natchez to be married, in February, 1845, Davis had as a fellow passenger on the river boat his onetime commander and father-in-law, General Zachary Taylor. During that voyage, all differences between them vanished.

The wedding was private—in deference to the fact that Davis was a widower—and the honeymoon began on a somber note: at Bayou Sara, the couple disembarked and placed flowers on Sarah Knox Taylor Davis' grave. After a month in New Orleans, they returned to the new plantation Joseph Davis had provided for them, Brierfield.

Delighted as Joseph Davis may have been by the marriage of his beloved younger brother to such a splendid woman, he got added pleasure out of Jefferson's willingness to run for the district's seat in the House of Representatives in 1845. The race was a hard one, but Jefferson Davis won it. On December 8, 1845, he took his place in the Congress of the United States.

John C. Calhoun took an immediate interest in the young statesman's career. Here, the aging South Carolinian saw, was a man whose breadth of intellect and deep convictions could be devoted to the struggle to maintain the rights of the several states within the framework of the Constitution in days to come.

Calhoun was not entirely correct in his judgment. Davis' first bill, which died in committee, called for the garrisoning of forts by forces furnished by states according to the proportion of each state's representation in Congress. Later, however, he objected to a rivers and harbors bill (even though it contained benefits for Mississippi) on the theory that his paramount obligation was to the national interest. "I feel, sir," he replied to a fellow Congressman who had solicited his support on the basis of *you scratch my back and I'll scratch yours*, "that I am incapable of sectional distinction upon such objects. I abhor and reject all interested combinations." Similarly, Davis opposed legislation which would have restricted immigration. "Do you gentlemen forget," he asked his colleagues in the House, "that among the signers of the Declaration of Independence, [there were] eight actual foreigners and nine who were the immediate descendants of foreign parents?"

Davis counseled caution when the question of admitting the Oregon territory came up for debate. War with Great Britain—which was the logical consequence of "54-40 or fight!"—was a last resort in his way of thinking. When the controversy in the House took on sectional lines, he made his position clear. "It is as the representative of a high-spirited and patriotic people," he said, "that I am called on to resist this war clamor. From sire to son has descended our federal creed, opposed to the idea of sectional conflict for private advantage and favoring the expansion of our union. If envy and jealousy and sectional strife are eating like rust into the bonds which our fathers expected to bind us, they came from causes our Southern atmosphere has never furnished."

When Davis finished his speech and yielded the floor, John Quincy Adams—the only man who served in Congress after having been President of the United States—took it. "That young man," he said, referring to Davis, "is no ordinary man. Mind me, he will make his mark yet. He will go far."

Adams was right, but—for the time being—in the wrong sense. War with Mexico over the annexation of Texas broke out in the early part of 1846, and Davis immediately offered his services to his fellow Mississippians. Before he left the House, however, he was compelled one day to rise to the defense of West Point graduates against the criticism that the citizen soldier was more than a match for a professional military man. In the course of Davis' remarks, he cited the example of General Zachary Taylor (who was not a West Pointer) and praised his professional skill in the conduct of the actions which had already taken place along the Rio Grande, and he asked—rhetorically—if "a blacksmith or tailor could have procured the same results."

Representative Andrew Johnson of Tennessee then took the floor and charged that Davis had insulted him: he was a former tailor, a man who had been taught to read and write by his wife, a pitifully insecure figure who loathed the "illegitimate, swaggering, bastard, scrub aristocracy" to which—in Johnson's enraged mind, at least—Davis belonged.

Davis was distressed over having unintentionally given offense to Johnson. He apologized at once, and two days later he amplified his heartfelt remorse and regret. "If I know myself," he told the House, "I am incapable of wantonly wounding the feelings, or of making invidious reflections upon the origin or occupation, of any man."

The wound Jefferson Davis had accidentally inflicted on Andrew Johnson would never heal. In time to come, it would fester and drive Johnson to acts of vengeance not only against Davis but against the people of the defeated and impoverished Confederacy as well.

— 6 —

Colonel Jefferson Davis assumed command of the Mississippi Rifles and took them to Mexico, but he left fresh controversy behind him in Washington. Percussion rifles were available, and Davis insisted that his troops be equipped with them even though General Winfield Scott maintained that flintlock muskets were still good enough. Davis got what he wanted, and the new weapons proved to be vastly superior to the ones Scott would have provided—but again history would eventually catch up with Jefferson Davis, for in 1861 Scott would be the man who would devise the grand strategy for crushing what the Union was to call "the rebellion."

In September, 1846, General Zachary Taylor's forces closed in on the outskirts of Monterey. While General William J. Worth led a division around the northern and western fringes of the city, Taylor sent the main body—including Davis' Mississippi Rifles—straight into town. Davis' objective was a tannery which had been converted into a fort. The building was covered by a heavily defended fortress not far away.

When the Mississippians were in position for an assault on the tannery, the second in command shouted "Follow me!" and led a wave of infantrymen over the wall. He was shot, and Davis took his place. The Mississippians continued the attack, and they were capturing a second fortified building when orders came for them to withdraw.

Having forced a breakthrough, Davis was infuriated by the thought of giving up the hard-won position, though he had no choice but to obey. He brought his men back, astonishing the soldiers with the virtuosity of his profanity.

Two days later, Davis led a force composed of Tennesseans and Texans as well as Mississippians through the same part of the city his men had cleared earlier. They pressed on toward the plaza despite heavy opposition: Davis saw that the Mexican troops were concentrated there, and he was certain that by nightfall the heart of the city would be under the American flag.

Once again he was ordered to withdraw. Other American units behind him had already pulled back, leaving a dangerous no-man's-land through which he would have to bring his forces. At each intersection, Davis was the first to cross so that he could test the volume of fire the men behind him would encounter.

That was to be Davis' last fight at Monterey, for the Mexican general, Pedro de Ampudia, asked for terms. General Taylor appointed three commissioners to work out the details of surrender, and one of them was Colonel Davis. Later, when other American officers expressed their fear of riding to the Mexicans' headquarters lest they be captured and held as hostages, Davis decided to go alone. General Taylor objected. "One man is as good as twenty," Davis explained. "If there is danger, nothing but an army will do." Finally, Davis and Colonel Albert Sidney Johnston made the trip—without any trouble from the enemy.

Davis returned to Mississippi during the armistice to see Varina, who was ill. The authorities in Washington rejected the terms Taylor had granted Ampudia, however, and Taylor was directed to resume the war. Davis got back to Mexico just in time to lead the Mississippi Rifles in the Battle of Buena Vista, which was fought south of Saltillo on February 23, 1847.

At Buena Vista, Taylor was obliged to halt the advance of 14,000 Mexican troops under the command of General Antonio López de Santa Anna. Earlier, Taylor had been forced to send all but about 5,000 of his men to join the force General Winfield Scott was assembling for an invasion along the Vera Cruz-Mexico City axis: moreover, the security of the units he still had was jeopardized when an American order fell into Mexican hands.

Santa Anna had every reason to be confident as he ordered his crack troops forward. They charged Taylor's thin lines, but American artillery broke up the assault. On the eastern end of the American position, the Mexicans massed for an attempt to get around Taylor's flank. For some unknown reason, an American commander ordered his men to fall back. Just as the senseless retreat was turning into a rout, Taylor's dragoons and Davis' Mississippi Rifles arrived from Saltillo and stopped the Mexican advance.

Buena Vista was to be Colonel Davis' finest battle. He rode ahead of his men urging them to follow him into the battle, and on they came. For a time, though, the Mexicans rallied. During the close combat a musket round slammed into Davis' heel, driving part of his spur into the wound. Davis ignored the pain and remained in command.

With the Mexican cavalry about to begin another attempt to smash the American line, Davis saw that he would have to repulse them without help from any other unit. His men were outnumbered by nine to one, and their supplies of ammunition were running low.

Davis put his men into an unorthodox and untried formation—a V with the opening facing the enemy. He ordered the men in the front rank to fire on his command, then the second rank would step forward to give the Mexicans a volley while the first rank reloaded.

The Mexican cavalry rode into the jaws of the V with bugles sounding the charge and banners waving from their lances and guidons—only to be cut down by the murderously effective cross fire of the Mississippians. Captain Braxton Bragg's artillery added to the slaughter, and before long the Mexicans who had been caught in the V littered the ground. Santa Anna was beaten. He collected the remnants of his army and retreated toward San Luis Potosi.

Taylor was told that Davis had been killed, but he refused to believe the report. When he found Davis at an aid station after the battle, he grasped the colonel's hand and said, "My daughter was a better judge of men than I." High as that compliment was, Taylor would have even more to say in his official report: he cited Davis for "distinguished coolness and gallantry."

President James K. Polk recognized the Mississippian's contributions to victory at Buena Vista by writing him a letter in which he said that he was promoting him to the rank of brigadier general of volunteers. Davis expressed his appreciation, but he reminded Polk that such appointments were the prerogatives of state—not national—officials, and declined the honor.

Davis had returned to Mississippi on crutches. News of his fine performance in Mexico had preceded him, and whatever he may have had in mind for his future, he soon discovered that other men had plans for him: one of Mississippi's seats in the United States Senate was vacant, and the governor—responding to popular demand—appointed him to fill it until the next election.

— 7 —

The Senate Jefferson Davis entered in 1847 was struggling with the question which would dominate its debates for many years: slavery. Closely akin to that agonizing subject, however, was the question of the rights of the states within the federal system. To both of these areas of serious concern Davis gave his full attention.

Military success in Mexico had added the southwestern quarter of the continental United States to the nation, thus opening vast new territories into which the institution of slavery could be extended. Jefferson Davis felt that slavery might be abolished at some future time, and he set forth the curious theory that the best way to accelerate its demise was to allow it to spread.

There were many reasons for Davis' attitude. He accepted some of the principles of fundamentalist religious preachers who argued that Noah had condemned the sons of Ham to everlasting servitude; he predicted economic ruin and social chaos as the inevitable consequences of abolition; and he maintained that since the founding fathers had not seen fit to prohibit slavery in the Constitution, the states reserved the right to deal with it as they saw fit. There might well have been a certain amount of self-interest in Davis' position, as well: even as he spoke in Washington, slaves were cultivating his acres back at Brierfield.

Jefferson Davis' stand on states' rights was not as clearly defined as his answer to the slavery question. He believed in the ideal of union, but the kind of association he had in mind differed sharply from the *status quo*. The continent was large enough, he felt, to allow two republics—one in the North, and another in the South. Once such a division had been made, each nation could deal with slavery, states' rights, and all other divisive questions with greater community of interest. Thanks to the right of secession each state had retained, as Davis interpreted the Constitution, such an experiment was possible.

In the course of developing his theory of dual nationalism, Davis could draw upon his vast knowledge of constitutional law—but there were a number of practical considerations to which he failed to give adequate weight. Virginia and South Carolina, which had been established as colonies long before the Revolution, had little in common with relatively new states such as Alabama and Mississippi, which had joined the Union years after the Federal government had come into being. Traditions of self-government ran deep in the older states on the seaboard, and the fact that a few prosperous men in the raw country to the west had created small islands of culture and refinement in the midst of generally primitive territories was not enough to create a bond between the diverse areas. In addition, the sharp cleavage between the haves in the broad and prosperous Cotton Belt and the have-nots in the southern mountains seems to have been overlooked or at least slighted in his thinking.

While controversies over slavery and states' rights raged, Davis —along with the rest of the nation—watched the Presidential election campaign of 1848 with great interest. He supported the Democratic candidate, Lewis Cass, even though the Whigs had nominated General Zachary Taylor. When Davis informed Taylor that he could not work in his behalf, the old general replied with gracious understanding. "I have your own advancement more at heart than my own," Taylor said. "You are now entering on the stage of action, while I must soon retire from it; you must therefore pursue that course which your good judgment will point out, as far as your honor and the good of the country are concerned, without regard to my advancement. It is sufficient to me to know that I possess your friendship, which is all I ask or wish."

Taylor was elected. His onetime son-in-law and Mexican War

subordinate, Senator Davis, was appointed to the joint committee of notification.

With the North and the South on what was clearly a collision course, Henry Clay of Kentucky—assisted by Senator Stephen A. Douglas of Illinois—worked out a solution to the question of extending slavery into new territory which was to become known as the Compromise of 1850. Clay's measure pleased neither the Southerners who believed that slavery should be allowed to follow the flag into the lands they had won with their blood, nor the Northerners who longed to see the institution abolished (or at least held within its prevailing bounds). It became the central issue for debate, and it brought forth eloquent statements of position from the Senate's giants—Daniel Webster, Clay, and John C. Calhoun.

Davis opposed the Clay proposal. "If I have a superstition which governs my mind and holds it captive," the Senator from Mississippi declared, "it is a superstitious reverence for the Union." He went on to deplore the thought that in order to be true to his constituents he would have to act against that solemn loyalty, but he went on to say that "if there is a dominant party in this Union which can deny to us equality . . . this would be a central government raised on the destruction of all the principles of the Constitution: and the first, the highest obligation of every man who has sworn to support that Constitution would be resistance to such usurpation." If such men want a standard bearer, he concluded, "in default of a better, I am at their command."

Words alone, Davis knew, might not be enough to defeat the Clay proposal. In order to solidify Southern opposition to the compromise, he became the leader of a group of prominent representatives of the Cotton Belt states which met at Nashville in June, 1850, to discuss secession as a means of forcing the Congress to allow the spread of slavery. The Nashville Convention's threat had little effect either in Washington or in the delegates' home states, however, and Davis' ideas of stretching the Southern empire into Mexico and even throughout Central America won even less support.

In the Senate, Clay received powerful assistance from Daniel Webster. The great Yankee statesman, delivering one of his most important services to the nation, spoke "not as a Massachu-

setts man, nor as a Northern man, but as an American" in pleading for unity. That spirit prevailed: the Compromise of 1850
was signed into law, and the country believed for a time that
the great controversy was settled.

In 1851, just as Davis was beginning a new six-year term in
the Senate, Mississippi Democrats asked him to make the race
for governor. Davis resigned from the Senate and went home
to oppose the Unionist who had served in the Senate with him,
Henry Stuart Foote. As before, Davis was stepping into the
campaign as a replacement for the original candidate; and once
again, time was short.

The differences between Foote and Davis were great. Unlike
Davis, Foote saw nothing but disaster and doom in the concept
of secession. He offered no dreams of Southern nationhood, no
ringing defense of slavery. Foote had supported the Compromise of 1850 at the time Davis—in Washington and at the
Nashville Convention—had tried to bring about its defeat.

To the burdens of a hard political fight, Davis now had to
add poor health. Facial neuralgia had been troubling him for
years, and it returned at the very time he needed maximum
vigor. As a result, he was obliged to curtail his already short
campaign schedule.

The struggle for the governorship against Foote had a personal side as well. Foote and Davis had never been friends.
Once, an argument at the dinner table in their Washington
boardinghouse had degenerated into a fistfight; and their
references to each other on the floor of the Senate had been
cutting.

Foote won the governorship by a narrow margin, and Davis
withdrew to Brierfield.

— 8 —

For a time it seemed as though Jefferson Davis' career had
ended. Repudiation by the voters was a bitter blow not only to
him, but to his brother Joseph as well. Earlier, the older man
had relieved his brother's sorrow by leading him into fields of
interest which had enabled Jefferson to make a new beginning;
this time, however, Joseph was sixty-seven years old, and the

failure of all his hopes for "Little Jeff"—coming as the blow did after so much success—almost crushed him.

The Presidential election campaign of 1852 drew Davis back into politics—and the man who came out of Brierfield that year was hardly the same person who had retreated to his farm some months before. Jefferson Davis set logic aside and tore into his enemies. "Fraud and falsehood and Free Soil and Foote and [President Millard] Fillmore have triumphed in Mississippi," he declared, "but success thus acquired must be as temporary as its means were corrupt." Davis' zeal was heightened by the nomination of General Winfield Scott as the Whig candidate: he recalled with a shudder the old soldier's refusal to arm Mississippi's volunteers with percussion rifles, the controversies between Scott and General Taylor during the Mexican War, and the man's obnoxious pomposity.

In addition, Davis saw in the Democratic candidate—Franklin Pierce of New Hampshire—renewed hope for preservation of the Union on a basis all Americans could accept. Despite the fact that the New Englander seemed to have little in common with the Mississippi planter, the two men had become close friends during Davis' service in Washington; Davis knew and respected Pierce's positions on the great issues of the time, and he worked for his election with real conviction.

Pierce won, and soon after the votes had been counted he invited Davis to come to Washington as his Secretary of War. Quite apart from Davis' high qualifications for the post, Pierce felt that the Mississippian could assist him in forging new unity in a nation that had become too divided for its own good. Davis did not reply immediately: Mrs. Davis was ill, and her views on the appointment were mixed. In the end, though, Davis accepted.

The years Jefferson Davis spent as Secretary of War—1853 to 1856—were highly important ones for him. He entered that post with more experience in both military and governmental affairs than most men who have held that position, and the outlet his work gave his talents eased his stiffness somewhat. Davis was never too busy to concern himself with even the most trivial problems; indeed, his tendency to become involved in matters he might well have delegated to others irritated many of his associates and took up time which he could have devoted to tasks in the realm of policy. By the end of his term, however, he had revised the Army Regulations and had modernized the weapons and tactical principles of the nation's troops. In addition, he had given the medical corps a permanent standing in the Army's tables of organization.

General Winfield Scott proved to be antagonistic to Davis, but the Secretary of War quickly and bluntly reminded the nation's top soldier that he was the superior authority. No peace between the two men was possible, and neither seems to have hesitated to lash out against the other once an argument began; but Davis had the last word, no matter how much Scott bellowed and raged. For Scott, this was something new—and he not only did not like it; he remembered it.

Pierce's son was killed in a train accident shortly before his inauguration, and that tragedy caused him to begin his Presidency in a retiring and despondent mood. He turned to Davis for both comfort and assistance, and the Mississippian was generous in the support he gave. For a time Davis loomed as the principal figure of the Pierce Administration: it was well known that no man had more influence with the President, and Davis' public statements were interpreted as official positions of his Chief.

During this period, many of Davis' actions and speeches gave some observers the impression that he had abandoned his views on states' rights and the possible desirability of forming a Southern nation. Actually, he maintained his old beliefs as fervently as he ever had: his circumstances had changed, but not his mind. Earlier, he had worked under the strain of having to represent Mississippi's interests at the same time that he was trying to take a statesmanlike approach to broad public questions. As a member of the Pierce Administration, however, his duties were clearly to the nation at large.

Davis' central position during Franklin Pierce's Presidency gave him an opportunity to see Federal government from a new and different perspective. On some occasions, he was able to act—directly or indirectly—in ways which would bring the nation into closer conformity with the philosophical concepts he had made his own during his seven long years of study after his first wife's death. The satisfactions he won from those successes encouraged him to hope that men in all sections of the

United States could continue to live and work in freedom *within* the scheme of affiliation the founding fathers had established, and it was to that end that he dedicated himself while he was Pierce's prime minister.

An example of Davis' statesmanship while he was serving as something more than Secretary of War was the Gadsden Purchase of 1853. Davis believed that national unity would be enhanced if the people in the Western territories could be linked to their Eastern countrymen by a railroad, but studies which had been made of such a project indicated that the route ought to pass through a region still claimed by Mexico. War was one way of getting the right-of-way, and there were some politicians who advocated that method. Davis disagreed. He was instrumental in having James Gadsden appointed Minister to Mexico for the purpose of negotiating the purchase of the land in question, and Gadsden carried out his mission with complete success. With the acquisition of those 45,000 square miles in the southern parts of present-day Arizona and New Mexico, the expansion of the continental United States came to an end.

Another of Davis' proposals met a different fate, however. He recalled that Napoleon had used camels in Egypt in his campaign against the Arabs, and he wondered if the United States Army could use them in the Western regions against the Indians. In 1856, thirty-four camels were delivered to a cavalry unit in Texas for an experiment. Davis' term as Secretary of War came to an end shortly thereafter, but the test went on. Nothing much either way had been proved by 1861, and after that men had matters of far greater gravity to worry about.

The Compromise of 1850 had averted secession at the time of its enactment, but the slavery issue did not remain entirely dormant during Franklin Pierce's Administration. In early 1854, Senator Stephen A. Douglas of Illinois asked Davis to arrange for him to see the President on a particular Sunday so that he could try to gain his support for the Kansas-Nebraska Bill, a piece of legislation which called for the separation of the region known as Nebraska into two territories—Nebraska and Kansas—and specified that the voters in each new unit would decide whether or not slavery would be permitted. Davis had mixed views as to the merits of the Kansas-Nebraska Bill, but he obtained an appointment for Douglas, and Pierce saw him.

The President's support bolstered Douglas' side in the controversy, and the bill became law.

Hindsight indicates that Davis may have been too obliging to Stephen Douglas, for the Kansas-Nebraska Bill canceled out the Compromise of 1850 and resulted in bitter fighting over the slavery question in Kansas. One of the prominent antislavery men in that territory was John Brown, a fanatical abolitionist whose name would be preserved in a war song a few years hence. In addition, Douglas' role in the enactment of that legislation boomeranged: he lost standing among Democrats in the North, and his opponents were spurred into forming the Republican Party.

Davis' personal life during the Pierce years was marked by tragedy—at first because of President Pierce's bereavement and need for consolation, later by the loss of his own son, Samuel. The boy's illness could not be treated with much effectiveness during the three weeks he fought for life, for the doctors could not determine what it was. Davis concealed his grief and tried to overcome it by work.

In 1855, life for Jefferson Davis and his wife was brightened by the birth of a daughter, Margaret. Later, there would be Joseph and Jefferson, too.

The aftereffects of the Kansas-Nebraska Bill were such that Franklin Pierce had to give way to James Buchanan as the Democratic candidate for the Presidency in 1856. Davis was asked by his fellow Mississippians to make the race for the Senate, and he consented. He was elected, and in March, 1857, he returned to his old battleground.

— 9 —

Once again, sectional disputes over the question of slavery were to be the primary concerns of the Congresses in which Jefferson Davis was to serve for the next few years. And once again, the strain of representing his constituents while attempting to lend his statesmanship to the national interest would break his health.

Almost as soon as his term as Senator began, the United States Supreme Court handed down a decision in a case involving a runaway slave, Dred Scott, which created a furor in the North. Scott, the Court held, did not cease to be another man's property when he fled across a state line into free territory. That ruling, however, had even greater significance: it said, in effect, that the Fifth Amendment to the Constitution (which, among other things, protects persons against being deprived of their property without due process of law) was paramount to legislative enactments such as the Missouri Compromise of 1830 which tended to make slavery legal in some states but not in others. The people of the North were enraged by the Dred Scott decision, and for a time some of *them* spoke out in favor of secession.

Judicial affirmation of Jefferson Davis' interpretation of the Constitution gave him an excellent opportunity to use his influence—which was extensive—to strengthen the Union or to provoke even further animosity. Here was the cue for opportunism, but Davis put his principles ahead of whatever enthusiasm he may once have had for Southern nationalism. Having witnessed a victory, he advocated no pursuit; instead, he called for unity within the *status quo*. "What Southern senator," he asked his colleagues, "has attacked any portion or any interest, of the North?"

Serious illness took Davis out of the Senate in the early part of 1858, and his recovery—part of which was spent in Maine— was slow. As strength returned, New Englanders sought Davis as a speaker. He appeared on a number of occasions, and he won the respect of his audiences even though he coupled his expressions of devotion to the ideal of union with candid admissions that if he was ever forced to choose between nation and state, he would side with Mississippi. "If one section should gain such predominance as would enable it, by modifying the Constitution and usurping new power, to legislate for the other," he said in New York, "the exercise of that power would throw us back into the condition of the colonies. And if in the veins of the sons flows the blood of their sires, they would not fail to redeem themselves from tyranny, even should they be driven to resort to revolution."

On his home ground, too, Davis called for fidelity to the Union but warned that there might come a time when men might have to provide for their own safety. He did not believe that abolitionists would win control of the Federal government or that Northerners would support a war to impose central control over their Southern countrymen, but he did not rule out those possibilities. His hopes of finding some way for Americans in all sections to resolve their differences remained high.

Events, however, gave many Southerners little cause to share Davis' optimism. In 1859, John Brown, the fiery Kansas abolitionist, led an abortive raid on a Federal arsenal at Harpers Ferry, was captured, tried, and hanged. In 1860, the Democratic Party split into sectional wings. The Republicans nominated Abraham Lincoln.

Irony and tragedy, the predominant themes of Jefferson Davis' life, were to have full outlet in that critical election year. Earlier, during debates in the Senate on the question of whether the Federal government should enact laws pertaining to slavery in the territories or leave that function to the territorial legislatures, Davis had differed sharply with his Democratic colleague, Douglas, who supported the concept of local sovereignty. That cleavage had carried over into the party's convention in 1860: Douglas' strongest opponent for the Presidential nomination was Jefferson Davis, who had not sought that honor. After fifty-seven ballots, neither man had won. Attempts were made to find a compromise candidate, but those efforts failed. Finally, the delegations from the Cotton Belt states ended the impasse by walking out of the convention, dooming it to adjourn without having selected a nominee.

Each sectional faction later found its candidate. In the North, Douglas was the obvious choice. The Southerners finally agreed to support John C. Breckinridge of Kentucky.

To complicate matters, the Whigs—who now called themselves the Constitutional Union Party in the hope of acting as peacemakers—nominated John Bell of Tennessee. The Presidential campaign of 1860, then, would have one strong contender, Lincoln, and three others who had to look to relatively limited regional enclaves for support.

Davis saw ruin ahead if Lincoln won, not so much because of the Republican candidate's own beliefs but because of the extreme abolitionist views of the men in his party who seemed to be dominating him. In order to mount unified opposition to the threat of disaster, Davis tried to get Douglas, Breckinridge, and Bell to withdraw in favor of someone who could bring together the Whigs and the dissident Democrats under one banner and beat Lincoln. He failed: Douglas, a longtime foe of Lincoln, refused to drop out.

The election results stretched irony to its limits. Lincoln won, but only by virtue of his strength in the electoral college. The majority of the men elected to Congress that year would be hostile to the platform on which Lincoln had campaigned for the Presidency. Under these conditions, and in view of the fact that the Supreme Court was still dominated by men who were pro-Southern, the impassioned Southern orators who mistook Lincoln for the beast with seven heads had little factual basis for arguing that the Republican victory meant that a vindictive North would now turn against the South and everything Southern. Lincoln had no great popular mandate, and he was not the kind of man who would ignore that circumstance; his first Administration might have been far more moderate than either his supporters or his enemies expected, but the temper of the times was such that he would not be given a chance to be his own man.

"The people are run mad," said Alexander H. Stephens of Georgia. "Men will be cutting one another's throats in a little while." As tensions in both the North and the South mounted alarmingly, President James Buchanan did nothing to meet the danger: his term was about to expire, and he was perfectly willing to let his Republican successor reap the whirlwind.

In the Congress, Jefferson Davis took part in the work of two committees which had been formed to deal with the deteriorating situation. The first was composed of men from nine Southern states who felt that some joint statement should be made to their constituents regarding the South's position. "The argument is exhausted," their report said. "We are satisfied the honor, safety, and independence of the Southern people require the organization of a Southern Confederacy—a result to be obtained by separate state secession." The second committee was a group of thirteen Senators under the chairmanship of John J. Crittenden of Kentucky which attempted to find a basis for compromise. Just as an agreement was being reached, news that South Carolina had seceded came; despite that development, however, Davis and the two Southern Senators who were serving with him tried to keep the Crittenden committee's work going forward. Lincoln, not yet inaugurated as President, advised the group's Republicans: "The tug has to come, and better now than at any time hereafter." That judgment doomed the committee's efforts to failure, to Davis' great regret.

With South Carolina out of the Union, the continued presence of Federal troops at Fort Sumter in Charleston harbor infuriated many Southerners. Davis urged President Buchanan to face the reality of secession and to withdraw the garrison, but the lame-duck Chief Executive not only refused but permitted a ship carrying provisions and reinforcements to Fort Sumter to proceed. South Carolinian shore batteries fired on the vessel and forced it to turn back.

Mississippi seceded on January 9, 1861. In a speech to the Senate the next day, Davis said: "If you will, the angel of peace may still spread her wings, though it be over divided States; and the sons of the sires of the Revolution may still go on in friendly intercourse with each other. . . . Thus it may be; and thus it is in your power to make it."

The tension which resulted from Davis' attempts to stop men from running mad finally broke his health. Sick and despondent, Davis rose to speak for the last time in the Senate of the United States on January 21. After he had given his colleagues formal notice of his state's withdrawal, he defended the right of secession by reviewing the principles of Constitutional law which—in his opinion—permitted it. His manner was legalistic, not emotional: he spoke not to the hearts of men, but to their minds. There was nothing new in what he said, and of course it was too late. He closed by saying that he carried no personal grievances away with him and that he hoped that he left none behind.

On the way home to Mississippi, people clamored for a speech wherever his train stopped. Davis was a very sick man, but he responded for as long as he was able. The Governor of Mississippi boarded the train at Jackson and told him that he had been selected to command his state's forces with the rank of major general, and Davis welcomed that challenge. Finally, he reached Brierfield.

— 10 —

It was characteristically ironic that Jefferson Davis, who had been one of the prominent advocates of Southern nationalism in earlier times, would have no direct part in the establishment of the Confederate States of America. Instead, the convention that was held in Montgomery, Alabama, for that purpose was composed of men such as Robert Toombs, Alexander Stephens, and Howell Cobb of Georgia; William L. Yancey of Alabama; and Robert Barnwell Rhett of South Carolina. They were able and experienced men, but their loyalties to their states were greater than their willingness to lend their talents to the creation of a truly viable federation of interests. As a result, they planted the seeds of the Confederacy's destruction even as they brought the new nation into existence.

The constitution the delegates at Montgomery produced resembled the one the founding fathers of the United States had written except for a few highly significant alterations. "We, the people of the Confederate States, each state acting in its sovereign and independent character . . . ," it began, in contrast to the more general language of its model: "We, the people of the United States, in order to form a more perfect union. . . ." The Confederate preamble invoked "the favor of Almighty God," while the Deity is not mentioned in the United States Constitution. The Montgomery delegates did not shrink from using the word "slave," as the founding fathers had, but they did prohibit the slave trade.

The most astonishing feature of the Confederate Constitution, however, was its silence on the subject of the rights of states to secede. Similarly, states were not authorized to nullify any laws which might be passed by the central government.

On the subject of finance, however, the Confederate Constitution was clear in ways that the older compact is not. Protective tariffs were specifically prohibited. Money bills had to originate with the President or the heads of his departments. The President had the right to veto any obnoxious part of an appropriation measure without jeopardizing the application of remaining authorizations. Finally, the Confederate government was barred from appropriating money for public improvements: that function was reserved by the states.

To preside over the new government, the delegates selected Jefferson Davis of Mississippi—through accident. Robert Toombs of Georgia was the popular favorite, but somehow the delegates from other states got the impression that Georgia would offer Howell Cobb, who had offended many of the Democrats among the Southerners by siding with the Whigs in an earlier controversy. Actually, the Georgia delegation had made no such decision. The result of the meetings held by other states, however, was that Cobb was rejected and Davis was selected—except by Mississippi, which hoped to retain him for service as commander of the state's military forces.

When the Georgians finally assembled to decide on a candidate, they knew that Toombs' chances were doomed by the decisions the other delegations had already made. They were also aware that it was the will of the convention that the Presidential appointment be made unanimously, in accordance with the precedent set by the founding fathers in calling George Washington to the post. With reluctance, they set Toombs aside and agreed to support Davis. The Georgians won some consolation from the appointment of Alexander H. Stephens as Vice-President.

When the news of his election reached him in the garden at Brierfield, Davis accepted. Within a few days he was in Montgomery listening as Yancey told a crowd that "The man and the hour have met." Davis responded to that welcome by reminding the men and women present that war might be ahead. Several days later, as he delivered his inaugural address, he expressed the hope that there would be little rivalry between the Confederacy and "the Northeastern States of the American Union" and that "mutual interests will invite to goodwill and kind offices on both parts."

"If, however, passion or lust of domination should cloud the judgment or inflame the ambition of those States," he added, "we must prepare to meet the emergency and maintain, by the final arbitrament of the sword, the position which we have assumed among the nations of the earth." He closed on a personal note: "You will see many errors to forgive, many deficiencies to tolerate; but you shall not find in me either want of zeal or fidelity to the cause. . . ."

— 11 —

The seven states which made up the Confederacy at the beginning—South Carolina, Georgia, Alabama, Florida, Mississippi, Louisiana, and Texas—were proud entities. For them, the act of secession from the Union had been a painful wrench. But having made it, having said—in effect—"we prefer to stand or die as Texans, or Alabamans, or South Carolinians," the amount of state pride they carried into the new government formed in Montgomery was enormous.

For Jefferson Davis to have assumed that he could expect the same loyalty from the Confederate states that they had rendered to the Union in earlier times, then, would have been a terrible mistake. For a time, he knew, the goodwill and cooperation of the states would be absolutely essential if anything of substance was to be accomplished by the fragile entity he headed. He could afford no slights to state pride, no feuds, no serious criticism. Accordingly, he had no choice but to defer to the sensibilities of the states even though this policy would oblige him to move with caution bordering on timidity during a period of critical danger.

In the selection of the members of his first Cabinet, for example, Davis was obliged to give one post to a man from each state despite the fact that he might have been able to form a more effective administration by using experience and capability as the criteria for his appointments. Inevitably, this expedient policy led to trouble—partly because of the errors Davis made in assigning the men he had, and partly because of the manner in which he utilized their services afterward.

The task of reconciling the requirement that each state be represented in the Cabinet, with the qualities of the men available, and the particular challenges of the departments to be administered, was a staggering one. It was complicated by the fact that some states could provide several acceptable ministers who would be well equipped for their assignments, while others could offer only one—or, possibly, none at all. Moreover, factors such as the prestige value of certain posts and variations in the political weights of the states could not be ignored. Under those circumstances, it is surprising not that Jefferson Davis made mistakes in selecting his Cabinet, but that he did not make more of them.

Once his Cabinet was formed, Davis often used it in a manner that was hardly orthodox. Having presented the group with a problem, he tended to pay more attention to *what* a man said than to *who* he was supposed to be within the government. This meant that the comments of the Attorney General on foreign policy, for example, might have greater influence on the President than those made by the Secretary of State. To the extent that this wide-open procedure resulted in Davis' receiving the best possible advice, the errors he had made in assigning men to offices tended to be canceled out. In addition, the sharing of concern during Cabinet meetings prevented undue compartmentalization of thinking. In the long run, however, Davis was to learn that he had not made enough allowance for the human element: no man relishes the knowledge that the position he holds is significant in name only, and if his counsel is rebuffed often enough he can be converted into a bitter and dangerous foe.

In some instances, Davis' original appointments proved to be the correct ones. John H. Reagan of Texas served as Postmaster General throughout the war and even operated his department at a profit. Stephen R. Mallory of Florida proved to be an excellent Secretary of the Navy, even though the Confederacy had no ships at the outset.

Cabinet ministers such as Reagan and Mallory whose areas of responsibility were remote from those in which Davis had personal experience were fortunate men, for the President had a definite tendency to interfere, to supersede, and often to contradict whenever he ran across a matter which seemed to be within his own competence. As a result, he overburdened himself and tactlessly estranged the executives whose functions he preempted. Moreover, he was not inclined to seek advice except on critical occasions, and whenever men tried to press their counsel upon him he grew extremely impatient.

To some extent, the military man in Jefferson Davis may have been responsible for his autocratic behavior. At West

Point, during his years of service as an officer on the frontier and later in Mexico, and as Secretary of War under President Franklin Pierce, Jefferson Davis had developed the capability of making his own decisions. In a military context, this was all to the good: in order to succeed, a soldier must be able to make up his mind. If he makes a mistake, he is expected to be man enough to bear the responsibility for it. Similarly, if he is unjustly charged with error, that same code demands that he defend himself.

There is nothing in military life, however, that precludes a soldier from admitting that he has been wrong—and indeed, it is in such facings-up to manhood that some have won their greatest honors. This, Jefferson Davis apparently never grasped, for whenever he was charged with having made a mistake—in the Army or out of it—he invariably launched an intensive effort to justify his actions. General Robert E. Lee, on the other hand, did not wait to be blamed for his defeat at Gettysburg. "It is all my fault," he said before anyone knew enough about what had happened to ask the question he had so readily answered.

Jefferson Davis' inability either to accept hostile criticism with easy grace or to ignore it hurt him both physically and in the performance of his duties. Periods of great stress were almost always followed by serious breaks in his health, and the strain of maintaining his end of countless disputes (many of which were utterly inconsequential) robbed him of time and energy he could ill afford to waste.

— 12 —

In late February, 1861, not long after Jefferson Davis had been inaugurated as the Confederacy's provisional President, a final effort was made to achieve reconciliation. On Virginia's initiative, representatives of twelve Northern and eight Southern states assembled for a "peace conference" in Washington. The compromise plan they developed was introduced in the United States Senate, but its fate hinged on what President-elect Lincoln thought of it. After study, Lincoln declined to lend his influence one way or another, and the compromise resolution was defeated—by one vote.

For a time, many Southerners felt that Davis was taking too gloomy a view of the future by warning them of war and dreadful sacrifice and battles ahead. Lincoln's inaugural address, however, caused them to share their President's grave misgivings. Although Lincoln said that he had no intention of interfering with the institution of slavery in the states where it existed, he reiterated his belief that "No State, upon its own mere action, can lawfully get out of the Union." Moreover, he gave the men in Montgomery the clear impression that he was willing to use force to put down the "rebellion."

For both the Union and the Confederacy, Fort Sumter soon became the focus of attention. Having taken the position that South Carolina's secession from the United States was not legal, Lincoln was not at all inclined to give in to that state's demand (which had long since been lodged with his predecessor, James Buchanan) that Fort Sumter's garrison be evacuated. Like Buchanan, Lincoln advised South Carolina that he intended to send provisions by sea to the fortress. If the Confederacy dared to fire on the flag of the United States, Lincoln may have reasoned, such an act would enrage and unify the North to such an extent that concerted action to force the return of the errant states would be possible.

Similarly, Jefferson Davis may have felt that the Fort Sumter situation could be used as a lever to bring other Southern states over to the Confederate side. During a Cabinet meeting on April 9, 1861, which Davis had called so that the question of the South's response to Lincoln's latest move could be considered, all but one of his ministers—Secretary of State Robert Toombs of Georgia—urged him to order resistance if the Yankee ship sailed into Charleston's harbor.

"The firing on that fort," Toombs warned, "will inaugurate a civil war greater than any the world has ever seen." The Secretary of State went on to say that "[such action] is suicide, it is murder, and will lose us every friend at the North. You will wantonly strike a hornets' nest which extends from mountains to ocean; and legions, now quiet, will swarm out and sting us to death. It is unnecessary, it puts us in the wrong. It is fatal."

Toombs had addressed his remarks to Davis: that was his function, and he carried it out with every bit of eloquent conviction he could muster. Even so, the President did not accept his Secretary of State's judgment. He expressed his decision (which reflected the will of his other Cabinet ministers) in the form of a telegram to General Pierre G. T. Beauregard, commander of the Confederacy's forces in the Charleston area, authorizing the bombardment of Fort Sumter.

A little over a month before that fateful Cabinet meeting, President Davis had personally sent Beauregard to South Carolina. If there was to be a battle over Fort Sumter, the Confederate President wanted to be sure that the South's forces would be commanded by an experienced professional soldier who represented the nation: state leaders, he feared, might act impulsively—without consulting the officials of the Montgomery government—and turn the crisis into a complicated and discouraging fiasco.

Beauregard proved to be an excellent choice for the post to which Davis had assigned him. He handled the delicate situation with great tact, kept Davis informed of all developments, carried out his instructions to the letter, and gave the Confederacy its first victory.

As Robert Toombs had predicted, Lincoln reacted to the bombardment of Fort Sumter by mobilizing the forces of the Union to put down the "rebellion." And as Jefferson Davis might have expected, Lincoln's intransigence in the matter of the supply ship and the fact of war precipitated the secession of Virginia, Arkansas, Tennessee, and North Carolina—states which had been reluctant to join the Cotton Belt Confederacy earlier.

Once Virginia had joined the new nation, the capital was moved from Montgomery to Richmond. Later, this decision would come under heavy criticism: Richmond was within easy striking distance of the North, and hundreds of thousands of men would die because of the Union's preoccupation with taking the city and the Confederacy's determination to defend it as a symbol even after its military significance was reduced to zero. By placing the new nation's center of government in the state from which so many of the founding fathers had come, however, Davis and his associates may have felt that the Revolution of 1861 might take on the distinction of being something more than an action taken by wealthy cotton planters of the deep South whose link with the revered traditions of the eighteenth century was tenuous, at best. The move also tended to solidify the fusion of the newly acquired northern tier of the Confederacy with the Cotton Belt region.

The shift of the capital from Montgomery to Richmond had no effect on the President's approach to his duties, however. He continued to be his own Secretary of War and Secretary of State, and he paid less and less attention to his Cabinet. His Vice-President, Alexander H. Stephens of Georgia, could not agree with Davis even when he was consulted, which was seldom, and he soon began spending most of his time at his home. As the war progressed, Stephens—who was a man of intellect rather than action—would compose devastating criticisms of Davis and his policies. The greatest service the waspish little man rendered Davis, ironically, was his absence.

By the end of the Confederacy's first hundred days, then, Jefferson Davis was in full control of a nation whose major problem—establishment as a viable entity with regard to the states which had formed it and the world powers among whom it would have to live—was compounded by a war.

— 13 —

For a time during the spring of 1861, Davis seemed to be involved with all of the operations of his government at once. He worked with Toombs to obtain diplomatic recognition from England, France, and Mexico. With Leroy Walker of Alabama, his Secretary of War, he sent purchasing agents to Europe and even into the North (of all places) to buy armaments. As state forces came into being, he issued orders for their disposition— and as Southern officers of the United States Army and Navy resigned their commissions and came home, he found assignments for them. When the Secretary of the Treasury, Christopher Gustavus Memminger of South Carolina, learned that a shipment of Confederate currency the American Bank Note Company in New York had printed had been seized as contraband, Davis helped Memminger establish an emergency printing facility which used the services of one of the very few engravers in the South and smugglers who brought the right kind of paper out of the North.

Because of Davis' tendency to concern himself with such matters, the burden of running the government was unevenly distributed and lines of responsibility became woefully tangled. It probably had to be this way, however: Davis had more experience in dealing with questions at the national level than any of his associates, many of the problems he faced were complex ones involving several departments, and time was of the essence.

Inevitably, Davis made a number of serious mistakes during the Confederacy's hectic early weeks. Some did only temporary harm, but one—his unwise decision with regard to the management of the new nation's cotton—was to damage the entire war effort.

Cotton was the only form of bargaining power or purchasing power the Confederacy possessed in abundance: accordingly, the problem was to use it to obtain diplomatic recognition, to convert it into credit which would enable the nation to buy the weapons it could not produce, and to maintain high production rates so that the internal economy would remain strong. It was not as good as gold; but in some ways, it was better.

Judah P. Benjamin of Louisiana, who was initially Attorney General in Davis' Cabinet, was an urbane man who understood the complexities of the cotton question, European politics, and international finance better than anyone else. Benjamin advised Davis to ship as much cotton as possible to Europe so that it could be sold there to generate the funds the South needed in order to buy ships, guns, and whatever else might be required. As subsequent crops became available, Benjamin suggested, they should be sent across the Atlantic to maintain the Confederacy's flow of credit and supply of war matériel. The Union blockade, he argued, was no problem: the Confederacy's coastline was long, and the Atlantic Ocean was vast.

Davis too was mindful of Europe's need for cotton, but he decided to use it for political leverage. The spinning mills of Great Britain and France employed millions of workers who would be thrown into panic if they lost their jobs due to a shortage of cotton: the pressure the unemployed mobs could bring against their governments, he knew, might force diplomatic recognition. And if the lack of cotton to supply British mills grew sufficiently acute, he reasoned, that great sea power might be persuaded to join the war on the side of the Confederacy.

Accordingly, Davis not only withheld shipments of cotton to Europe but ordered great quantities of it to be burned. Planters refused to send their crops to ports, and warehousemen and longshoremen refused to handle the "white gold" available for shipment. Vigilance committees were formed in the principal ports to enforce Davis' embargo. Such actions, however, were not publicly proclaimed as policy: to Europe, Davis said—in effect—we are unable to trade with you because of the Union blockade.

In the first full year of the Civil War, the United States Navy had exactly three ships with which it attempted to patrol 3500 miles of Confederate coastline. Between 500 and 700 vessels called at Southern ports during that time, but most of them were turned away without cotton cargoes. Had Davis accepted Benjamin's counsel, he might have exported at least two million bales of cotton to use in generating the funds he needed so desperately in order to buy what his own pitifully inadequate arsenals could not produce.

As the critical blunder ran its course, tragedy piled on tragedy. Lincoln was delighted, for he had imposed the blockade to prevent the Confederacy from enjoying the full benefit of its most important financial resource even though he was hardly in a position (at the outset) to enforce it. The Europeans took their economic disruptions and civil unrest in stride without giving Davis any real hope of diplomatic recognition. Confederate armies went into battle poorly equipped and won—when they won—despite their lack of adequate armament. Agriculture was virtually suspended. Compensation to planters drained the Confederate treasury. Inflation of a currency which had always been based mostly on hope got completely out of control.

Ironically, some shipments of cotton reached Europe despite Davis' policy and the Union blockade. They were used exactly as Benjamin had suggested, and the results were excellent.

— 14 —

In the conduct of military operations, Davis had some success —but not enough.

In the North, his old enemy—General Winfield Scott—had devised what he called the Anaconda strategy for beating the Confederacy into submission. Scott's assumptions were that the South lacked strong national administrative direction of the war; that state forces dispersed along the long periphery of the new nation would be weak and poorly led; and that the Union's superiority in men and weapons, together with better transportation systems and communications facilities, could overcome the Confederates' advantage of a central geographic position (which he may also have expected them to fritter away by trying to hold every portion of their territory). Accordingly, "Old Fuss and Feathers" urged the younger generals who would have to fight the Union's battles to press the Rebels everywhere at once. That they did.

Davis may have recognized the validity of Winfield Scott's assumptions, if he perceived them at all—but whether he did or not is beside the point, for he was in no position to do much to offer an effective rebuttal to them. He was doomed by the very nature of the Confederate adventure to maintain a defense of states' rights with states' forces. Governors might release their states' units to Confederate control when they felt that they could be spared, but they retained the right to recall them in the event of a Union invasion threat or for any other reason— including disagreement with the way in which Davis or his military subordinates intended to use them.

Similarly, Davis was handicapped by the lack of any means of assuring his forces logistical support. Once state units had been turned over to Confederate control, some governors felt that supply was Davis' problem—which it certainly was, in view of the difficulty his purchasing agents had in finding food, clothing, and other goods at any price. Even in those relatively few instances in which surpluses of any needed item existed, Davis was unable to establish a system for distributing them. His greatest problem in the area of logistics, however, grew out of the old dichotomy which had been built into the Confederacy:

the people in the highlands who had never had anything in common with the Cotton Belt kept such produce as they had from the Confederacy at gunpoint, and plantations which had been ruined by his cotton policy could not grow enough turnip greens or anything else in time to make any difference in the outcome.

Hindsight indicates that Davis ought to have established the equivalent of a modern general staff in order to cope with his military challenges; and some historians have been surprised that he did not, in view of his background as an educated soldier, warrior in Mexico, and Secretary of War under Franklin Pierce. As it turned out, Davis did not even use the men who served him as Secretary of War—Leroy Walker, Judah Benjamin, George W. Randolph, and James A. Seddon of Virginia, and John C. Breckinridge of Kentucky—effectively. Despite his background, or possibly because it was so strong, Davis not only ran that vital department of government but immersed himself in routine details which clerks could have handled. When positions he had taken developed into controversies, he insisted on defending his actions—thus compounding the error of having usurped the functions of others in the first place.

Secretary of War Leroy Walker—who had been obliged to turn away volunteers for the Confederate Army at the outset because he could provide neither cadres to train them nor facilities to house them—finally gave up, and Judah Benjamin took his place. Benjamin wisely left the great decisions to Davis, but he almost lost the considerable services of General Thomas J. "Stonewall" Jackson to the Confederacy by an inadroit attempt to interfere with the operations of troops under Jackson's command, and Benjamin later was blamed (in part unjustly) for the loss of an island off the North Carolina coast. Davis then promoted him to the post he probably should have had all along, Secretary of State. Seddon was the workhorse who kept the War Department going through the times of greatest strain, and Breckinridge performed his most important service by helping General Joseph E. Johnston surrender his forces at the very last.

In the meantime, Davis was his own general staff—although for a time he kept General Robert E. Lee near him as an adviser and later gave heavy weight to Lee's counsel. At First Manassas (also known as Bull Run) Davis would ride up on his

bay horse in time to order a pursuit which could not be accomplished by troops who were too green and too tired to get
out of their own way, and on another occasion he would solicit
criticisms of General Braxton Bragg from his subordinates in
Bragg's presence. He would anger and misuse Generals Joe
Johnston and Pierre Beauregard, and he would never work out
a coherent strategy to counter the Anaconda old Winfield Scott
had thrown around him.

— 15 —

During the war years, Jefferson Davis and his wife enjoyed
the warm acceptance of Richmond's aristocracy. To the extent
that the President's duties and health permitted, they took part
in the busy social life of the Confederate capital. Personal
tragedy saddened the First Family when their son, Joseph, fell
from a porch rail while playing and died; but on happier occasions, Jefferson and Varina Davis made themselves very much
at home in a city which at the time was noted more for ancestor
worship than anything else. For a man who had been born in
a log cabin in Kentucky and who did not know who his grandfather was, this was something of a personal accomplishment.

Jefferson Davis had assumed the Presidency of the Confederacy with deep misgivings, and he had not been indulging in
mere rhetoric when he had said that there would be many
mistakes to forgive—but as they mounted, and as their effects
became more apparent, his courage remained intact. In the
spring of 1862, during the Union's invasion thrust toward
Richmond up the narrow peninsula formed by the James and
the York rivers, he went out each day to see how the battle was
going; and when the Yankees came again two years later, this
time to stay, he remained at his seat of government for as long
as General Lee felt that he could.

One day in 1863, Jefferson Davis had to demonstrate his
powers of leadership in a peculiar and perhaps unique way. A
mob of women and boys, outraged by the shortages of food and
clothing in Richmond's stores and the high prices which prevailed for the thin supplies the merchants of the city still had,
staged a riot in the streets of the capital. The women broke

into stores and took what they wanted while Richmond's police and home guard mobilized to put down the rebellion within a rebellion.

Davis heard the commotion and went over to see what he could do to stop it. He mounted a wagon and started to speak. None of the women could hear him at first, but he kept talking —and soon the frail figure of the President of the Confederate States of America drew the harridans out of the hat shops and into respectful silence. He explained that the people of Richmond could hardly expect suppliers to send in merchandise for sale unless they could be assured of orderly markets—which certainly was true—and the riot subsided, never to recur.

He could rise to such occasions and perform admirably, but there was always a price he had to pay—his old curse of neuralgia and (at times) complications from it. Government went on, from his bedroom. There were able men to whom he might have delegated responsibilities, but he would not or could not relinquish the control he had over his beloved but doomed Confederacy.

Part of Davis' difficulties as President stemmed not so much from the fact that he made decisions which might have been left to others as from inherent flaws in the Confederacy's structure, economic shortages, and plain bad luck. The currency his government issued was easy to counterfeit, and some of the bogus bills were more impressive than the genuine ones. His minister to Mexico was fool enough to write two sets of reports —one official, and one private (which was sharply contradictory and critical)—both of which fell into the hands of first the Mexican government and then the United States' consular officers; and when that minister reconstructed the official set at New Orleans and handed the document to the local postmaster for transmittal under his personal supervision, he unwittingly entrusted it to a Union spy.

Similarly, the Conscription Act that Davis won from the Confederate Congress was a faulty law which caused great dissension throughout the South without producing the manpower Davis needed for the Army. The clergy, railroad workers, employees of munitions factories, and certain other groups were exempt from the draft, and governors had the right to broaden the range of exempt occupations. Governor Joseph Brown of

Georgia, for example, who had drawn his political support from the hill country and whose enthusiasm for Davis was negligible, considered the Conscription Act an arrogant attempt to consolidate military power in the hands of a strong central government; frustrated in his efforts to have the law nullified in the Georgia legislature and in the state's Supreme Court, Brown emasculated the act by placing local officials, schoolteachers, and even druggists in the exempt category—with the result that there was a sudden increase in the number of men who took up those callings.

Governor Brown's reaction to the Conscription Act was not unique. His counterparts in North Carolina, Alabama, Mississippi, and Texas followed his example. Those governors did not neglect their state forces, however, and on many occasions such units fought with distinction.

As the war wore on, the split between national and state loyalties within the Confederacy grew so acute that Jefferson Davis was forced to adopt many of the measures which Abraham Lincoln had used—suspension of the writ of habeas corpus, imposition of martial law, virtual confiscation of property. Many men who had once been great supporters of the Davis who had spoken so eloquently on states' rights now looked upon him as a tyrant; members of the 1861 Montgomery Convention who had insisted that the Confederacy model itself on the nation the states had left now damned their own creation because the President they had selected was using the very powers they had given him.

When disaffected mobs created disorders which interfered with the war effort, and local law enforcement agencies proved to be unable or unwilling to carry out their duties, Davis had little choice but to declare martial law. The Confederate soldiers who were sent in by the national government to restore order drew the resentment—even the hatred—of the proud citizenry who vented their anger by calling Jefferson Davis a traitor, a usurper of states' rights, and worse.

Organizations to oppose the actions of the central Confederate government were formed throughout the South at the very time the embattled country's need for unity was absolutely vital. Even men who stayed aloof from such groups cooperated with their aims by keeping their crops off the market, refusing to pay taxes, ignoring the Conscription Act, hiding deserters, and in some instances actively assisting Union troops. The more rampant such practices became, the more Davis was obliged to use his police powers on his own people: and with each new application of Confederate force, local resistance intensified.

Davis had been able to quiet the mob of women in Richmond, but he had no real hope of being able to persuade millions of men in his vast nation to cope with the demands of the harder right instead of giving in to the easier wrong. Few paid any attention to him anymore: instead, they applauded the acid criticisms Alexander Stephens, Governor Joe Brown, and others hurled against him. "I shall be justified in any extremity to which the public interest would allow me to go in hostility to his illegal and unconstitutional course," Robert Toombs—who was then a general in command of troops at the front—wrote. "The energy [of Davis' government] I discover now seems to me like that of a turtle after fire has been put upon its back," Stephens observed, failing to add that he had done his part in kindling the flame. Nothing much was ever said by Davis in rebuttal: he was inclined to strike back, but he was too busy.

— 16 —

Even if Jefferson Davis was doomed to fail in his administration of the civilian aspects of the Confederate government, it might seem that a "military despot" could at least salvage some glory for himself in the eyes of his countrymen through his direction of the defense his armies mounted against the Union invaders.

At the beginning, such a thing seemed possible. Confederate victories at Fort Sumter and First Manassas buoyed Southern enthusiasms and hopes, but they also engendered complacency.

By mid-1862, however, the Union had beaten Confederate forces at Forts Henry and Donelson in northwest Tennessee, captured New Orleans, and moved into Virginia's rich Shenandoah Valley granary and up the peninsula to the gates of Richmond itself. During the battles east of the capital, Davis contributed to the eventual victory only by being wise enough to place Lee in command when Joe Johnston was wounded. Gratitude went to Lee and sympathy poured in for Johnston: Davis had only made himself seem ridiculous by making his daily trips out to inspect the battle.

The war in the west was a problem that always eluded the Confederate President's grasp. In part, he failed to provide coherent direction because he had something less than complete faith in the men he sent out as commanders—Beauregard and Joe Johnston. Davis probably ought not to be blamed for the way in which he divided his country into military districts— state feelings hobbled him into designating impractical zones— but there is little excuse for the running fight he had with Joe Johnston over whether Confederate forces should attack or re- treat in instances where Davis' information was woefully in- complete.

Toward General Lee, however, Davis maintained a warmth of feeling that bordered on worship. After Lee had suffered defeat at Gettysburg, he wrote Davis a long and personal letter in which he suggested that if public confidence in him had been shaken to the detriment of the Southern cause, a younger and abler man should be sent to replace him. "To ask me to sub- stitute you by some one in my judgment more fit to command, or who would possess more of the confidence of the army, or of the reflecting men of the country, is to demand an impossibil- ity," Davis replied.

Lee embodied, in person and in action, many of the qualities Jefferson Davis might have displayed as a commander in battle if he had only been given the chance. Like Lee, Davis was a believer in bold, aggressive action: his record as a regimental commander in Mexico had been excellent because of his quick grasp of battlefield realities, his imagination, and his daring. Splendid though his conduct as the leader of a relatively small unit was, however, he was never to have the opportunity to grow into the stature of even a minor strategist, much less that of a supreme commander. Lee, though, would go on to win respect even when he lost battles, gaining in ability while giv- ing up ground, becoming the warrior-saint Davis may have wanted to be.

But fate—for Davis—had decreed otherwise. Having accepted the role of President when he already held a commission as commander of Mississippi's forces, he had condemned himself to fail as commander-in-chief, a position for which he was hardly equipped. Despite his service as Secretary of War under Franklin Pierce, he did not realize that the principles of warfare which had been valid a generation earlier in Mexico had been made obsolete by improvements in ordnance, increased mobility due to railroads, and improved communications over the telegraph wires which spanned the country by 1861. Despite his desperate need to make maximum use of the best leaders available to him, whether he liked them personally or not, he kept men such as Joe Johnston and Beauregard idle while a favorite, Braxton Bragg, was left to pursue incompetence to its limits, and natural leaders such as Nathan Bedford Forrest were ignored. Despite his lifelong familiarity with the geographical characteristics of the Southern nation, he underestimated the significance of the Mississippi River and put undue importance on holding Richmond; sent John Hood northward from Atlanta while Union General William T. Sherman went rampaging eastward from that city to the sea; and still thought in terms of rallying his forces when Yankees had taken every significant communications center in the South.

Could any other prominent Confederate politician have been a better commander-in-chief? No clear answer is possible, but it is remarkable that none of them came forward with constructive ideas which might have been useful. Toombs, the man who might have been elected President but for a misunderstanding among the delegates at Montgomery in 1861, quit his post as Secretary of State after six frustrating months and took a field command in which he not only failed to distinguish himself but seems to have spent a great deal of time in writing letters in which he roundly denounced Davis' every action. Stephens, a frail man who knew nothing about the conduct of military operations, would almost surely have been crushed by the responsibility.

There remains the fact that Davis *was* commander-in-chief. It is to his credit that he retained that role, imperfectly though he may have performed it, to the very end.

— 17 —

When the Union Anaconda had done its work and Jefferson Davis was in irons in a dungeon in Fortress Monroe, the stage was set for the Great Remembering. It would go on for the next hundred years or so, at least—glossed over with romantic fantasy, clouded by inaccuracies, stirred from time to time by the revival of bitter controversies, but never less than fascinating and often the source of brilliant insight into the American character.

The spotlight of history caught the handsome figure of General Lee in defeat, and it does not seem to have searched very far beyond him. He bore his fate with consummate gallantry, and he had more than enough nobility to lend the lost cause virtue it did not always deserve.

Just as lost causes produce their saints—and the intersections of Monument Avenue in Richmond are still guarded by their statues—they also require scapegoats. It is this ignoble role that has too often been assigned to Jefferson Davis, whose tortured, vacant eyes and goatee gave him even the physical qualifications for the part. But inside that stiff body was the spirit of a man who saw his fate and accepted it anyway: and therein lies his glory.

For a man to look defeat squarely in the eye—as Jefferson Davis did that day in the rose garden at Brierfield when he accepted the summons of the delegates at Montgomery, feeling that he was doomed—and for him to fight on for as long as he is able, knowing how it all may end, requires the expenditure of an enormous amount of raw courage. This, Davis had. For as long as he could, he shared it and imparted it. When the war was reduced to a private matter between him and his jailers at Fortress Monroe, he retained it.

"We will not run," Jefferson Davis had said to his sister when the heavy-antlered buck had stood in their path as they walked through the Mississippi woods on their way to a log cabin school. That buck had reappeared in many guises, at many times, during his long life—but his response had been consistent: he had never fled.

Other men had, with no great loss of honor. Stephens, the

Confederacy's absentee Vice-President, pronounced this savage benediction:

> Never did a people exhibit higher virtues in patriotism, in courage, in fortitude, and in patience under the severest trials and sacrifices. The disasters attending the Conflict are chargeable to their leaders, to their men in authority, to those to whom the control of public destiny was confided, and to no one is it more duly attributable than to Mr. Davis himself. He proved himself deficient in developing and directing the resources of the country, in finance and in diplomacy, as well as in military affairs. . . . His greatest failure in statesmanship was either in not understanding the popular aim and impulses, or in attempting to direct the movement to different ends from those contemplated by the people who had entrusted him with power. If he did not understand the purpose of the people, he is certainly not entitled to any rank as a statesman. If he did understand them and used his position to abuse confidence, then he equally forfeits the title to honest statesmanship.

There is some truth in this venomous appraisal, rendered though it was by a man who had contributed so much to the creation of a government whose inherent flaws virtually insured its downfall. That Stephens inadvertently damned himself in condemning Davis is beside the point: given the fact that a man Stephens described as "weak and imbecile" at one time, and "vacillating, petulant, [and] obstinant" at another, was becoming a "despot," the disaffected Vice-President does not seem to have done anything either to carry out his own obligations or to provide his countrymen with any realistic alternative. Still, it is probably fair for Stephens to have said that Davis had his share of deficiencies: he did. Indifference to duty, personal cowardice, and hypocrisy, however, were not among them.

So it was that Jefferson Davis would go down in history—as in life—as the unsuccessful leader of a lost cause, a tragic figure who became what other men (his brother Joseph and ultimately the men at the Montgomery Convention) destined him to be. As he prophesied at his inauguration as President in February, 1861, there were many mistakes to forgive—and they were remembered, magnified, and thrown back at him for as long as he lived.

Time erased some of the bitterness, however, and when he died in 1889 Richmond would compete for—and win—the distinction of being his final resting place. The people of that proud city buried what was mortal and fallible in Jefferson Davis, honored what he was rather than what he might have been, and gave him the peace he had never found in life.

2

Joseph E. Johnston

A Professional's Professional

1807—1891

ONE afternoon in late May, 1862, as the chaotic Battle of
Seven Pines was nearing an end a few miles east of Richmond, General Joseph E. Johnston rode out to Fair Oaks to find
out for himself whether the fighting there was likely to prove
decisive. He had an eye and an ear for combat, and it took him
only a little while to decide that his men would have to sleep
where they were that night and complete the victory early the
next morning; he gave his staff officers the necessary orders, and
they departed.

Suddenly, a bullet smacked into his right shoulder. A moment
afterward, a shell fragment tore into his chest, knocking him off
his horse. An aide ran over, picked Johnston's frail body up,
and carried him back to a relatively safe spot. The general was
unconscious, and it seemed that he was dying.

After a few minutes, a tall, gaunt man came over to see about
Johnston. The soldiers who had gathered around the fallen
commander made way for the visitor, the President of the Confederate States of America, Jefferson Davis.

General Johnston opened his eyes and recognized the President. They had known each other since their West Point days,
nearly forty years before—but they had never been close, and
lately they had hardly been friends. Even so, Johnston held up
his hand. The President took it. Johnston said that he did not
know how seriously he was hurt, but that he thought the fragment had injured his spine.

Davis understood: Johnston was merely reporting the facts he knew the President ought to have in order to make the necessary decision—he was not conceding that he could no longer command, nor was he asking to be relieved. The President, who knew that a stretcher was on the way, said that Johnston should be taken to his house. Someone told Davis that another place had already been found.

Johnston noticed that his sword and pistols were gone, and he grew uneasy. "That sword was the one worn by my father in the Revolutionary War," he said, "and I would not lose it for ten thousand dollars. Will not someone please go back and get it and the pistols for me?"

His aide, paying no heed to Union fire, returned to the spot where Johnston had been hit. He picked up the sword and the pistols and took them back to the general. Johnston showed his gratitude by giving the man one of the pistols.

Johnston's wounds were serious, and the inept treatment he received was almost as damaging as the Yankee steel had been—but he was determined to recover so that he could fight again. He was a pine knot of a man, a soldier every inch, a professional's professional. He had taken blows in battle before, and he had every reason to expect that he would suffer others: but wounds were of little consequence to him, for the important thing was to serve.

Nearly thirty years later, long after the Civil War was over, General Johnston's attitude was precisely the same: he would serve. The occasion was the funeral of one of his old foes, General William T. Sherman, in New York. The day was dismal, and Joe Johnston's duty as a pallbearer was purely honorary, but he stood bareheaded in the cold rain as the coffin was carried from Sherman's house out to the caisson. "General," someone said, "please put on your hat. You might get sick." Johnston refused. "If I were in his place and he were standing here in mine," he said, "he would not put on his hat."

Such an attitude, reflecting as it did Joe Johnston's stubborn insistence on doing what he believed was right rather than what was expedient, was typical of the man. He had been behaving in this manner all his life, and even though he was eighty-four and tired, he could not let concern for his own health prevent him from paying his deep respect to Sherman. Earlier, his strict adherence to the principles of a strict profession had cost him glory, the support of his superiors, and command of the Army of Tennessee. Now his fidelity to custom—based on utter sincerity—was to cost him his life: he caught a cold that day, and five weeks later he died.

Joe Johnston was an old-fashioned man in his own time. It was inevitable, perhaps, that his actions and beliefs would be misunderstood by men who were more in tune with the era in which he and they lived. Johnston knew full well how the winds of change were blowing, but he was no weather vane to be knocked this way and that by forces not in accordance with the code of conduct he had long since adopted.

So it was that he could worry about the safety of his father's sword at a time when his own life seemed to be ebbing, and provide the respect that he felt was due General Sherman when the February rain threatened to ruin what was left of his resistance to death. Tradition and honor were not to be set aside, no matter what the cost. With Johnston, there could be no compromise—and in that fact reposes both the explanation for his failure to have accomplished more than he did and the essence of his greatness as a man.

— 2 —

Peter Johnston, who had fought in the Revolutionary War under the command of General Richard Henry ("Light-Horse Harry") Lee, became a judge and settled at Abingdon, in southwestern Virginia, in the early 1800's. His eighth son, Joseph Eggleston Johnston, was named for a captain with whom he had served—and it was to young Joe, who seemed to be on his way to a military life, that he gave the sword he had carried throughout the war.

The country around Abingdon was ideally suited for Joe Johnston's main boyhood interests—hunting, riding, leading war games which were based on the stories told by men who lived nearby who were veterans of the Battle of King's Mountain. At the Abingdon Academy, young Joe showed a special fondness for the classics and the novels of Sir Walter Scott; he was a good student, and he had no difficulty in being accepted as a cadet at West Point in 1825.

Joe Johnston entered the Military Academy with many soldierly qualities already implanted, partly because he had always been capable of handling himself outdoors and partly because of the traditions he had absorbed from his father. Robert E. Lee, Light-Horse Harry's son, was a classmate and close friend—but another cadet, Jefferson Davis, took a dislike to Johnston for reasons that have never been established: one story suggests that Davis and Johnston may have had a fight over the daughter of a Highland Falls tavern keeper, but there is no evidence that such an incident ever occurred.

Some of the animosity Davis felt for Johnston may have been due to the difference between their fortunes as cadets. Davis was the principal figure in one disturbance after another, while Johnston and Lee managed to have their fun without incurring official wrath. Johnston was nicknamed "The Colonel," which implies that the dignity and scrupulous concern for the proprieties which were to become his distinguishing characteristics in later years must have been recognized even then in a kidding way by his fellow cadets. By contrast, Davis had to face a court-martial charge at one point and was never very far from being dismissed.

Eye trouble kept Johnston from establishing an outstanding academic record, but even so his standing at graduation in 1829 was relatively high—thirteenth in a class of forty-six. He was commissioned as a second lieutenant in the artillery and spent the next seven years at various posts along the eastern seaboard. During most of this period his duties had to do with the removal of Indians to reservations which had been provided for them.

Trouble with the Seminoles in Florida from 1836 to 1837 gave Joe Johnston his first experience in the two kinds of combat he was later to face in full measure. He went to Florida as an aide to Major General Winfield Scott, who failed to satisfy his civilian superiors and was obliged to face a court of inquiry. Johnston's career was not put in jeopardy, but the episode taught him that the military service is not as free from politics as he had imagined. Another commander succeeded where Scott had failed, and with the signing of a peace treaty in 1837

Johnston resigned from the Army with the intention of becoming a civil engineer. Warfare broke out again only five months later, however, and Johnston volunteered to serve in a civilian capacity. In January, 1838, he was caught in an ambush and took command when all of the military leaders were wounded. "The coolness, courage, and judgment he displayed at the most critical and trying emergency was the theme of praise with every one who beheld him," a companion later reported. In that engagement he took a slight wound on his forehead, and his clothing was cut in a number of places by arrows.

The taste of battle Johnston received that day prompted him to apply for return to active duty, and in mid-1838 he was commissioned as a first lieutenant in the Corps of Topographical Engineers with no loss of seniority. In addition, he received brevet (or honorary) promotion to captain in recognition of his gallantry in Florida.

When Johnston learned that the United States was at war with Mexico in 1846, he asked for assignment to that theater immediately. He was ordered to join the invasion force General Winfield Scott was assembling for the thrust he planned to make from Vera Cruz westward to Mexico City. At first, Johnston was assigned as an engineer—along with Robert E. Lee, Pierre G. T. Beauregard, George McClellan, and other promising officers—but once Scott's army was ashore, his request for a combat command was granted: he was made a lieutenant colonel and placed in charge of a regiment of skirmishers known as the *voltigeurs*.

Lieutenant Colonel Johnston led his gray-clad troops up the invasion corridor with audacity and skill. His mission was to advance until he made contact with the Mexicans, to develop the situation, and to hold the enemy in place until Scott could put his main body into the action. The *voltigeurs* met resistance at a place called Cerro Gordo, and during that initial brush with Mexican General Antonio López de Santa Anna's forces Johnston was wounded twice. Lee and Beauregard went on to scout out the Mexican defenses and trails in the Cerro Gordo area, and before long Scott was able to claim a major victory.

Johnston recovered from his wounds in time to lead his *voltigeurs* in the battles of Padierna, Contreras, Churubusco, Molino del Rey, and Chapultepec, all of which took place just outside Mexico City in August and September, 1847. During the *voltigeurs'* bold advance up the slopes of Chapultepec, Johnston was hit three times, but he kept leading his men forward. Promotion to brevet colonel came afterward, along with citations for bravery under fire which included this comment from General Scott: "Johnston is a great soldier, but he has an unfortunate knack of getting himself shot in nearly every engagement."

In 1848, Johnston came home to relatively prosaic duties as an engineer—but the thrill of combat and the allure of Mexico remained fresh in his mind. George McClellan had become one of Johnston's closest friends. In 1855 Johnston transferred to the cavalry; and two years later, when McClellan left the service, Johnston said in a letter to "Beloved Mc" that "there is no one left in the regiment or army to take your place. I wish I was young enough to resign too."

Transfer to Washington came in 1858, but Johnston's duties frequently took him elsewhere. When the post of Quartermaster General became vacant in 1860, Johnston was considered along with Albert Sidney Johnston, Robert E. Lee, and Charles F. Smith. Joe Johnston won it, and was made a brigadier general. He now outranked his contemporaries, and in time he could reasonably expect to become the United States' senior Army officer.

General Johnston carried out his assignment as Quartermaster General as though the great controversy over secession did not exist. When Virginia left the Union in April, 1861, however, his moment for decision came.

The Union's senior soldier, Winfield Scott, pleaded with Johnston to stay at his post. Scott even tried to get Mrs. Johnston, who had been born in Baltimore, to restrain her husband from resigning. "[He] cannot stay in an army that is about to invade his native land," Lydia Johnston told Scott.

The old man replied, "Then let him leave our army, but do not let him join theirs."

Mrs. Johnston had doubts of her own, quite apart from her Baltimore background, as to the wisdom of her husband's desire to offer his services to the Confederate States of America. For the past few years, she had been a friend of the wife of the United States Senator from Mississippi, Jefferson Davis. Lydia

Johnston knew that Davis, who had since become President of the Confederate nation, hated Joe Johnston. "[Davis] has power," she told her husband. "He will ruin you."

Johnston, however, considered himself bound to defend his native Virginia, and he submitted his resignation to General Scott. Once he had completed his duties for the Union, as though he were merely leaving for another post, Johnston left everything but his father's Revolutionary War sword behind him in Washington and headed for Richmond.

— 3 —

Joseph Johnston, at fifty-four, was as seasoned a soldier as either side possessed, with the possible exception of old Winfield Scott, whose first fighting had been done nearly fifty years earlier during the War of 1812. A soldier, however, was all that Joe Johnston was. He had no instinct for politics and no desire to acquire one.

Johnston volunteered for service in Virginia's state forces and was promptly commissioned a major general. General Robert E. Lee, who had been given the task of commanding Virginia's defense against invasion, asked Johnston to organize and train the recruits who were responding to the Old Dominion's call to arms.

With Virginia's decision to join the Confederate States of America, however, there came a subtle change in the command system. To the officers in charge of military forces in many states, the creation of a national rank structure made little or no difference. In Virginia, though, it created a problem—particularly for Joe Johnston, who saw the inherent weaknesses of the states' rights theory as it was being applied to the Southern nation's military problem of winning a war it had not sought.

Johnston set aside all personal considerations and placed himself at the disposal of President Davis. In doing so, Johnston acted in accordance with principle, and nothing more: he had his doubts as to Davis' ability to create the kind of military structure that would be effective enough to meet the Union's challenge, and he conceded none of his primary loyalty to Virginia by accepting a Confederate Army commission, but

some critics still charged him with the sin of being an oppor-
tunist. If he was, he had his reasons.

President Davis respected Johnston's Virginia origin by placing him in command of a unit that was composed for the most
part of troops from his home state. At the same time, Davis
assigned Johnston to the very location at which action seemed
most imminent: Harpers Ferry.

Johnston's appraisal of the situation at Harpers Ferry left
him with the conviction that the place could not be defended
with the relatively small forces he had. He advised his military
superiors of his misgivings, asked for clarification of his mission,
and got nothing much in reply. It was his best judgment that
the men under his command could be put to better use in the
defense of the Shenandoah Valley if they were moved southwestward to Winchester; to stand and fight at Harpers Ferry
might be a gallant act, he conceded, but at best his unit would
be cut out of the war—and that, he argued, would do no one
any good.

Finally, after an exchange of messages with the Confederate
War Department which had to do mostly with where the burden of responsibility for a retreat would lie (a consideration
which bothered Johnston not at all), he pulled back to Winchester and occupied a position from which he could move with
relative ease to block Union attempts to invade the valley. His
reading of the realities of the situation at Harpers Ferry and
his decision to withdraw to the superior site at Winchester
ought to have marked him as a commander with an exceptional
grasp of strategy; instead, he was tagged by men in authority
who knew little or nothing about war as a leader who seemed
reluctant to fight.

Thus, at the outset, a pattern was set. General Johnston, a
consummate realist, recommended actions which he considered
prudent not only for the safety of his command but in the
larger context of the military policy the Confederacy ought to
adopt for the conduct of the war. Places, as such, were of importance to him only to the extent that they had bearing on
the success of his mission; he was vastly more interested in
strategic position. President Davis, and the Secretaries of War
who for the most part served only to communicate the Confederate Commander-in-Chief's views, believed that every point

within the embattled nation's limits ought to be held. So it was that military questions posed by Johnston were always doomed to be subjected to consideration in tactical terms when they reached the attention of the Confederate President.

In one sense, it had to be that way. Davis' problems were enormously complex, and Johnston was in no position to understand them. It was no easy thing to weld a nation into a unit capable of fighting a major war. The President's task was complicated to an incredible extent by the necessity of observing the rights of the states within a governmental system that contained numerous serious flaws, most of which were beyond his power to correct.

Johnston, however, had little inclination to concern himself with such matters. His professional standards required him to stick strictly to military considerations. Moreover, he needed no formal tradition to guide him: loyalty to Virginia and to the cause his state had adopted, together with his fidelity to the antique notion that a man should conduct himself in the right way, were enough.

Quite often, though, the orders Johnston received seemed to be worded in vague terms. A more sophisticated general might have refused to carry them out on the grounds that the politicians were being deliberately imprecise, so that they could blame any failure on the military commander. Johnston may have seen traps of that kind before him, but he took his assignments as they came. As a soldier who had been wounded in combat at least six times, he could hardly understand how anyone could take a selfishly defensive attitude in the midst of a war for survival. If the Confederacy won, quibbles over who was right and who was wrong at a given time would scarcely matter; and if victory went to the Union, he doubted if such questions would make the slightest difference in the lives or minds of those left alive.

Both Davis and Johnston were wrong, as it turned out. Davis' insistence on holding specified towns precluded the application of sound strategic concepts, and no amount of gallantry or tactical skill on the part of the Confederate armies could make up for that fundamental blunder. Johnston erred in believing that it was enough to do what he believed was right: he could not foresee that many of the surviving leaders of the lost cause would continue the conflict in bitter words for as long as any of them lived.

Given the vast differences between their stations in the Confederacy and their views as to how the war should be fought, then, it was inevitable that Jefferson Davis and Joseph Johnston would clash. There remained only the questions of when and where the critical breach would occur and how detrimental to the war effort it would be.

— 4 —

Although Johnston's withdrawal from Harpers Ferry to Winchester had roused intense criticism, the soundness of that decision quickly became apparent. He had concluded—correctly— that there would be a certain amount of sparring before the two sides started to slug it out in earnest, and now he had enough maneuvering room to match probing blows with his Union opponent. Cavalry screens under the command of Colonels J. E. B. Stuart and Turner Ashby kept the Potomac River frontier under close surveillance, and the early warning of Union advances they gave enabled Johnston to rush troops forward to block each enemy thrust.

If Johnston's detractors in Richmond remained unimpressed —and they did—his Federal adversary, General Robert Patterson, took an entirely different view. So effective were the Confederate cavalry operations and defensive shifts that Patterson seriously overestimated Johnston's strength and thus deprived himself of a splendid opportunity to strike what might have been a murderously effective blow to open the Shenandoah Valley (which was Virginia's granary) to Union raiders.

Invasions which do not occur seldom attract the attention of journalists, however, and Johnston's critics continued to fill the columns of Richmond's newspapers with their expressions of dismay. For his part, President Davis was man enough to support Johnston. "The anxiety of the reckless and the shortsighted policy of the selfish may urge you to fight when your judgment decides otherwise," he wrote; and he advised Johnston to "follow the dictates of your own good judgment and true patriotism" in dealing with the situation in his sector.

In order to protect the railroad system in northern Virginia and to block the obvious invasion route from Washington to Richmond, Davis had placed another Confederate force under the command of General Pierre G. T. Beauregard—the hero of Fort Sumter—near the town of Manassas, roughly fifty miles to the east of Winchester. Reports furnished by the Confederacy's crude intelligence system indicated that Federal troops were massing in the Washington area and suggested that they would be used in an offensive drive which would smash through Manassas toward Richmond. Beauregard filed appeal after appeal for reinforcements, submitted complicated and impractical plans for offensives of his own, and made such preparations as he could to meet and repel the Union assault.

Those who knew enough about the growing threat from the North to think about what ought to be done to cope with it agreed that some concentration of the forces led by Johnston and Beauregard would have to be made, and Manassas seemed to be the likely place: there remained only the question of timing. If Johnston were to be moved eastward prematurely, the Shenandoah Valley would be left open to Patterson—or Patterson might strike Johnston's army while it was en route to Manassas. If the shift did not occur in time to contain the Washington-to-Richmond invasion thrust, however, Johnston might have to fight two enemy armies at once.

Union forces under the command of General Irvin McDowell made contact with Beauregard's outposts on July 17, 1861, and Beauregard immediately appealed to Johnston for assistance. An order from the War Department at Richmond to move to Manassas reached Johnston at one o'clock on the morning of the eighteenth, and he lost no time in getting his men started. To screen the movement he sent his cavalry forward: Patterson, the scouts reported, showed no signs of being in a fighting mood.

Johnston's shift from Winchester to Manassas was the first instance of any consequence in which the railroad was used, and the results left much to be desired. The trainmen failed to appreciate the urgency and importance of their role, and they refused to work after sundown. Even so, a substantial portion of Johnston's army rode to war on the Manassas Gap Rail Road.

As General Johnston neared Manassas, he worried about the

fact that a commander for the unified force had not been designated. Moreover, he was worn out: for nearly three days he had been devising schemes to hold Patterson in place, supervising the movement of his units, and thinking about what could happen once the battle opened. He outranked Beauregard, but he had to face the fact that Beauregard knew the ground on which the fight would occur. There would be no time in which he could make his own inspection of the terrain. And at some point, his frail body told him, he would simply have to get some rest.

The question of who would command was answered soon after Johnston arrived at Manassas on the night of July 20. A message from the Confederate War Department assured him that he was considered the senior general.

Even so, some doubts remained in Johnston's mind as to how he should use his authority. Beauregard, he noticed, seemed to have a realistic grasp of the situation. The plan Beauregard had outlined for the next day's battle made sense, although Johnston was dubious about parts of it. A reasonable way of handling the command problem, Johnston decided, was for him —as the senior commander—to allow Beauregard to go ahead and execute the orders he seemed so ready to issue. As soon as the delighted Beauregard left, Johnston went to bed for the first time in three days.

The battle opened very early on the morning of July 21, 1861. Johnston's decision the night before had doomed him to allow it to be Beauregard's fight, at least in the initial stages.

The attacks Beauregard had ordered failed to develop, in part because some of his couriers never reached subordinate commanders to deliver his instructions. Union General Irvin McDowell had better luck in starting his drive. From the outset it seemed that McDowell's troops would have little difficulty in getting around the northern end of Beauregard's lines at a creek called Bull Run.

Johnston quickly perceived that the initiative had gone over to the Union commander. He was distressed by Beauregard's strange inability to react, but he restrained himself from interfering in the hope that the junior commander's lapses were only temporary. To set Beauregard aside at such an early stage was distasteful to Johnston, especially since they were operating on a battleground he hardly knew. Moreover, Johnston was mindful of the fact that some of his own men were still en route to Manassas from Winchester. He may have reasoned that it would be better for him to remain aloof for as long as he could so that he would be able to supervise their commitment to exactly the right place in the battle area when they arrived.

As the morning's fighting dragged on, however, Beauregard showed few signs of responding to the threat McDowell's advance posed to the security of the northern end of his long battle line. Even worse, Beauregard failed to gain any significant control over his forces in the southern sector, where an attack was supposed to have been launched.

Johnston bridled his impatience for as long as he could. Finally, it snapped. "The battle is there," he said, pointing to the north. "I am going."

— 5 —

On the four-mile ride northward, Johnston came across confused batches of stragglers who had been thrown out of their positions. He found new leaders for the dazed men and ordered them back into the fighting. When he reached Henry House Hill, which was under heavy Union artillery fire, Johnston worked feverishly to build a defense line around the troops commanded by General Thomas J. Jackson (who at that moment was earning his immortal nickname, "Stonewall"). Beauregard, too, was re-forming broken units and placing them along the front.

Beauregard, greatly concerned about General Johnston's safety, finally persuaded him to move about a mile to the rear. This was no easy task for Beauregard, for Johnston disliked the thought of leaving the scene of the hottest action—but Beauregard seemed to be in full control once more, and there remained the need for Johnston to direct the units which would be arriving from Winchester.

Johnston's decision to shift his command post proved to be an excellent one, for in mid-afternoon General Kirby Smith brought three fresh regiments to the battle. Smith's brigade, together with another one commanded by Colonel Jubal A. Early, joined the fight as Johnston ordered and attacked just as the Union forces were throwing their last gallant charge. As a result, the battle became a rout: the Confederates smashed the Federal troops and sent them eastward in near panic. Johnston called for a pursuit, but it failed to carry very far because the troops were green or tired or both.

President Davis arrived too late to see anything of the action. The stragglers and wounded he encountered near Manassas gave him the impression that the Confederacy had lost the battle. Although Davis was happy to learn otherwise, he complicated life for Beauregard and Johnston by taking part in the routine decisions the two generals had to make.

Actually, First Manassas, or the Battle of Bull Run, had not been the great Confederate victory people on both sides considered it to be. Neither army had been ready for such a massive encounter, and the arrival of General Kirby Smith's forces at precisely the right moment had been a matter of luck rather than planning. Johnston's decision to ride to the north was probably the key act of the day—but he had restrained himself for a long time before he made it, and even when he moved he was almost too late to exert his influence. Had he tarried for another hour, the outcome might have been sharply different.

Even so, Confederate public opinion was buoyed inordinately by the success at Manassas. An army which had beaten the Yankees so decisively in one engagement, people believed, was surely capable of pressing northeastward to capture Washington and liberate Maryland. Such judgments were hopelessly shallow. Only the families of soldiers lost in the fight realized that the victory had been terribly expensive, and hardly anyone could appreciate the fact that Johnston's men were neither sufficiently trained nor adequately supplied for the kind of military adventures the press demanded.

Johnston knew that it was vastly more important for his army to be built into the fighting force it would have to become than it was for them to furnish new headlines for the Richmond newspapers. An army, even if it is stationary, exerts a certain amount of deterrent power simply because it exists—and it was this function that Johnston believed his troops could best serve for the time being. Moreover, the Confederacy's moral position rested on the fact that the new nation was fighting a war for survival, not undertaking the conquest of territory lawfully belonging to the United States. In addition, Johnston was convinced that the Union generals he knew so well would soon launch another offensive, and he devoted his energies to preparing his men to meet it.

Beauregard thought otherwise, and so did many of the more influential politicians in Richmond. Johnston's attitude was difficult for them to understand, and it was complicated by the running disputes he had with Davis and Secretary of War Judah P. Benjamin over his rank, supplies for his army, control of subordinate units within his command, and variations in reports of what had happened. For the rest of the summer, that fall, and through the winter the paper war between Johnston and Richmond continued—with Johnston usually on the losing end of the exchanges of messages—but the same kind of thing was going on north of the Potomac, and no significant Union threats developed.

During the winter of 1861–62, Johnston—professional soldier that he was—resolutely refused to enjoy a standard of comfort higher than that of his men. He lived in a tent, but he slept on the ground wrapped in the same blankets he had used back at Winchester. When he complained to Richmond about the inadequacies of the supply system, he spoke with complete authority—but, usually, in vain.

Johnston had great respect for the principle of civilian authority over military commanders, but Secretary of War Benjamin's legalistic way of coping with operational problems put his fidelity to that tradition to a severe test. Complicating an already vexing situation, President Davis consistently upheld Benjamin in the controversies which reached his attention. Ironically, however, it was Johnston who saved the services of General Stonewall Jackson for the Confederacy after Benjamin's awkwardness had infuriated Jackson to the point of submitting his resignation: Johnston persuaded his fellow Virginian to put patriotism before pride, and the crisis passed.

With the coming of spring in 1862, Johnston began to feel uneasy about being in such a forward position. He could fight a creditable battle at Manassas if the Union high command chose to try that invasion route again, but he was not so sure that he would be able to move from the old Bull Run lines quickly enough to meet and block a Federal thrust if it came

at any other place. Johnston's old friend, General George Mc-
Clellan, was now the commander of the Union Army of the
Potomac, and he knew that the brilliant man he used to call
"Beloved Mc" in his letters would not be foolish enough to
repeat Irvin McDowell's mistake.

When Johnston recommended a withdrawal from the Manassas area, however, the politicians in Richmond were appalled,
and a fresh wave of bitter controversy swept over him. They
interpreted his carefully wrought and highly professional counsel as a cowardly request for permission to retreat—and such a
show of weakness, they protested, was unthinkable.

Davis finally decided to approve Johnston's proposal, but the
shrill criticism of his ignorant compatriots had jarred his confidence in Johnston. A very real side effect of the Confederacy's
victory at Manassas in July, 1861, had been the massive buildup
of Union troop strength, and Davis was still enough of a soldier
to realize that the next Federal strike would be a maximum
attempt to crush his nation. With many misgivings, the President allowed the move he knew Johnston believed it mandatory
to make: and Johnston, Davis may have thought, had better be
right.

Johnston withdrew from the Bull Run positions without attracting the attention of Union forces, and he managed to take
along the greater portion of the supplies he had accumulated.
His first assembly area was forty miles or so to the southwest of
Manassas behind the Rappahannock River at Culpeper Court
House, but he later moved south of the Rapidan to a better
location.

McClellan had assumed that Johnston would not move that
far, and his old friend's sudden and drastic shift upset his plans
and forced him to make new ones. President Abraham Lincoln,
disappointed by this turn of events, began to take a greater
interest in what his key commander intended to do.

Johnston needed every man he could get, but he knew that
concentration of forces is not the answer to every military problem. Accordingly, he left Stonewall Jackson's command in the
Shenandoah Valley to act as a magnet to draw Union units away
from the Manassas-Fredericksburg-Richmond invasion corridor.
He assumed that McClellan would launch his drive from Chesapeake Bay and require him to commit his main body to the

east of Richmond. He disliked the idea of having to meet his old friend with anything less than full strength, but he hated even more the notion of leaving his northern flank unguarded.

McClellan took advantage of the toehold the Union had at Fortress Monroe on the narrow peninsula formed by the York and James rivers stretching southeastward from Richmond, and he put a major invasion force ashore at that point. Johnston responded by moving his army to the Richmond area. McClellan moved up the peninsula toward Richmond in early April, and the battle was on.

Johnston soon incurred the wrath of his horde of critics in Richmond by arguing that it was foolish to try to stop McClellan until the Union invasion force neared the capital. He was quickly overruled, and against his better judgment he sent more troops into the Yorktown-Williamsburg area than he ever expected to see again. He managed to delay McClellan, but that was about all; his major achievement was in extricating his outnumbered forces from one trap after another without suffering serious losses.

Here the difference in the thinking of Johnston and Davis came into clear focus. Davis wanted local victories as far distant from Richmond as possible; Johnston advocated conservation of the Confederate forces' few advantages so that—at the right time and under circumstances of his own choosing—a really significant defeat could be inflicted upon the invaders. Davis thought in terms of places, while Johnston's main concern was battle position.

As it turned out, McClellan slowly pushed the Confederate line back to the place Johnston had long since selected for the critical battle. Over in the Shenandoah Valley, Stonewall Jackson was doing a superb job of drawing Federal forces away from Richmond in the brilliant series of actions that would later be known as the Valley Campaign. Every mile McClellan moved up the peninsula added strain to his supply lines (while Johnston's own logistic problems were made just that much easier). Johnston felt he was winning—but few shared his optimism.

With Union troops setting their watches by the church bells of Richmond, President Davis adopted the habit of paying daily visits to Johnston's command post. Johnston was too busy to appreciate such honor as there was in the Chief Executive's attention; moreover, he deplored the habit Davis' aides had of going back to the capital and talking about the condition of the Confederate forces despite the presence in Richmond of Union spies. Accordingly, Johnston became unusually reticent about discussing his plans with the President, and their relations—which had never been cordial—became severely strained.

For a time in mid-May, it seemed that Union General Irvin McDowell might be able to strike southward from Fredericksburg against Richmond after all, and Lincoln was pressing him to do just that. Stonewall Jackson responded by drawing McDowell westward once again during the next week or so, but Johnston was unable to make realistic plans (except on a day-to-day basis) because of the threat McDowell's forces still posed. This seeming uncertainty on Johnston's part nettled Davis, who by this time was virtually out of communication with his senior commander.

On May 31, 1862, Johnston launched the attacks which resulted in the battles of Fair Oaks and Seven Pines. There was too much confusion and delay for the assaults Johnston had ordered to have the effect he desired, but the audacity of the Confederate drive shocked the Union troops and they fell back. Johnston was trying to figure out his next moves when he was hit first by a bullet and then by a shell fragment and had to be carried out of the action.

On a statistical basis, McClellan had won the battle by a narrow margin—but in a more significant sense, Johnston had achieved his purpose: the Union invasion had been stopped.

— 6 —

Lee, who had been appointed to succeed Johnston as commanding general of the Army of Northern Virginia, wrote Mrs. Johnston a message of sympathy in which he said: "The President has thought it necessary that I take his place. I wish I was able, or that his mantle had fallen on an abler man."

Johnston, upon learning that Davis was sending reinforcements to Lee, said: "Then, my wound was fortunate; it is the concentration which I earnestly recommended, but had not the influence to effect. Lee has made them do for him what they would not do for me."

There was no bitterness in Johnston's remark, only recognition of an important truth. Although Lee had never curried the favor of the officials in Richmond, he had managed to keep from antagonizing them. Davis was in awe of him—and none of the lesser authorities in the Confederate government dared cross the President in any matter regarding the general who was clearly his favorite. Johnston, on the other hand, would not have known how to begin to mend his political fences. Louis Wigfall, a Texan who was an old friend, became a Confederate Senator—but Wigfall was more energetic than influential, and he was never able to give Johnston much help. Johnston was doomed to be out of favor in Richmond for the rest of the war, to be put more and more in Lee's shadow.

While Johnston was recovering from his wounds, however, he enjoyed a few weeks of public approval. In early June, 1862, the Richmond *Examiner* had this to say about him:

> He is the only commander on either side of this contest that has yet proven, beyond all question, a capacity to manoeuvre a large army in the presence of one yet larger; to march it, fight it, or not fight it, at will, and while so doing, to baffle the plans of the ablest opponents in every instance. Time may yet produce another, but no living man in America is yet ascertained to possess a military knowledge so profound, or a decision of character so remarkable. He is one of those who can take responsibility; who is never a nose of wax; and who can hold out with the solidity of a rock against all foolish projects formed for him by others.

And even Davis remarked, "I wish he were able to take the field. . . . He is a good soldier, never brags of what he did do, and could at this time render most valuable service."

Lee, in the summer and fall of that year, went on to fight— and win—the Seven Days Battles east of Richmond and the Second Battle of Manassas, but a drive he led north of the Potomac into Maryland was stopped at Sharpsburg with heavy losses to the Confederates. For a time, Lee may have considered himself only a temporary replacement for Johnston—but no one knew whether or not Johnston would ever be able to resume command, and in the meantime the Army of Northern Virginia became Lee's Army.

Johnston was aware of that fact when he reported for duty in mid-November, and he was the first to recognize the wisdom of leaving Lee in charge of the army they both loved. But there remained for Johnston an assignment which the Davis Administration considered a promotion—command of the vast Western Department, which consisted of the states of Tennessee, Alabama, Mississippi, and that portion of Louisiana east of the Mississippi, and included two field armies.

From the beginning, Confederate forces in the Western Department had taken one defeat after another. In April, 1862, Union General Ulysses S. Grant had defeated Generals Albert Sidney Johnston and Pierre G. T. Beauregard at Shiloh, near the Tennessee-Mississippi boundary; Federal troops had taken New Orleans later that month; and now Grant was trying to gain complete control of the Mississippi River by moving against Vicksburg, which was virtually the only remaining crossing site that afforded communication with Texas, Arkansas, and western Louisiana. Confederate Generals Braxton Bragg and Kirby Smith had led twin drives into eastern Kentucky in August and September, but by mid-October they had been driven back to Murfreesboro, southeast of Nashville.

President Davis, believing as he did that every point in the Confederacy ought to be held, was entirely sympathetic to the complaints he had received from the governors and legislators of the Western states. Moreover, he saw the threats posed by Grant in Mississippi and General William S. Rosecrans in Tennessee for what they were—attempts to slice the Confederate nation into a series of compartments—and he realized that if their strategy succeeded, the end would not be long in coming.

The naming of a new commander was hardly the answer to the Western Department's problems, and Davis knew it—but the appointment was both good politics and an excellent morale booster. Johnston was admired and respected by the citizens of the Western states, some of whom remembered him from Mexican War days.

Johnston was glad to learn that he might yet be of some service, but he approached his new duties with caution. Almost at once he spotted several serious flaws in the plan he had been given to carry out, and he remained in Richmond for about two weeks in the hope of getting some of its less realistic aspects eliminated.

In effect, he saw, he was to have operational responsibility for both the Army of Mississippi and the Army of Tennessee, which were then at least 360 miles from each other, but he was not to be in direct command of either of them. His role, then, would only be advisory—if he could find some way of keeping in contact with both forces.

In addition, it was not clear that for him to have operational control in the Western Department really meant anything. Both armies had been taking their orders directly from Richmond; and as far as he knew, that practice would continue. This meant that his headquarters would not necessarily serve even as a clearing point in the communication system, and he feared that it might only lead to confusion if some commanders reported through him and others used their existing lines to Richmond.

And then there was the ironic fact that the Western Department was both too large and too small. Johnston needed control of Confederate forces just west of the Mississippi River in order to develop an effective defense against Grant's attempt to capture Vicksburg, but Davis refused to put the troops in Arkansas and western Louisiana under his command. The whole point of sending Johnston to the western theater was to provide the on-the-scene leadership Richmond could not supply except through him—and yet any use he cared to make of Confederate units west of the Mississippi in blocking Grant had to be coordinated by Davis and the War Department from the capital.

Mrs. Johnston, basing her judgment on feminine instinct, was certain that Jefferson Davis was luring her husband into a vicious trap. If things went wrong, she warned, Joe Johnston would be the obvious scapegoat.

General Johnston, who had won little clarification of his vaguely worded orders, conceded that the situation was not to his liking. As a soldier, however, he felt that he had no choice but to go west and see what he could do.

Johnston assumed his new command in early December, 1862. Only a few days after he arrived in Tennessee, and before he could learn anything about the condition of General Braxton Bragg's Army of Tennessee (which was still near Murfreesboro, facing a numerically superior Union force), Johnston was ordered to meet President Davis at Chattanooga and to accompany him on a two-week inspection tour of the western states.

If anything, the situation in Mississippi was worse than Johnston had expected. General J. C. Pemberton had assigned labor battalions the task of preparing Vicksburg to withstand siege—not as a compact bastion, but as a huge fortified area. Pemberton and most of his troops, however, were at Grenada, about 150 miles to the north, digging in along an overly extended front to block Grant's advance. At Port Hudson, about 150 miles to the south of Vicksburg, there was another Confederate garrison, and Davis made it clear to Johnston that he meant it to remain there.

To Johnston, all this was madness. Davis and Pemberton were thinking in terms of places, when the task at hand was simply to destroy Grant's forces. In order to do that, Pemberton should forget about constructing defenses and keep himself free to fight Grant wherever he could catch him at a disadvantage and annihilate him. But if Grant succeeded in trapping Pemberton at Vicksburg or General Franklin Gardner at Port Hudson, Johnston pointed out to Davis, it would be only a matter of time until both garrisons would be taken. In that event, he argued, the Army of Mississippi would cease to exist. Regardless of the number of troops that might be gathered elsewhere in Mississippi and nearby states, the western wing of Johnston's command would be reduced to little more than a guerrilla force.

Davis emphatically disagreed with Johnston. He found no fault at all with Pemberton's obvious fondness for defensive warfare and considered the preparations he was making at Vicksburg to be in strict accordance with his "hold everywhere" policy. To Johnston's astonishment, Davis even ordered the

War Department at Richmond to send Pemberton more heavy guns—weapons that were suitable only for the defense of a citadel-type position.

The trip also reinforced Johnston's conviction that he could not possibly provide effective command in both Tennessee and Mississippi, and he repeated his request that the district be split in conformity with the realities of geography and military necessity. Davis still believed that someone in high authority outside Richmond ought to be in the theater of operations to shift troops from one army to another—regardless of the fact that both of the major field forces were sadly understrength and likely to remain that way, regardless of the staggering time and distance factors. Accordingly, he rejected Johnston's recommendations. Johnston asked Davis to transfer him: Davis refused.

Soon after the President departed for Richmond in late December, Braxton Bragg fought and lost a battle at Murfreesboro, Tennessee, and had to retreat to Tullahoma. Bragg's losses were very heavy, and for a time Johnston had no idea of whether any part of Tennessee could be held. Pemberton, too, was in trouble at Vicksburg: Federal forces were forcing their way past the city and seemed to be heading down the river. The Confederate War Department responded by ordering Johnston to shift his forces from one army to the other as the situation demanded, and the Secretary of War expressed his regrets that Johnston had not been in actual command either at Murfreesboro or in the fighting around Vicksburg.

To these maddening complexities, the President now added a fresh one. Bragg's defeat at Murfreesboro and retreat to Tullahoma had set off considerable criticism of the Davis Administration. In addition, Bragg's subordinates had been free in expressing their lack of confidence in him as a commander. Davis ordered Johnston to investigate the matter and take the necessary corrective action.

Johnston did as he was told, found no immediate cause for relieving Bragg, and so reported to the President. He added, however: "should it . . . appear to you necessary to remove General Bragg, no one in this army or engaged in this investigation ought to be his successor."

The weight of opinion in Richmond was against Bragg

despite Johnston's report, and the controversy soon shifted to the question of who should take command of the Army of Tennessee in his place. Davis took the position that Johnston was already the army commander by virtue of his theater responsibility and that no further orders were required. Johnston, though, could not accept either that rationalization or the idea that he, a superior, could possibly allow himself to benefit from Bragg's removal as a consequence of his own investigation.

Here, the old-fashioned side of Johnston's character was thrown into the harsh light of a day more modern and more inclined to expediency than he had imagined. He had yearned for assignment as commander of either army, and he had been completely candid in expressing his discomfort as nominal leader of both—but if he was to get his wish, he considered it necessary for the War Department to make the decision and send him his orders. For him to assume the leadership of the Army of Tennessee at another man's expense was unthinkable, especially when he had found no serious fault with the subordinate and only political pressure remained as a cause for removing him.

Johnston's attitude amazed and irritated Davis, and it prompted Senator Wigfall to write his old friend to ask him what he really wanted. The solution Johnston suggested in his reply to Wigfall was a curious one: if the assignment as theater commander was really as important as the President insisted it was, Davis should give the responsibility for the Western Department to Lee—and Johnston could then be returned to the Army of Northern Virginia in Lee's place.

Finally, Davis ordered Johnston to relieve Bragg and take over his command in addition to his present responsibilities. Johnston complied, but he made no announcement of the change because Mrs. Bragg became critically ill just at that time and Johnston wanted to spare Bragg's feelings. Under Johnston, the Army of Tennessee showed quick improvement in morale and combat readiness. Johnston's own health deteriorated, however, and he had not made a full recovery by early May, 1863, when Grant broke loose south of Vicksburg and Davis ordered Johnston to take charge of the battle for Mississippi. The man Johnston left behind in command of the Army of Tennessee was Braxton Bragg.

— 8 —

From the beginning, Joe Johnston had been pessimistic about the chances for holding Vicksburg. Without the authority to concentrate Confederate forces and to fight a war of maneuver, and obliged as he was to defend Vicksburg along with every other place in his district, Johnston could hope only to keep the disaster to minimum proportions.

General J. C. Pemberton's actions merely deepened Johnston's discouragement in the opening months of 1863. Pemberton had ignored Johnston and had kept in touch with Richmond instead; accordingly, his tendency to disperse his troops and to maintain his defensive attitude had encountered little opposition from anyone—including Union Generals Ulysses S. Grant and William T. Sherman who had succeeded in hooking to the south and east of Vicksburg with a major force. Pemberton seemed to be fascinated with the idea of withstanding a siege inside Vicksburg's lines: the Federal commanders were bent on giving him just such an opportunity.

Johnston took charge of about 6000 Confederate troops at Jackson, Mississippi, in mid-May and quickly ordered Pemberton to move eastward to join forces with him. He did not intend to abandon Vicksburg to Grant, but he realized—as hardly anyone else did—that the only way to save that city was to defeat the Union invasion force in open country. If Pemberton moved quickly to complete the consolidation, Johnston would be able to face Grant with almost as many men as the Federal general commanded.

Soon, though, Johnston was to learn that cooperation on Pemberton's part was too much to expect. Pemberton was indecisive by nature and changed his mind with dismaying rapidity. To some extent, the conflicting orders he received from Davis (to hold Vicksburg) and from Johnston (to move eastward and consolidate) contributed to his inability to act in a positive manner. Rather than carry out either of those directives, however, Pemberton worked out a plan of his own—and then modified it. His carefully prepared fortifications at Vicksburg, moreover, seemed to have a magnetic appeal for him, and this strange fascination may have been an important reason for his poor performance.

Even if Pemberton had been eager to comply with Johnston's orders, however, it is doubtful if he could have done so because of the lack of any quick or reliable system of communication between the two commanders. Johnston was forced to rely on couriers who faced a ride of forty miles or more through country in which Union forces were becoming more numerous by the hour, and most of the messages he sent Pemberton arrived two days later—if they arrived at all. The replies Pemberton sent back were useless, for by the time Johnston got them his associate usually had changed his mind and was doing something directly contrary to what he had said he meant to do.

Despite these handicaps, Johnston kept trying to arrange a junction with Pemberton. His intention of moving westward from Jackson was blocked on May 14 when a strong Union attack captured the town and forced him to withdraw to the northeast. Pemberton, meanwhile, had decided to abandon the attempt to move eastward to join Johnston and had angled off to the southwest in the vain hope of cutting the supply lines Grant had long since decided he could do without. Without knowing where Pemberton was, Johnston headed westward on May 18, but before he had made much progress he learned that his advance was useless: Pemberton was inside the defenses of Vicksburg, and Grant was building a steel ring around him.

With Pemberton penned inside Fortress Vicksburg, all Johnston could do was to collect as many Confederate units as he could in preparation for an attempt to drive a corridor through Grant's lines and open an escape route for the garrison. That effort led to another controversy with the authorities in Richmond and made a bad situation worse: the War Department reminded Johnston that he had the authority to draw troops from the Army of the Tennessee, and Johnston replied that he was astonished that they still considered him in command there, quite apart from the fact that he hardly felt authorized to make what amounted to a political rather than military decision—that is, to give up the people of one state to try to save the citizens of another.

As usual, Davis and the Secretary of War paid far more attention to documenting the case against Johnston than to what he was trying to tell them. To their credit, however, they made about 20,000 troops available to him: by the end of June, Johnston's strength had grown to about 31,000.

Early in July, Johnston advanced toward Vicksburg, only to find that Union forces under General Sherman were waiting to block him. He managed to get close enough to the besieged city to hear the sounds of the fighting, and he got his men ready for the attempt to crash through the Federal lines. Just as his attack was about to be launched, though, he learned that Pemberton had surrendered on July 4.

Johnston withdrew to Jackson to await the next Union move. By July 9, Sherman had made it: Johnston now faced a victory-flushed Federal army of 50,000. To his surprise, however, Sherman did not attack. Instead, he settled down and made preparations for a siege. Johnston held for several days, but he finally decided that there was nothing to be gained by staying at Jackson and took his army out on the night of July 16.

By that time, Johnston was clearly marked as the Davis Administration's scapegoat for the Vicksburg disaster, which—along with Lee's defeat at Gettysburg, which had also occurred on July 4—had crushed Confederate morale. Most of the criticism was easy for Johnston to ignore, but he was astonished to realize that the Confederate President would turn away from more constructive tasks for long enough to write a vitriolic fifteen-page letter to him in which all of his "lapses" were recited in damning detail. As Mrs. Johnston described the bitter document in a letter to Mrs. Wigfall, it consisted of "such insults as only a coward or a woman could write." Her advice to her husband was to resign. The general, though, replied that he was serving not Davis, but a people who had never been anything but kind to him.

Now that it was too late for the action to mean anything, Davis accepted the suggestion Johnston had made repeatedly months before and cut what was left of the Western Department into two commands. Whether the belated change came as a rebuke or as the result of a rare flash of realism, Johnston was at least spared the added burden of Davis' wrath for Bragg's retreat from Tullahoma to Chattanooga and then into northwestern Georgia. For Johnston's part, the new arrangement meant that he would have an opportunity to rebuild the army he had brought out of the ill-fated Vicksburg campaign. He was even able to lend Bragg two divisions for the Battle of Chickamauga which Bragg fought and won in mid-September, 1863, at a time when the Confederacy was in dire need of a victory.

Despite his success at Chickamauga, Bragg soon found himself the object of a personal investigation by President Davis. Bragg's disaffected subordinates pleaded with Davis to replace him with Joe Johnston, but in vain: the President left Bragg in command.

By the end of November, 1863, however, Grant had whipped Bragg at Chattanooga and had driven the Army of Tennessee back into northwest Georgia. Bragg asked Davis to relieve him, and his request was granted. Davis offered the command to Lee, but Lee declined the honor. Finally, after the President realized that there was no one else to whom he could turn, he appointed Johnston as commander of the Army of Tennessee.

— 9 —

As 1863 was drawing to a close, General Johnston arrived at the little railroad town of Dalton, Georgia, which is located about twenty-six miles southeast of Chattanooga. To some, it might have seemed that a defeated leader was taking charge of a beaten army: the record, so far, indicated as much. But such generalizations had no foundation in fact, for Johnston's fighting spirit was as high as it had ever been, and he knew that the Army of Tennessee was fully capable of the greatness he meant for it to achieve.

Johnston, seasoned soldier that he was, saw that his troops needed vigorous training. Men at war often adopt the shallow attitude that it is enough for them to be in combat—that efforts to sharpen their skills are just a silly nuisance—but Johnston made it clear that the problem was the Confederacy's survival, and the toughening program produced excellent results.

The communications Johnston received from Richmond, however, suggested that neither the President nor the Secretary of War knew what to think about the condition of the Army of Tennessee as 1864 opened. Davis said that the units Johnston had been given were in good shape and added that the government would provide whatever was needed to launch an offensive. Secretary of War Seddon wrote that the army's low morale and weak troop strength were deplorable, but that Johnston would have to find his remedies himself: Richmond could not help. Seddon, Johnston knew, was closer to the truth than Davis—but in any event, he had long since learned that he would have to solve his own problems.

Fortunately, General Grant—who had beaten Bragg at Chattanooga—was not inclined to put pressure on Johnston's army during the winter and early spring of 1864. Sherman launched a drive in Mississippi that seemed to have Mobile, Alabama, as its objective, and Davis ordered Johnston to send a major portion of his forces westward to Confederate General Leonidas Polk to stem the Yankee offensive—but the threat dissipated with the capture of Meridian, and the Confederate President returned Johnston's men to Dalton.

Braxton Bragg, who had become Davis' military adviser, informed Johnston that the Administration expected him to lead the Army of Tennessee back up into the territory from which it had drawn its name—and beyond. Johnston knew that his forces were far too weak to undertake such an adventure, and he said so. But as the weeks went by, the pressure on him mounted. Several authorities, including General Beauregard over in Charleston, offered plans for aggressive action. Davis emphasized his desire for a bold advance.

Johnston was not—as his critics maintained—afraid to fight: rather, he saw no worthwhile purpose in exposing the Army of Tennessee to senseless slaughter. Sooner or later, he knew, Sherman would attack. Once he had defeated the Union forces and depleted their strength, a Confederate offensive might be possible. For the time being, though, and until he received significant reinforcements, he could only stay where he was.

In addition, Johnston understood the importance of having adequate sources of supply and dependable systems of transportation. This fact made him almost unique, for neither the Davis Administration nor very many other Confederate generals appreciated the relationship of logistic requirements to success in battle—and that being the case, Johnston's concern over shortages of food, ammunition, and wagons could be (and was) easily mistaken for unwillingness to drive the Yankees out.

Still another reason for not launching an offensive through Tennessee into Kentucky was the capability the Union army had of stopping such a thrust dead in its early stages. Unlike Davis, Abraham Lincoln did not have to think about stripping troops from one army to reinforce another. Desertions were serious problems for both Presidents, but by this point in the war Union supremacy in manpower and industrial resources was beginning to make a profound difference wherever Federal forces were committed. Johnston grasped this truth at once; Davis never did. A commander can respect the overwhelming strength of his enemy without fearing it—as Johnston did at Dalton—but that does not make him a coward, even if ignorant men say otherwise. But as Johnston might have expected, his realism was branded as craven weakness of will.

General John B. Hood, a gallant fighter who had already lost an arm and a leg while serving the cause, came to the Army of Tennessee just as the authorities in Richmond were putting maximum pressure on Johnston to attack. Hood had little difficulty in winning Johnston's friendship and confidence, and he gave his commander every indication of being in wholehearted agreement with him regarding the necessity of remaining on the defensive. The letters Hood sent to Davis and others in Richmond, however, would hardly have pleased Johnston if he had known what they contained. Hood reported that the Army of Tennessee was perfectly capable of invading Tennessee and Kentucky and expressed his own impatience with Johnston for not ordering an offensive.

While Johnston did what he could to rebuild his army for the fighting he knew it would soon experience, Ulysses S. Grant was settling into his new assignment as Lincoln's general-in-chief. Grant conceived a plan that was wonderfully simple: General George Meade's Army of the Potomac would drive into Virginia, and Sherman's forces would strike Johnston in Georgia *on the same day*. Thereafter, both armies would carry out a gigantic pincer movement which would destroy Lee's Army of Northern Virginia and Johnston's Army of Tennessee and end the war. Here was the kind of grand strategy neither side had employed before—and Grant had both the political backing and the resources to put it into action.

Sherman massed troops and accumulated supplies for a long and expensive campaign. By May 5, the date Grant had set for the opening of the Union's dual offensives, Sherman was ready.

— 10 —

General William Tecumseh Sherman was as able a commander as the Union could place in charge of an important campaign. He is best remembered for burning a path from Atlanta to the sea, and this suggests a degree of ruthlessness which is not admirable—but at other times in his career he proved to be shrewd, careful, and even cautious in his conduct of military operations.

For Grant to have put Sherman up against Joe Johnston amounted to an excellent matching of brilliant soldiers, but the odds clearly favored the Union. Sherman's numerical advantage over Johnston was almost two to one, and his logistical situation was far superior to that of the Confederates. Each commander meant to destroy the other if possible, but Sherman was in a position to live off Georgia's strategic resources to the extent that he could advance. Even if Johnston somehow broke up Sherman's army and managed to drive northward, however, he would be operating in ruined country until he reached Kentucky.

At first, the authorities in Richmond thought that Johnston's reports of the massing of Union troops above Dalton reflected only a show of strength on Sherman's part to divert attention from Meade's preparations for his drive into northern Virginia. When sharp cavalry skirmishes on May 2 near Dalton made it clear that Sherman was getting ready to open a battle of major proportions, Davis and Bragg responded by ordering General Polk—a remarkably fine fighter who had earlier been a bishop in the Episcopal Church—to move eastward and join Johnston's army.

For several days, Johnston watched Sherman build his combat power opposite the Confederate positions along Rocky Face Ridge just west of Dalton. Before long, however, he discovered that Sherman had sent forces southward to outflank him—and Johnston withdrew about twelve miles to a little town called Resaca.

Such were the opening moves of the Atlanta campaign, and they seem simple enough. Actually, Sherman and Johnston were locked in a battle of brains as well as blood. Sherman was certain that his thrust southward would cut Johnston's line of communication and open the way for a classic entrapment. Johnston saw that possibility in time to shift enough units into the Union flanking force's path to delay it. In addition, he made good use of the Dalton-Atlanta railroad in moving his main body down to Resaca. As a result, Sherman gained real estate but failed to accomplish anything beyond that. The situation at Resaca was roughly the same as the one at Dalton—but Sherman had lost nearly two weeks.

Again Sherman tried the combination of direct pressure to hold Johnston in place at Resaca and an attempt to envelop his enemy. Union columns drove southward along back roads, but Johnston's cavalry sent back reports of Federal progress. Johnston withdrew from Resaca during the night of May 15 and was ready to meet Sherman once more near Cassville, about twenty-five miles to the south of Resaca.

On the way to Cassville, General Polk resumed his duties as a bishop long enough to baptize General Johnston. The service was spartan and brief. As soon as it ended, the generals returned to the tasks of reading reports of actions and preparing orders for the next day's fighting.

By this time, Sherman and Johnston had learned a great deal about each other. Sherman knew that Johnston was placing heavy dependence on the railroad, and he had noticed the Confederate commander's tendency to keep his main body of troops near it. Johnston saw that Sherman was hesitant to launch a frontal assault even though the success of his envelopments depended upon his holding Johnston in place until the flanking element was ready to join in the final phase of the battle. Sherman had to concede that Johnston's timing had been excellent; Johnston had gained new respect for his foe's knowledge of the country through which he was operating.

The logistic factors still favored the Union force, but Sherman's advantage diminished with each mile as Johnston drew him deeper and deeper into Georgia. Johnston could not spare enough cavalry units for raids of his own against the Federal supply line at points deep in the enemy rear, but he sent one urgent appeal after another to Richmond to order General Nathan Bedford Forrest or other Confederate cavalry commanders to strike blows in Tennessee which would help him defeat Sherman in Georgia.

Cassville was no place for making a major stand, Johnston quickly realized, and he abandoned it as soon as it was of no further strategic use to him. He built a strong position at Allatoona Pass a few miles to the south of Cassville, but Sherman saw the futility of trying to storm it: instead, Sherman cut loose from his own line of communication and sent his main body westward in the hope of luring Johnston away from the railroad. Johnston obliged Sherman by being at New Hope Church, about fourteen miles west of the rail line and Marietta, to meet him.

Now the fighting began to take on a savage aspect. Sherman had drawn the main body of Johnston's army onto a battleground of his own choosing, and he meant to get maximum results from that success. The men of the Army of Tennessee, though, were spoiling for the chance to punish the Yankee invaders. Sherman threw assault after assault against Johnston's lines, but the determined Confederates held.

Sherman then tried another idea. He ordered action to hold Johnston where he was and used his superior strength to stretch his battle line over toward Marietta and the railroad. Johnston caught on quickly, and he made his opponent's sideslip as costly as possible for him. Both sides, in effect, were digging their way to Marietta. May gave way to June while the eastward extension of the lines went on. Good fighting weather was replaced by steady rain.

Johnston, of course, had won no glory for himself by giving up nearly a hundred miles of Georgia—but he had saved the Army of Tennessee, and he had drawn his enemy so far into dangerous country that Sherman was having to keep looking over his shoulder most of the time lest Confederate cavalrymen slice his strained supply lines to Chattanooga and Nashville. Moreover, the eastward shift of both armies had resulted in Johnston's seizure of a superior battle position just to the north of Marietta, and this in itself amounted to a major victory over Sherman—though few would ever realize it.

Bad as the news from Georgia was, the reports from the battles Lee was fighting—and losing—in northeastern Virginia were even worse. In the minds of Jefferson Davis and certain other observers in Richmond, though, there was a qualitative difference between the kinds of defeats the two major Confederate field armies were suffering. Lee and Grant had been fighting a series of furious actions all the way from the Wilderness through the bloody tragedy of Spotsylvania to Cold Harbor, where the Union had lost over 7000 men in a single half hour. Johnston, meanwhile, had given up mile after mile of Georgia without having fought a single serious engagement. Lee, at least, was trying to stop Grant—or so the stories in the Richmond newspapers implied. Why couldn't Joe Johnston do as much? Why was he always pulling back before a battle could develop? Could it be that he was afraid to fight?

War takes on a bewildering number of forms, wherever it is fought—and it is grossly unfair to compare the performance of one commander in one campaign with that of another who is conducting an operation some distance away, even if the two actions are going on at the same time. Davis ought to have known that; but if he did, he set that bit of knowledge aside and made bloodshed the criterion it should never be.

Lee and Grant stormed into each other in the Wilderness on the day the Union's twin offensive opened, and the viciousness of that encounter was sustained as the killing moved along a blood-drenched arc toward Richmond. Grant lost enough men to earn fame of a sort as "The Butcher" from Northern newspapers; but Lee, too, was suffering casualties. Lincoln could replace Grant's dead and wounded. Jefferson Davis was able to send Lee only encouragement.

Johnston had been on the defensive in Georgia from the outset: for him to have slammed into Sherman's forces above Dalton would have been suicidal. He had fought the only kind of campaign that was left open to him, given the realities of his situation—and he had fought it with rare brilliance. Like Lee, he needed reinforcements in order to stop the invading army and launch a counterattack. But in contrast to Lee, Johnston did not need those men to replace the losses he had taken in battles he had not been able to avoid.

Such were the facts. Lincoln, Grant, and Sherman took them for what they were, and so did Lee and Johnston—but the use Jefferson Davis would make of them was to be quite another thing.

— 11 —

If the readers of newspapers or even official reports in faraway cities are often poor judges of a commander's real worth, and frequently they must be, the men in the line are in a splendid position to show by their performance the degree of respect they have for the man in question. General Polk's troops had always been one with him, and when he was killed by Union artillery fire while he and General Johnston were inspecting a forward position on Pine Mountain north of Marietta one day in June, they were all shocked and saddened by their loss. If anything, though, Polk's death made them appreciate Joe Johnston all the more, for they knew that the blast that had caught one general might just as easily have deprived them of the leadership of the other.

This is not the kind of thing soldiers say much about. Either such a feeling exists, or it does not. In the cases of Polk and Johnston, it was a very real force. In days—and years—to come, it would make a significant difference.

Most of June was used up by both sides in strengthening their positions, for Sherman feared a Confederate attack as much as Johnston expected his Federal opponent to launch one against him—so evenly were the commanders matched, despite the Union's superiority in troop strength and supplies. Finally, though, Sherman's desire to accomplish something resulted in an attempt to break through Johnston's defenses on Kenesaw Mountain above Marietta. In scorching weather, he sent his men forward—only to have them thrown back with losses that Johnston later estimated as 6000—against Confederate casualties of 552 dead and wounded.

Davis, fearing that Johnston would retreat all the way to the sea, was ready to remove Johnston from command of the Army of Tennessee—or so Senator Wigfall reported to his friend when he arrived at Kenesaw Mountain the day after the battle. Johnston acquainted Wigfall with the realities of the situation, and the Texan did his best to rally political support for him—but by this time Davis had become something of a dictator as far as military affairs were concerned, and Wigfall must have known that he could only postpone the inevitable. Even so, he tried.

June gave way to July with Johnston still holding Kenesaw Mountain and Marietta. Sherman ran out of new ideas and reverted to an old one: envelopment. He sent enough troops southward to the Chattahoochee River to give Johnston something to think about, and Johnston moved—not, as Sherman expected, south of the river, but into a strong position just to the north of it (with six bridges behind him in case they might be needed).

Davis sent Bragg to Georgia in early July to get a firsthand report on General Johnston's conduct of the campaign. Now the roles of the two generals were reversed: a year and a half earlier, Johnston had been obliged by the President to render judgment on Bragg. This time, there was to be no charity. Bragg started filing reports long before he reached Johnston, and they suggested that a catastrophe was in the making. When Bragg finally saw Johnston, he was less than candid in expressing the purpose of his visit. With General John B. Hood, however, Bragg was much more open—and Hood facilitated Bragg's mission (which was really to select a replacement for Johnston) by writing a letter to Bragg which was a bid for command.

Sherman, meanwhile, was still reluctant to assault Johnston's carefully prepared main line of resistance and was trying to find an unopposed crossing site to the east. Johnston knew that it was only a matter of time before the Union scouts provided their commander with what he wanted: then Federal troops would come pouring over Peachtree Creek, and the Army of Tennessee would have to withdraw once more.

Johnston, though, was ready. His stand on the north bank of the Chattahoochee had bought time for the completion of defense lines around Atlanta. Moreover, Sherman would get a rude surprise when the battle for the city opened: the fortifications had been laid out in anticipation of the move he was making, and Confederate forces would be there to cut his columns to ribbons.

On the night of July 17, 1864, as Johnston was talking to his chief engineer about the Atlanta defenses, he received a message from President Davis: "You are hereby relieved from command of the Army and Department of Tennessee, which you will immediately turn over to General Hood."

— 12 —

General John B. Hood now had what he had worked so long and so deviously to get—but the responsibility of being the army commander frightened him. This was not what he had expected: he had pictured himself as the leader of an offensive which would recapture lost territory and renew the glory of Confederate arms—but instead, he would have to fight a defensive action against a strong and determined foe. He ought to have been more careful in his prayers—for they had been answered.

Hood's first reaction was to go to Johnston and beg him to forget that he had received the order. A change of command in the midst of a withdrawal, he argued, was an invitation to disaster. Johnston refused, and then he told Hood everything he would need to know in order to conduct the impending battle. Later that night, John Hood returned to Johnston's tent and repeated his appeal. Again Johnston rebuffed him.

Johnston's insistence on complying with Davis' instructions was motivated solely by his old-fashioned belief that a soldier must obey. He was not aware of any disloyalty on Hood's part at that time, and he felt no bitterness or envy toward his successor: if anything, he was inclined to do as Hood suggested out of compassion for the younger man. In addition, Johnston wanted nothing more than the chance to vindicate himself by inflicting a stunning and decisive defeat on Sherman at Atlanta. After all those vexing weeks of always having to pull back, after all the bitter criticism, after the magnificent response the Army of Tennessee had given him time and again, he was to be denied the satisfaction of seeing the campaign through. He had every reason in the world to pocket Davis' order but one—the duty of obedience. And for Johnston, that one was enough.

Seasoned soldier that he was, Johnston knew that the sooner he departed, the better it would be for Hood and the Army of Tennessee. He informed Richmond of his compliance, sent a farewell message to the men, and left. Those who watched "Old Joe" go by saw him through their tears.

News of the change spread quickly. The troops were dismayed. Several senior commanders immediately requested transfer or relief. Some sent messages of protest to the President. Sherman, of course, was jubilant: Jefferson Davis had given him the victory Johnston had denied him for so long. Moreover, Hood was a known quantity to many of Sherman's subordinates: they had served with him in the old Army, and they were certain that he would attack—thus insuring the destruction of the Army of Tennessee as Johnston had known it.

Hood lost Atlanta without forcing Sherman to pay much of a price, and then he addressed himself to the task of doing what President Davis wanted. By the middle of December, 1864, Hood had taken the Army of Tennessee back to Nashville, where it was roundly defeated. In the meantime, Sherman scorched the Georgia earth from Atlanta southeastward to Savannah. As Sherman was turning his army northward to give South Carolina the same kind of treatment, Hood brought the weary survivors of the Nashville fiasco back into northern Alabama and asked to be relieved of his command. The remnants of the once-proud Army of Tennessee were soon scattered throughout what was left of the Confederate nation.

Johnston, a general without a command, remained aloof from the intense controversy that followed his removal. The thing was done, and he had no regrets to plague him or magical solutions to advance. As a man of honor, he offered along with his official reports a spirited defense of the actions he had taken —but since most of them had been defensive in nature, and because Grant was pounding away at Lee's thin lines only twenty miles to the south of Richmond at Petersburg, no one paid much attention.

If he had been a petty man, Johnston might have gloated over Hood's tragedy. Davis had got the offensive he wanted, but —as Johnston had warned from the beginning of the Atlanta campaign—at a price the Confederate nation could not afford to pay. Johnston mourned the fate of Hood and the Army of Tennessee in silence: their loss was his own.

Richmond gossip in the early part of 1865 had it that Davis' days were numbered and that a military dictator—Lee, most likely, but possibly Johnston—would take over the government. Such talk was nonsense, of course, but it indicated Johnston's stature in the minds of the people who prided themselves on being the best-informed citizens in the Confederacy.

Demand for the reappointment of Joe Johnston to a major command mounted during the opening months of 1865, but Davis angrily rejected each new appeal. Johnston took up temporary residence in South Carolina, worried about the safety of his wife, volunteered his services to the state's governor, but remained very much on the shelf.

Sherman, meanwhile, was burning his way northward through the Carolinas. General Beauregard had been put in charge of a resistance force too weak to bear any memorable name, but his health was precarious and his efforts to stop Sherman had been futile.

Davis put Lee into the position of general-in-chief in February, 1865, and Lee quickly took the action Davis had resisted: he appointed Johnston to the command of the scattered units that had been serving under Beauregard. Late though the hour for the Confederacy was, Johnston attempted to concentrate his forces so that something might yet be done to blunt the point of Sherman's advance. He scored a brilliant success at Bentonville, North Carolina—but it was to go down in history as no more than a gallant effort in which, to Johnston's great satisfaction, elements of his old Army of Tennessee performed with distinction.

President Davis was obliged to take his government from Richmond to Danville in early April, and before long the Confederate capital had been moved again to Greensboro, North Carolina. Lee surrendered to Grant on April 9 at Appomattox. Johnston's army was the only major Confederate force left to protect the dying nation.

Davis ordered Johnston to meet him at Greensboro, and on April 12 and 13 they discussed the possibilities for continuing the war. In the concluding session, Davis asked Johnston for his opinion. Johnston gave Davis and the members of his Cabinet who were present an analysis of the military situation; reminded his civilian superiors of how deficient their nation was in terms of manpower, financial resources, and war matériel; and recommended that negotiations for peace be opened at once. General Beauregard, who had won the Confederacy's first battle and was as reluctant as a man could be to give in, told Davis that he agreed completely with General Johnston's views. With great reluctance, Davis gave Johnston authority to ask Sherman for terms of surrender.

Johnston contacted Sherman immediately, and they met in a farmhouse near Durham, North Carolina, at noon on April 17. Once they were alone, Sherman handed Johnston a telegram and watched the Confederate general's expression closely as Johnston read the news that President Lincoln had been assassinated. Johnston, visibly shaken by the tragic message, said that he hoped Sherman did not believe that the Confederate government had anything to do with the crime. Sherman replied that he could not imagine that Johnston or Lee could be involved in such a hideous act, but he added that he was unable to say as much for Jefferson Davis.

Lincoln's assassination made it imperative that the negotiations be completed as quickly as possible. Sherman had kept the telegram's contents secret lest his men break the truce in his absence, but he knew that news of such importance could not be withheld for much longer. Both generals were able to find a broad area of agreement, however: neither wanted any more killing, and the terms Grant had given Lee at Appomattox some days earlier provided an excellent basis for bringing the war to a close. The only unresolved question was whether Johnston could surrender for the entire Confederate Army (as he desired) or only his own Army of Tennessee.

Since Johnston was virtually certain that President Davis would challenge any document of surrender he might sign, he asked Secretary of War John C. Breckinridge of Kentucky (who was also a major general) to join him in the negotiations. Breckinridge, who had a great fondness for bourbon whiskey, was delighted beyond measure when Sherman produced a bottle and poured the Confederates a drink. Once the discussions began, Johnston and Breckinridge argued with such eloquence that Sherman was forced to interrupt. "See here, gentlemen," he said, "who is doing the surrendering anyhow? If this thing goes on, you'll have me sending a letter of apology to Jeff Davis."

While Sherman was writing a draft of the agreement, he got up from the table, walked over to his saddlebags, found the bottle, and helped himself to a swig. Still deep in thought, he replaced the cork and returned to the task of finding language that both sides could accept.

After Johnston and Breckinridge had signed the agreement—which could not become effective until both governments had approved it—they rode back to the Army of Tennessee's camp. When Johnston asked the Kentuckian what he thought of General Sherman, Breckinridge replied: "Sherman is a bright man, and a man of great force, but, General Johnston, General Sherman is a hog. Yes sir, a *hog*. Did you see him take that drink by himself?" Johnston replied that he had. "No Kentucky gentleman would ever have taken away that bottle," Breckinridge complained. "He knew we needed it, and needed it badly."

Rumors of the war's end led to desertions from Johnston's ranks, but he was not sorry to see the men leave. If, for any reason, nothing came of his efforts to negotiate a peace with Sherman, any further military action would be senseless and tantamount to murder—and in that case, the weaker and more dispersed his forces were, the better. Officially, however, he had to maintain the fiction that the Army of Tennessee still existed.

The Johnston-Breckinridge-Sherman agreement was reluctantly approved by Davis, but the authorities in Washington refused to ratify it. Johnston met Sherman again, and this time they worked out a pact which was acceptable: the Civil War was over.

— 13 —

At the end of the war, Joseph Johnston, like countless other Confederate veterans, was financially a ruined man. After a few months, however, he joined other Virginians in forming an express company; the venture failed eventually, but at least a beginning had been made. Johnston went on to become the president of a railroad, an insurance broker, and a member of the United States Congress from Virginia for one term—but the great days of his life were over for him.

The respect Johnston had earned during the war, though, was not forgotten by men on either side. Wherever he went, he was honored. When he paid a call on General Grant, for example, to request that Union authorities be more diligent in recognizing the paroles of Confederate veterans, Grant promised to take the necessary action—and then asked his visitor to remain so that he could present the members of his staff.

The controversies with Jefferson Davis and other Richmond authorities which had plagued Johnston all the way from First Manassas to the surrender near Durham were kept alive as the memoirs of one former officer or politician after another came off the presses, and finally Johnston felt compelled to write his own version of what had happened. The book he published in 1874 was exactly what he intended it to be—a report of the operations he conducted. It reveals almost nothing of the man, and it had little effect on the thinking of his critics.

Johnston was always a popular figure at Confederate reunions. When he went to Atlanta in 1890 for such a gathering, veterans of the Army of Tennessee broke through police lines to shake his hand—and before long, they had unhitched the horses which pulled his carriage and were hauling him forward themselves.

One by one, though, the great men of Joe Johnston's era died, leaving him standing by as pallbearer. He performed that saddest of duties for General Grant, General McClellan, and General Sherman—his onetime foes—and yet when his own death occurred in 1891, he was buried in Baltimore with only a few veterans of both armies there to pay him honor.

History has tended to overlook Joe Johnston, for he was destined to stand in the shadow of his beloved friend and classmate, Robert E. Lee, whose majestic nobility in defeat set the tone for the finer aspects of the Great Remembering. Johnston and Lee, however, were the kind of men who gave little thought to fame: instead, they gave life what they had and left it to others to appraise their worth. They were the closest of friends, no matter how widely they were separated by time, distance, and duty. Johnston maintained that link as best he could after Lee died in 1870: he raised funds for the Lee Memorial at

Lexington after Mrs. Lee declined his offer to try to create a trust for her support, and one of the great honors of his life came in 1890 when he was asked to unveil the equestrian statue of Lee which now stands on Monument Avenue in Richmond.

The most valid measure of Johnston's merit as a soldier came from the men he commanded, both in their performance during the campaigns he led and in their spontaneous tributes to him whenever they saw him after the war. They were the proper custodians of his memory, for they knew him for what he really was. And for Johnston, their respect was enough.

3

Nathan Bedford Forrest

Nature's Soldier

1821–1877

A UNION cavalry force of about five hundred troopers was moving toward the village of Sacramento, in western Kentucky, on December 28, 1861. Their mission was to destroy a ragged band of Confederate raiders which had been stripping the countryside of livestock and to teach the enemy that it was certain death to try to operate in that region.

Scouts brought news of the Federal cavalry column's position to Lieutenant Colonel Nathan Bedford Forrest, and the Confederate commander immediately ordered his 200 men to follow him with all possible speed. Before long, he had overtaken the rear of the Union force. The Yankees halted, but they seemed to be confused over whether the troops behind them were friends or foes: Forrest took a rifle, fired at a blue-clad soldier, and clarified the situation.

The Federal rear guard withdrew to alert the main body, and Forrest tore after them at a gallop. Soon he reached a clearing and signaled a halt, for just ahead—along the edge of the woods on the other side, two hundred yards away—the Union force stood in line of battle. The Yankees opened fire, but Forrest paid no attention to the danger and rode among his soldiers shouting orders.

Forrest split his unit into three sections. His plan was simple: while dismounted skirmishers, some of whom had no weapons, moved forward through the stumps and brush piles in the clearing, one force on horseback would move around the left flank of the Union line while another mounted outfit circled the right end.

Finally, the golden moment came. Union troops, confused and disconcerted by the attacks which were striking them from their sides and rear, slackened the fire they had been pouring into the bold Confederate skirmishers. Forrest, at the forefront of the men in the clearing, stood up in his stirrups, waved his saber over his head, and shouted "Charge!"

With a Rebel yell, his men shot forward into the demoralized Yankee line. Forrest's face was flushed with excitement and there was a strange, savage gleam in his eyes as he led his warriors through the Union position. Panic seized the Federal troopers: those who could make it to their horses rode away as fast as the frightened animals could carry them. Forrest gathered his cavalrymen and pursued the fleeing enemy through Sacramento and for a mile or so beyond the town, firing and slashing all the way.

Some Union officers finally managed to pull enough men together to form a roadblock. Forrest charged into their midst and killed or wounded three Yankees in the desperate hand-to-hand struggle which raged until every Federal soldier was disabled, killed, or captured.

— 2 —

General Albert Sidney Johnston, in his report of operations in his department for December, 1861, said: "For the skill, energy, and courage displayed by Colonel Forrest [at Sacramento] he is entitled to the highest praise, and I take great pleasure in calling the attention of the general commanding and of the government to his services." Albert Johnston was a West Point graduate, a veteran of many skirmishes, an expert judge of men. The commander who had won this great soldier's admiration and respect had never had a day's instruction in tactics or any other military subject, and Sacramento had been his first battle—but he knew how to fight.

Actually, Nathan Bedford Forrest had broken virtually every rule in the book that day at Sacramento. His mission was to gather supplies and to do some scouting, not to engage the enemy. Having learned of the Union column's presence and superior size, he could easily have slipped away without attracting the Yankees' attention. Even after he caught up with the Federal rear guard, there was no justification for him to show his hostile intent by firing at the enemy troopers. By pursuing the Union force, he accepted the risk of riding into a trap: as it was, he was obliged to fight on ground selected by his adversaries. In splitting his inferior force in the face of the enemy, and by attempting to combine the efforts of three untrained and untested bodies of troops in an attack against a unit which had every possible advantage, he exposed his command to piecemeal destruction. Once the battle was opened, there was no way in which he could exercise control over his maneuvering elements, for he was in the thick of the fighting where only the skirmishers could hear his orders. By engaging in hand-to-hand combat, he abandoned all hope of exerting his influence on the movement or fire of any other soldier. The mounted pursuit he led after the field was won was almost inexcusable: he had no idea of where most of his men were, he was completely unprepared to resist a Union counterattack, and there was no clear need for him to be the first to cut and shoot his way into the desperate Yankee defenders.

But Forrest did one thing right: he won.

"War means fighting," Forrest said once, "and fighting means killing." That was as close as he ever came to expressing the principles by which he conducted his battles, but those seven words were enough. They were to guide him—and the thousands of men he inspired—until the very end.

The same brutally simple idea undoubtedly occurred to many other leaders on both sides of the Civil War at one time or another, but few of them translated that concept into action as consistently, as ruthlessly, and as effectively as Nathan Bedford Forrest did in the brilliant series of campaigns he waged in the western area of operations during those four bloody years.

Although he was certainly unorthodox in his approach to leadership, Forrest was no madman. In many ways, he was a model commander: he never asked his men to undertake any task he was unwilling to perform, he was just and considerate in matters having to do with the welfare of his troops, and he held the shedding of blood to a minimum whenever skill or even chicanery enabled him to win the victory he sought. When all else failed, however, when only a fight to the death could produce a decision, he did not evade the duty of seeing the horror through.

Against this background, the Battle of Sacramento was not as grossly mismanaged by Forrest as it may seem. Without knowing that he was conducting what is now called a spoiling attack, he eliminated the threat the Union cavalry force posed to his unit's security. In the process, he struck terror into the hearts of other Federal soldiers who were likely to be sent out to destroy him. Confederate soldiers who went into the fight without weapons or horses came away fully equipped: in no other way could Forrest have obtained those necessities for them, for Richmond was a long way off and requisitions had a habit of getting lost. Similarly, there was an astonishing amount of common sense in the plan of attack he devised under enemy fire. Outnumbered and outgunned as he was, he realized that he could win only by creating the impression that his force was large enough to surround and crush the Federal position. What he lacked in troop strength and firepower, he gained by shock effect and surprise and aggressiveness and valor—and as a result, he inflicted a stunning defeat on an enemy outfit which was fully capable of chopping his unit to pieces.

For many reasons, the Battle of Sacramento—along with the man who won it—would be lost to history. It was, after all, a border action which involved less than a thousand men; it was hardly a turning point, except for Forrest and the men on both sides who were wounded or killed; and Sacramento, along with the rest of that part of Kentucky, remained under Union control. Still, the forgotten fight at Sacramento had an importance that far transcended its actual scope.

— 3 —

Henry Steele Commager has pointed out:

The South had one categorical advantage, one which—had it been properly exploited—might have been decisive. It was this:

that she did not need to win battles in order to win the war. If the Union was to win, it had to conquer the South—that is to invade and hold an area as large as all western Europe except Italy and Scandinavia—an achievement without parallel in modern history. But the Confederacy had a far less exacting task. She was under no obligation to carry the war to the North; she demanded neither territory nor tribute nor even terms, except the elementary term that she be left alone, to go her own way. Hence the paradox that the Confederacy might lose all the battles and campaigns and still emerge victorious. She had merely to hold the field long enough to weary the North with fighting; merely to persuade the North that she was unconquerable, or that the price of Northern victory was too high.

Such a strategy meant that the Confederacy ought to have avoided pitched battles, to have conserved her resources, and to have done everything possible to buy time: the major problem was to endure, not necessarily to prevail. Given the relatively easy victory Generals Joseph E. Johnston and Pierre G. T. Beauregard won at First Manassas (Bull Run) in September, 1861, however, President Jefferson Davis was emboldened to think beyond mere survival. If the Confederacy could meet the Union's armies on roughly equal terms and win major battles, he may have reasoned, there was no need to trade space for time.

In any event, Davis' major policy decisions had the effect of meeting the Union's challenges on the Union's terms. He attempted to hold everywhere at once by putting masses of Confederate troops in opposition to Federal concentrations, thus insuring the inevitability of pitched battles—many of which his forces were able to win. The strategy of inflicting punishment on the Yankee invaders in such a way as to make maximum use of the men he had within the Confederacy's vast open spaces was adopted—when it was adopted at all—not by design, but because it was applied by natural leaders such as Nathan Bedford Forrest who knew of no other way in which they could keep their small forces in the war.

The great battles—Manassas, the Seven Days, Sharpsburg, Fredericksburg, Chancellorsville, Gettysburg—have attracted so much attention that the other war—the one Forrest fought— hardly seems to belong to the same conflict. Many of the engagements Forrest turned into victories were on a scale only slightly larger than that of Sacramento, and most of them followed the same pattern: he won the field, only to give it up at the end of the day's work so that the Union troops could bury their many dead. Accordingly, at first glance there seems to be little to note in what he accomplished, especially when a Sacramento must be evaluated alongside Sharpsburg.

Still, one wonders what might have happened if Jefferson Davis had tried to do for the Confederacy what Nathan Bedford Forrest actually did for the nation's northwest corner. Such a line of curiosity leads to another interesting but unproductive question: What might Forrest have become if he had been a Virginian who was educated as a soldier?

As it was, Shadrach Forrest—the general's great-grandfather—had left Virginia for Tennessee as early as 1740. In 1821, when Nathan Bedford Forrest was born near Tullahoma, conditions in the Duck River country were still primitive and only the basic skills—reading, writing, and arithmetic—could be acquired. As the oldest boy in a growing family, Nathan's duties around the homeplace took most of his time and energy. The death of his father made him—at sixteen—a leader whether he wanted to be one or not: his five brothers were his first troops, and four of them were later to follow him into battle.

Once the family farm was producing something more than a bare living and his brothers could manage it in his absence, Nathan Forrest went out to Texas to join the Republic's army. When he got there, he found that there was no need for his services and that he would have to work his way back to Tennessee. This he did, moving from farm to farm, always earning his meals and shelter. By 1842 he had joined a relative in Hernando, Mississippi, in operating a store. During the next nine years he invested his profits in land and cattle and amassed something of a fortune. After he moved to Memphis in the early 1850's, he engaged in the slave trade for a time—but his wealth was such that he could afford to keep Negro families together, provide them with new clothes and decent food, and treat them in a manner that was far more humane than the kind of care they usually received. Toward the end of the decade, however, he closed out his businesses and concentrated on developing his large plantations.

In growing up, Nathan Forrest accumulated the respect of

his fellowmen as well as money. As a boy, while he and some other children were gathering blackberries one day, a rattlesnake broke up the party; Forrest, who stayed when the others ran away, found a stick (which he held in his fighting hand, his left) and flailed away at his enemy until he could land the killing blow. Later, in Memphis, an angered mob gathered to lynch a prisoner in the city's jail: Forrest rushed through the crowd, waved a knife in his left hand, threatened to strike the next man to make a move, and persuaded the astonished throng to let the law take its course.

When Tennessee seceded from the Union and joined the Confederate States of America, Forrest enlisted as a private in Captain Josiah White's Tennessee Mounted Rifles Company. Private Forrest's standing in west Tennessee was such, though, that in July, 1861, he was asked to recruit a battalion of five hundred "mounted rangers." Men were eager to serve under his leadership, but not many of them could bring even a shotgun or a pistol with them when they reported for duty, and the Confederate government was not able to provide any weapons, horses, or equipment to an outfit so far away from Richmond. Forrest took a group of purchasing agents northward and bought supplies for his men. The funds came from his own fortune.

By contrast, some of the great-grandsons of the neighbors old Shadrach Forrest had left behind in Virginia had been graduated from the United States Military Academy at West Point, had served in the Mexican War of 1846–47 and in the old Army, and were now being commissioned as generals in the Confederate field forces. They were able and accomplished gentlemen who would win much glory for the cause, but the war they were to fight was to be the kind they knew best—the massed engagements, strategic maneuvers, and concentrations of firepower which had been characteristic of formal combat since the invention of gunpowder.

Out west, where Forrest was to do his fighting, there would be dashing movement and the ignition of gunpowder—but in most respects, the similarity ended there. He would lead as he had lived, by fitting his resources to the problem at hand, but he would do that with a mind that was free from inhibitions imposed by classical precedents and formal rules. Fortunately, he brought to his new calling precisely those traits of character West Point strives to develop; shrewd warrior though he was, authentic military genius though he may have been, Forrest was first of all an honorable man. And ultimately he would win the respect of the Union's most seasoned and skillful commanders—Ulysses S. Grant and William Tecumseh Sherman.

In the century of the Great Remembering, which began in 1865 as soon as the guns were silent, some would claim that Lieutenant General Nathan Bedford Forrest was the greatest soldier on either side in the Civil War, greater even than General Robert E. Lee. Perhaps he was. No one will ever know for sure, for it is impossible to rank the performance of leaders when the challenges each of them had to face were not identical. Comparisons of Forrest and Lee are especially difficult to draw: the two men had almost nothing in common except the will to win and fierce loyalty to the cause they both served, each according to his capabilities, with such gallantry.

— 4 —

Not long after the Battle of Sacramento, Colonel Forrest was ordered to take his cavalrymen to Fort Donelson, a Confederate strong point on the Cumberland River in northern Tennessee. In early February, 1862, a Union general called Ulysses S. Grant brought a Federal force down from Illinois and captured Fort Henry, ten miles or so to the west of Fort Donelson. Grant then turned eastward to complete his campaign.

Fort Donelson, Grant's new objective, was commanded by General John B. Floyd and garrisoned by about 15,000 troops under Generals Gideon J. Pillow and Simon Bolivar Buckner. Albert Sidney Johnston, the general commanding the Department of Tennessee, had ordered the fort held if possible but evacuated if necessary: even at that early stage of the war, he recognized that the Confederacy could not afford to lose even a company merely to hold a piece of ground.

First contact was made on February 11, 1862, by Forrest about three miles west of Fort Donelson when he turned back a Union cavalry column. As at Sacramento, Forrest had to use shock and surprise to cover his relative weakness in numbers.

The next morning he took a larger force out over the same route, checked the Union advance for a time, then withdrew to the Confederate trenches outside Fort Donelson.

On February 14, with Grant's men drawn up against the trenches on the west, Flag Officer Andrew Foote brought a flotilla of gunboats up the Cumberland River in the hope of silencing Fort Donelson's batteries. After a vicious artillery duel, which Forrest watched with excited interest, Foote's gunboats had to withdraw. During the day, however, Grant had received enough reinforcements to bring his strength up to about 25,000 men.

General Floyd, aware of the Union buildup but mistaken in his belief that Grant now had at least 50,000 troops, decided to attack the southern end of the Union line in order to open an escape route. This was his only possible course of action, for the Cumberland River to the east was too deep to ford and he had no other means of getting his command across.

On the morning of the fifteenth, while Grant was riding off to spend the day in a conference with Flag Officer Foote a number of miles away, General Pillow gave the signal for the attack to begin. Forrest led the advance. Union resistance was stubborn at first, but by mid-morning a Confederate cyclone was pressing the Federals back. The Union commander of that portion of the line sent a plea to Grant for reinforcements, but Grant was gone and none came.

Just as confusion and dismay reached a peak among the Yankees, Forrest led his troops in a powerful assault against the Union flank and rear. "Charge!" Forrest shouted, and his men routed the enemy: panic broke out among the Federals and spread northward rapidly.

While his cavalrymen rampaged through the remnants of Union troops, Forrest found General Bushrod Johnson and begged him to order a general assault to complete the destruction of Grant's entire army. Johnson declined, saying that he lacked authority. Forrest, baffled and irate after this encounter with a man who would let victory slip away simply because of some rule, could not reach General Pillow—who was at the other end of the Confederate line—and so he returned to try to accomplish with his own men a task that ought to have been undertaken by the whole garrison.

Forrest, his face red with anger and his saber swinging, led his men in the capture of a Union battery of six guns which had been vexing him. His horse was shot, but it did not fall until Forrest was attacking a second battery: Forrest got another mount, took his men onward, then was thrown to the ground when a cannonball struck the second animal who was unfortunate enough to have him for a rider. Just as Forrest was getting up from that spill, General Pillow ordered him to gather all of the arms and equipment his men could carry and to retire to the trenches.

If General Floyd had meant for the attack on the fifteenth to open the way for a breakout, that part of the order had been ignored or misunderstood by those who were supposed to begin the withdrawal from Fort Donelson once Forrest had opened the way: in any event, no Confederates had left while the opportunity existed. That night, Floyd called Forrest, Buckner, and Pillow into a council of war to discuss the situation. To Forrest's amazement, the subject Floyd really wanted to explore was the surrender of the garrison.

Forrest immediately protested that the men were not hemmed in and were certainly not defeated. Pillow agreed, but Floyd and Buckner favored giving in. While the argument ran on, Forrest slipped out. He found two men and a citizen of the nearby village of Dover, sent them on a scouting expedition to see if the Clarksville road was open and if Lick Creek could be forded, and waited. When they returned with good news, he returned to the meeting and urged his superiors to begin the evacuation of the fort. But he was too late: the other generals had already decided to surrender.

For his part, Forrest intended to get his men out. He even offered to conduct the rear-guard action so that the entire garrison might escape via the Clarksville road and the ford across Lick Creek, but his offer was rebuffed. Forrest then announced that he would not surrender himself or his command, and he left. By morning, all of his men were twenty miles south of Fort Donelson.

Generals Floyd and Pillow had passed the command of Fort Donelson to Buckner, and by daylight they had crossed the Cumberland in boats and were gone. Buckner accepted Grant's demand for "unconditional surrender" and went into captivity along with more than 10,000 Confederate troops.

Forrest was openly disgusted. He was convinced that at least two thirds of the garrison could have escaped, and he was willing to believe that the entire force might have withdrawn. His first exposure to men who fought according to the book had left him unimpressed, to say the least; but to his chagrin, he was ordered to report to Nashville to serve once more under General Floyd.

Nashville, Forrest found, was a city gone berserk. The disaster at Fort Donelson three days before had unhinged the population, and even the soldiers who were supposed to defend the place had been infected by the panic. Floyd, who had already exhibited his dislike for disintegrating situations, turned command of Nashville over to Forrest and fled.

Forrest moved quickly to place guards over the enormous quantities of supplies no one else had bothered to protect or remove—except by looting. At one point he had to turn back a mob that was bent on plunder: with his saber drawn and the look of battle on his face, he rode into the unruly crowd, hammered one opponent into unconsciousness with the butt of a six-shooter, and restored order. Next, Forrest assembled every mule and wagon in the region and started the shipment of the supplies to the south. He did not abandon the city to Federal troops until all public property had been removed.

Once Forrest had reported to General Albert Sidney Johnston at Murfreesboro, he was ordered to take his men to Huntsville, Alabama, where he was to grant them a furlough. On March 10, the day on which they were to return, every man was present for duty.

By early April, Johnston's Army of Tennessee—of which Forrest's command was a part—was moving northward from Corinth, Mississippi, toward the bend in the Tennessee River near Pittsburg Landing, Tennessee, where General U. S. Grant's army was concentrated. Johnston knew that Grant was about to receive reinforcements from General Don Carlos Buell at Nashville, and he meant to strike before his chances of eliminating the forces at Pittsburg Landing ran out.

Johnston launched his attack on the morning of April 6. Confederate troops stormed through the Union bivouac area near

Shiloh Church and charged on toward the banks of the river in the hope of winning a quick and decisive victory, but before long Federal resistance stiffened and a bloody stalemate seemed to be setting in. In the confusion, Forrest could find neither General Johnston nor General John C. Breckinridge, the commander to whom he had been assigned, so he made up his own orders and took his men into that part of the battle in which it appeared he could do the most good.

General B. F. Cheatham's division had been thrown back because of Union artillery batteries which dominated the zone in which he wanted to make his thrust. Forrest reported to Cheatham and asked him for orders to charge the Federal guns. "I cannot give you orders," Cheatham replied. "If you make the charge, it will be on your own responsibility."

"Then I'll do it," Forrest answered. In a matter of minutes, the Yankee artillery pieces had been captured.

Forrest then took his men over to join in the battle against Union General Benjamin Prentiss' troops in one of the fiercest fights of the day. He arrived just in time to seal off the demoralized Yankee force from the Tennessee River, then he pushed on toward Pittsburg Landing. The deeper he got into the Federal positions, the more convinced Forrest became that one more major assault by Confederate units would clinch the victory. He sent a report of the deteriorating situation by courier to General Leonidas Polk, but the orders he received were to withdraw. He had no choice but to comply.

During the night, Forrest went out on a scouting expedition of his own. After moving along the bank of the Tennessee for some distance, he was able to see Buell's men pouring across the river to reinforce Grant. Forrest hurried back to report the news to General Beauregard, who had assumed command after Albert Sidney Johnston had been killed that afternoon, but he did more: he urged the launching of a night attack to destroy the enemy. If the Confederates did not act, Forrest warned, the Army of Tennessee would be "whipped like hell before ten o'clock tomorrow." Forrest was told to return to his regiment.

Forrest was entirely correct in his prediction. The reinforced Union army counterattacked with a vengeance the next morning, and by afternoon Beauregard was in full retreat. The commander of his rear guard was Colonel Nathan Bedford Forrest.

As Beauregard withdrew toward Corinth, Forrest and his men lagged behind to punish any Union columns Grant might send out in pursuit. Near Monterey, about halfway between Pittsburg Landing and Corinth, a unit from General William T. Sherman's division marched into an ambush Forrest had prepared. At the critical moment, Forrest shouted "Charge!" and his men tore into the flanks of the bewildered Yankees. As always, he was at the forefront of the advance. Suddenly, he found himself surrounded by Union soldiers who were determined to kill him. A Federal infantryman shoved the muzzle of his rifle almost against Forrest's side and fired. Other Yankee soldiers hit his horse in two places. Forrest stayed in the saddle, urged his wounded horse to leap ahead, and shot his way out of the trap.

Sherman, stunned by the ferocity of Forrest's attack, called off the pursuit of Beauregard's beaten army. It was his first brush with the rugged Tennessean, and he was impressed.

— 5 —

Forrest was sent to his home in Memphis to recuperate from the wound he had received at Monterey, but he could not stand enforced idleness and returned to his command at Corinth only three weeks from the day he had been shot. To his vast displeasure, he was forced to undergo an operation and to spend several more weeks in bed after he reported for duty.

He had a right to be impatient, for there was much work ahead. General Braxton Bragg was about to lead a thrust into central Tennessee, and Forrest's cavalry was to have a part in that operation.

In mid-June, when Forrest reported to Bragg at Chattanooga, he learned that his troops would have to stay behind and that he must build a new outfit. He was disappointed, and so were his men—but the change had to be made, or so the superior officers who had read the book claimed. The soldiers who had fought under his command since Sacramento never forgot him; years afterward, when their grandchildren pestered them with questions about what they did during the Great War, they replied: "I was with Forrest." So, incidentally, did thousands of other

Confederate veterans who had no right to make that proud claim.

Forrest quickly assembled a fighting force to replace his old "mounted rangers." While he was whipping his new unit into shape, he sent scouts northward to locate the enemy. By July 12, acting on the reports his scouts had brought back, he was just outside Murfreesboro and ready for action.

The three Union detachments in the Murfreesboro vicinity were completely unaware of Forrest's presence. Even after some of his men had opened their assault against one Federal unit, the others were unable to move to the assistance of their compatriots because Forrest's troops had rushed through the village to pin them in place. After making sure that the isolation of the first Union force was complete, Forrest called for a truce and demanded the surrender of the defenders: he stated that the other Federal units in the area had been captured and that he was concentrating his entire force around their position, but that he desired to avoid further bloodshed and would accept their immediate capitulation. If his offer was refused, Forrest added, he would give no quarter to those who resisted. The Union commander gave in.

Forrest quickly shifted the bulk of his troops to the next Federal strong point. Once again he presented his demand for surrender during a truce, and the Union officer in command saw the futility of holding out. This led to the capture of the third Union element and brought the battle to a close.

A report on this action was filed by Confederate General J. P. McCown. It said:

> Forrest attacked Murfreesboro at five o'clock Sunday morning, July 13th, and captured two brigadier-generals, staff and field officers, and 1200 men; burned $200,000 worth of stores; captured sufficient stores with those burned to amount to $500,000; 60 wagons; 300 mules; 150 or 200 horses, and field-battery of four pieces; destroyed the railroad and depot at Murfreesboro. Had to retreat to McMinnville owing to large number of prisoners to be guarded. Loss of 16 or 18 killed, 25 or 30 wounded.

To his old standbys—shock and surprise—Forrest had added a new tactic: bluff. He was to use it time and again, and his subordinates would too: in several instances they won the surrender of superior Union forces merely by sending in demands for capitulation in Forrest's name even though he was miles away.

At one point during the Battle of Murfreesboro, someone suggested to Forrest that it was enough to capture the commanding general and his staff, to free the Confederate prisoners held in the town's jail, and to rattle the Yankee troops in the besieged detachments. "I did not come here to make half a job of it," Forrest retorted, "I'm going to have them all." This mood lingered on after Murfreesboro: Forrest advanced to within sight of Nashville, burned a number of railroad bridges, disrupted communications, captured supplies and a few Union soldiers, and dared the Federal commander to come out and stop him.

For the next few weeks Forrest kept up his series of strikes against trestles, outposts, supply trains, and Union detachments that blundered across his path. "Destroy Forrest," Union General Don Carlos Buell ordered his commanders in central Tennessee, but he added: "if you can." They could not, and one by one they ruefully admitted it, blaming their failure on the hot weather, a surly native population, and comparatively slow horses. General George H. Thomas almost caught him once, but Forrest's scouts gave timely warning and Forrest merely moved his men into the woods and watched the Union column ride past; later, when about half of Forrest's men were detected near McMinnville, they turned about, outran their pursuers, and rejoined the main body after marching cross-country for some hours.

For the rest of September, 1862, Forrest led his cavalrymen into eastern Kentucky as a part of Braxton Bragg's invasion force. As before, he tore up railroads, raided Union supply points, and raised general hell. When he was ordered to report to Bragg on the last day of that month, he got his reward: he was directed to turn the command of his cavalry over to another officer and to recruit another body of men.

— 6 —

By this time, Forrest had become famous among Confederate sympathizers in central Tennessee. He fought as they liked to see a man fight, and he was one of them—his boyhood had been spent in the Duck River country. When he asked for volunteers to fill a new regiment, men poured in to serve under his command.

Grant had selected Vicksburg, Mississippi, as his next major objective, and he was massing troops and supplies in the northern part of that state during the fall and winter of 1862. To the east, around Nashville, Union General William Rosecrans faced Braxton Bragg's Army of Tennessee. Railroads in western Tennessee served both as Grant's principal means of supply and as a means of moving troops back to Rosecrans if Bragg became too much of a problem.

In mid-December, Forrest took his new brigade into west Tennessee on a raiding mission that was to serve several purposes. He could not have picked a more miserable season in which to launch his campaign: winter had come down early and with savage ferocity. But he paid no attention to the cold, the snow, or the freezing rain that would have driven many another commander into winter quarters. The time had come to strike, and he did not mean to let the opportunity pass.

Forrest took his men across the Tennessee River at Clifton at night on December 15 and 16. Once the ferrying operation had been completed, he gave the order to sink the boats and he pressed northwestward about thirty miles to Lexington, where he met and defeated a small but determined Union blocking force on the eighteenth. News of his presence in Tennessee was spread to all Federal commands; telegraph wires carried the urgent message: "Get Forrest!"

On December 19, Forrest made a feint toward Jackson, about twenty-five miles west of Lexington, and drove the Union garrison into that town's defenses while some of his men tore up the railroad that connected Jackson and Corinth, Mississippi. From Jackson, Forrest led his men northward along the railroad for more than seventy miles to Union City—a town he captured without having to fire a shot. During that rapid advance, Forrest's men systematically destroyed bridges, culverts, stations, and even lengthy stretches of track.

Forrest pressed northward into Kentucky and destroyed the railroad as far as Moscow before turning back to Union City. By Christmas Day, Union commanders were frantic: 125 Union transports were sent down the Mississippi to obtain troops from Grant, and detachments throughout Tennessee and Kentucky were rushed into position to trap the bold Confederate.

At Dresden, about twenty miles southeast of Union City, Forrest had to cross the north fork of the Obion River if he was ever to get southward to safety. Union troops had destroyed all but one of the bridges over the stream, but Forrest's scouts found it. A great deal of repair work had to be done on the structure before it could be used, however, and Forrest grabbed an axe and helped his men cut reinforcing timbers. When the bridge was ready, he drove the first wagon across to test the span's strength. By December 29, his entire command—except for two captured wagons loaded with ammunition, which slipped off the narrow causeway—had reached the south bank.

Scouts then brought in reports that two formidable bodies of Union troops were closing in—one from the east, the other dead ahead. To the south, another Federal force was waiting to annihilate him if he made it to the Tennessee River. Along the river itself, Union gunboats were making sure that he would have no means of crossing.

Forrest had to decide whether to make a run for the river or to try to defeat first one nearby Union detachment and then the other. Most of his objectives had been achieved. The Mobile & Ohio Railroad was in ruins. His men, many of whom had carried flintlock rifles and squirrel guns when the campaign began, were now armed with the latest U. S. Army weapons. Grant had been forced to send troops northward from Mississippi, and Rosecrans was nervous about his western flank. To run would not be ignoble, but he knew that he would have a fight at the Tennessee River if not before: that being the case, he elected to eliminate what could be a vexing pursuit force by striking the Federal unit at Parker's Crossroads.

Since time was of the essence and Forrest had to be prepared to fight the second Union detachment at any moment, he made maximum use of his artillery in attacking the first Federal ele-

ment at Parker's Crossroads so that the major portion of his
men would be available to meet a new threat if necessary. Success came quickly, and flags of truce brought a halt to the fighting while Forrest sent in a message demanding immediate surrender.

Suddenly, the second Union detachment arrived and attacked
Forrest's rear. "What will we do, General?" an astonished soldier asked.

"We'll charge both ways," Forrest replied.

Unfortunately, the Union attack had struck the place where
some of Forrest's men were holding the horses for others who
were taking part in the battle. Forrest realized that he had to
withdraw at once. He organized a rear guard, pressing into
service every man he could get. "General," one man protested,
"I am unarmed—I have neither gun, pistol, nor sword."

That made no difference to Forrest. "Get into line and advance on the enemy with the rest," he ordered, "I want to make
as big a show as possible." He charged with sufficient ferocity
to discourage the Federals from all thought of pursuit, ex-
tricated his command from what could have been a crushing
disaster, and headed for the Tennessee River.

The jubilant Union commanders claimed a great victory.
Forrest, they reported, had been whipped: there remained only
the task of hunting down the scattered remnants of his brigade.

The rejoicing proved to be premature. As soon as Forrest
reached Lexington that night, which was New Year's Eve, he
sent a detachment of scouts under his brother, Jeffery, to the
Tennessee River near Clifton to bail out the sunken ferries.
After a brief skirmish with Union cavalry the next morning,
Forrest brought his troops to the crossing site. He first sent
the artillery to the south bank to cover the operation; next
came the wagons filled with supplies captured from the Federals. The men were ferried across, but most of the horses had
to swim. By the morning of January 2, 1863, the entire brigade
was on the south bank in friendly territory once more.

Between December 15 and January 1, Forrest had taken his
men on a march which covered three hundred miles in the
worst possible weather. Roads along his route had been terrible.
Enemy opposition had been constant: he had fought at least
one skirmish a day, and on some there had been two or more.

With only 2500 men, he had disturbed the peace of Union troops from Mississippi almost to Nashville. Grant was forced to abandon the rail system in west Tennessee and shift his line of communication to the Mississippi River, thus accepting delay in the buildup for his Vicksburg operation and giving up the hope of drawing reinforcements from Rosecrans.

— 7 —

At the end of January, 1863, General Joseph Wheeler, chief of cavalry in the Department of Tennessee, directed Forrest to move to a position along the Cumberland River from which he could attack Union waterborne traffic. Forrest established an ambush near Palmyra and waited for an opportunity to use it.

In the meantime, Wheeler had what he thought was a better idea—an attack against Fort Donelson. Forrest saw little merit in Wheeler's plan and said so, but Wheeler insisted. "If I am killed in this fight," Forrest told his chief of staff, "you will see that justice is done me by officially stating that I protested against this attack, and that I am not willing to be held responsible for any disaster that may result."

Despite his gloomy forebodings, Forrest gave Wheeler his full cooperation once the order had been issued. On February 3, in bitter cold, the assault was opened. Forrest saw a detachment of Union soldiers leaving the fort, assumed that they were the vanguard of a breakout attempt, and charged into them. The Federals broke and ran for the safety of the fort, and Forrest pursued. Suddenly, Forrest's men were cut down by withering rifle and artillery fire. His horse was hit, and he fell. While Union artillery poured canister and grape into the shattered Confederate ranks, Forrest led his men out of the danger and reorganized them.

Forrest then took his men through the village of Dover, cleared most of it, captured a generous supply of blankets which his men needed desperately, and ordered a second charge against the Federal breastworks. Once again his horse was shot, and Forrest was badly shaken up by the fall. Wheeler finally called off the attack and ordered a retreat.

That night, Generals Wheeler, Forrest, and John A. Wharton gathered in a farmhouse to discuss the day's work and to prepare an official report. Major Charles W. Anderson, Forrest's chief of staff, rode up outside, but he was so nearly frozen he could not dismount. Forrest went out, helped him slide down from the saddle, and took him into the house. Two officers were sleeping in a bed: Forrest ordered them to get up, then he pulled the covers over Anderson. That done, he stretched out on the floor by the fire.

Wharton had just said something about the performance of Forrest's men in the assault. "I have no fault to find with my men," Forrest said. "In both charges they did their duty as they have always done." Wheeler assured Forrest that he would say as much in his report. "General Wheeler," Forrest replied, "I advised against this attack, and said all a subordinate officer should have said against it, and nothing you can now say or do will bring back my brave men lying dead or wounded and freezing around that fort tonight. I mean no disrespect to you; you know my feelings of personal friendship for you; you can have my sword if you demand it; but there is one thing I want you to put in that report to General Bragg—tell him that I will be in my coffin before I will fight again under your command."

Joe Wheeler understood. "Forrest," he said quietly, "I cannot take your saber, and I regret exceedingly your determination. As the commanding officer I take all of the blame and responsibility for this failure."

Forrest's brigade camped near Columbia, Tennessee, for the next few weeks. During this interlude, Forrest—who knew almost nothing about drill—insisted on holding two dress reviews a week in order to tighten the troops' sense of organization. Forrest's scouts brought in a report that there was only a light Union guard around 2000 mules at Nashville and he requested permission to lead a force in to capture them, but permission was denied. After some grumbling, Forrest turned his attention back to drill.

Action came in early March, 1863, when Forrest was ordered to join General Earl Van Dorn's wing of the Army of Tennessee in an operation to block a probe Rosecrans was sending southward from Nashville. In the Battle of Thompson's Station on March 5, Forrest's artillery caught the Yankees in their flank and saved a portion of the Confederate line; later that day he had another horse shot from beneath him while leading the charge which resulted in the surrender of the Federal force.

By the twenty-fifth, Forrest was striking at Brentwood, nine miles or so north of the Union base at Franklin and only ten miles south of Nashville. The plan of attack called for him to join Colonel J. W. Starnes' troops—a brigade Forrest had recruited and led—at Brentwood at daylight, but he was late. Starnes, thinking that a major change in the scheme must have been made, withdrew; actually, Forrest was approaching Brentwood by a side road. Forrest arrived, noted Starnes' absence, made a quick estimate of the situation, and decided to attack anyway.

Starnes had aroused the Union garrison at Brentwood, and the Federal commander politely declined Forrest's demand that he surrender. Not long after Forrest's men intercepted a Yankee wagon train as it was attempting to get away, the artillery went into position and prepared to open a bombardment. Forrest scattered his men in a wide circle around the town. This was enough to convince the Union commander that he had no chance of surviving: Forrest had won without losing a man.

From Brentwood, Forrest pressed on to the stockade that guarded the bridge over the Harpeth River. After one round of artillery had been fired at the Yankees, Forrest ordered Major Anderson to take in a flag of truce with the usual message. Anderson, it turned out, could not find a white handkerchief to tie to the tip of his saber. "Strip off your shirt, Major," Forrest commanded. The flag was hardly white, but it served its purpose: the 230 officers and men in the stockade were added to over 500 who had been captured earlier that day at Brentwood.

Forrest's luck seemed to run out as he was returning south that afternoon. A Union pursuit force created a panic in his rear guard, and for a time it looked as though the unseemly emotion might spread throughout his column. Forrest rode back, grabbed a shotgun from a soldier, ordered the fleeing troops to halt and reassemble, and fired into them when they failed to heed his sharp command. The panic ceased at once. Forrest reorganized the men and turned them against the Yankee cavalry, and the march continued.

Another combined operation at Franklin on April 10 required Forrest's services, but his role in the fight was relatively minor. Captain S. L. Freeman, Forrest's artillery commander, was captured, however, and Union soldiers shot and killed him when he proved to be too tired to run as they commanded. This atrocity enraged Forrest and his men: from that time onward, they fought with Freeman much on their minds.

— 8 —

While Forrest was operating in central Tennessee in early April, 1863, Union Colonel Abel D. Streight was preparing a task force which he would lead through northern Alabama into northwestern Georgia to cut the vital Confederate rail supply line that enabled Braxton Bragg at Chattanooga to draw support from Atlanta. Federal commanders put a high priority on Streight's mission and saw to it that he had ample escort until he reached the hilly country around Tuscumbia, Alabama, in which a large number of Union sympathizers lived.

Forrest was ordered southward to deal with Streight as soon as the venture became known to Bragg. Soon after Forrest reached northern Alabama, his scouts located Streight's column and reported back. Forrest understood at once what Streight was attempting to do and planned his counterstroke immediately.

Streight, aware that Forrest had been sent to stop him, moved quickly—but Forrest made better time. The two forces met at the top of Sand Mountain on the morning of April 30 and fought a bloody skirmish which neither side really won. Streight pressed on to the east, Forrest pursued, and a running fight—marked by frequent ambush actions—developed.

During the battle atop Sand Mountain, an artillery lieutenant incurred Forrest's wrath by losing two guns to the enemy. It was not unusual for Forrest to become irate over such incidents, and no one paid much attention at the time. Later, however, the consequences would be tragic.

Although Forrest would have relished a chance to stop Streight at any point, he felt that he had his enemy under firm

control and could afford to let him drive eastward until the
Union troops were exhausted and supplies were running out.
For his part, Forrest had made sure at the outset that his own
men were adequately provided with rations and ammunition,
and he regulated his pursuit in such a way as to give his cavalrymen slightly more rest than the Yankees were able to enjoy.

From Sand Mountain, Streight drove eastward through
Blountsville, captured all of the area's horses and mules as replacements for his jaded animals, and continued the march
when Forrest's men struck his rear guard. Streight crossed the
Black Warrior River east of Blountsville and burned the bridge
behind him: for a time, he assumed, he was safe.

Forrest galloped up to the burned bridge just in time to
capture a Yankee soldier who had tarried on the west bank of
the Black Warrior a moment too long. Once the prisoner was
out of the way, Forrest noticed a farmhouse not far away. A
widow and her two daughters lived there, he learned, and one
of the girls—Emma Sanson, who was sixteen—offered to show
him a ford which might enable his men to cross the river without having to take a long and time-consuming detour. Her
mother was shrill in her objections, but Emma was determined
to do what she could to help.

Emma Sanson climbed on the back of Forrest's horse, put
her arms around the general's waist, and told him which way
to ride. When they neared the ford, she told him that they had
better go the rest of the way on foot. She started to lead the
way, but Forrest insisted that she stay behind him lest a Union
sharpshooter notice their advance. When he had inspected the
ford, he took Emma back to the farmhouse. Her mother was too
grateful to have her back safely to realize that Emma had just
become a heroine.

Forrest took his men across the ford the brave girl had
pointed out, struck Streight a surprise blow, and chased him on
through the rugged country past Gadsden toward Rome, Georgia, which was Streight's objective. While his men kept pressure
applied to the Union rear guard, Forrest sent a courier to Rome
to alert the Home Guard to the possibility that Streight was
coming: he asked that the bridge over the Coosa River be
either defended or burned so that the Federal raiders could not
reach the railroad and cut it.

By May 1, Forrest's troops were few in number. Streight had done a magnificent job of gathering up all of the serviceable horses along the route, and Forrest had no choice but to let men and animals drop out of his column whenever a horse threw a shoe or went lame. With only a little over 500 men, Forrest was outnumbered by Streight by roughly three to one. Moreover, the running fights had depleted Forrest's ammunition supply, and nothing could be done about that.

Streight anticipated that the bridge at Rome might be destroyed. He sent ahead a picked force of 200 men under Captain Milton Russell to secure the crossing, but in vain: Russell was repulsed by the Home Guard. Streight was no quitter, and he ordered a nightlong march in the hope of reaching Russell in time to defeat the bridge's defenders.

At Lawrence, ten miles or so west of Rome, Streight called a halt at about nine o'clock on the morning of May 3 so that his men could feed the animals and get a short rest. His troops were utterly exhausted, and many of them could not stay on their feet long enough to take care of their horses.

While Streight was trying to rouse his weary men, he heard Forrest's hoofbeats in the west. Forrest had given his troops ten hours of rest while Streight had been slogging eastward during the night, and he had been able to overtake his enemy with no strain at all. Streight deployed his men for battle, but as soon as they got to their positions most of them went to sleep.

Forrest quickly called for a truce and sent in a message demanding that Streight surrender. Out of respect for the gallantry the Union force had displayed, he omitted the "Murfreesboro provision"—the warning that the survivors would be given no quarter if a battle had to be fought.

Streight and Forrest sat down together. Forrest observed that further resistance on Streight's part would be suicidal, for Confederate forces (Forrest said) stood between Lawrence and Rome, and (Forrest said) the men he had with him could easily annihilate the Union raiders. Streight consulted his officers who advised surrender. Finally, he agreed.

The effort Streight had made to reach and cut the Chattanooga-Atlanta railroad had put Forrest and his men to a maximum test. In order to bring Streight's raid to a halt, Forrest had led his troops well over 150 miles; during one fifty-seven-hour stretch, he had kept them in the saddle for fifty-two; and along the way, Streight had obliged him to fight one skirmish after another. At the last, Forrest had been forced to make maximum use of bluff in order to win: fortunately for both sides, he had been able to make his 500 men seem as powerful as 5000 to the worn-out but still game Union commander.

After Streight's surrender, Forrest took his men back to central Tennessee. At Columbia, the artillery lieutenant he had scolded at Sand Mountain asked to see him, and Forrest left the room in which he was engaged in a conference to join the young officer in the hall. In his right hand, Forrest carried the pen-knife he had been toying with while the discussions droned on.

The lieutenant, it turned out, was furious because Forrest had directed that he be transferred to another outfit. Forrest had not taken any other action against the young officer, but that made no difference: the transfer, the lieutenant maintained, was a reflection on his courage. When Forrest refused to rescind the order, the lieutenant drew a pistol and fired. Forrest stepped aside, but the large caliber round struck his left hip. He reached out with his left hand and prevented the lieutenant from firing a second shot, and he raised the penknife in his right hand to his mouth: with his teeth he opened the knife, and a moment later he plunged the blade into the lieutenant's stomach. The young officer ran out of the building, reached a nearby store, and collapsed.

Forrest, bleeding profusely, calmly walked down the street to a doctor's office and asked if the wound seemed fatal. The doctor could not say for sure, but he admitted that he thought that it was. Forrest borrowed a pistol from a staff officer and went in search of the lieutenant.

Several men tried to restrain Forrest. "Get out of my way," he ordered. "He has mortally wounded me, and I intend to kill him before I die." A crowd had gathered around the lieutenant, however, and someone stopped Forrest by telling him that the officer was dying. Forrest's rage passed, and he directed that the lieutenant be taken to the hotel and given medical aid. By this time Forrest was about to collapse from loss of blood: friends carried him to a house and got him into bed.

Two days later, when the lieutenant realized that he was about to die, he asked General Forrest to come to him. Forrest came, on a stretcher. "General," the young man said, "I was not willing to go away without seeing you in person and saying to you how thankful I am that I am the one who is to die and that you are spared to the country. What I did, I did in a moment of rashness, and I want your forgiveness."

Forrest took the lieutenant's hand in his and assured him that he was forgiven. The general wept like a child.

— 9 —

In the mid-summer of 1863, General Rosecrans decided that Bragg's Confederates had held Chattanooga long enough. Using Nashville as his base, he began a careful offensive to the southeast. Shelbyville, a town at which most of Bragg's wagon trains were concentrated, was one of Rosecrans' first objectives.

General Joe Wheeler was given the mission of protecting Shelbyville, and Forrest was ordered to join him there. When they were to rendezvous, Wheeler fought off one Union assault after another not only to protect the wagons but in order to buy time for Forrest, but the pressure of the Federal attacks was too great: he finally had to give up the bridge he had been holding all day, and he even forced his horse to leap into the Duck River when he saw that he was cut off.

Forrest's men took a wide detour around Shelbyville, found another place to cross, and joined the main body of Bragg's Army of Tennessee at Tullahoma the next day. Wheeler's gallant delaying action had enabled the wagons to clear Shelbyville even though he had not been able to hold the way open for Forrest—and the fact that he had risked so much to save Forrest was not overlooked.

During Bragg's retreat to Chattanooga, Forrest fought a series of rear guard actions against Union cavalry detachments. After one of these, as Forrest was making sure that all of his men had fallen back, he noticed a woman standing outside her cabin. She was irate: she shook her fist at the retreating soldiers and showered all of the abuse she could muster upon them. As Forrest rode by, she shouted: "You great big cowardly rascal, why don't you turn and fight like a man instead of running like a cur? I wish old Forrest was here, he'd make you fight!" Forrest laughed, and moved on.

Rosecrans' offensive was a plodding affair which dragged on through July and August while his superiors in Washington vexed him with messages which called for more speed and asked him for reports on Forrest's location. He had dispersed his forces in order to force Bragg out of Chattanooga, and he was extremely vulnerable to the kind of lightning battle Forrest liked to wage.

Forrest saw many possibilities for chipping Rosecrans' army to pieces, but none of his suggestions were accepted. Even so, he fought whenever he could—and in a fight at Tunnel Hill, not far from Dalton, Georgia, he was wounded slightly on September 3. That day, suffering from shock and loss of blood, Forrest consented to take a drink of whiskey: otherwise, he had no use for the stuff.

At Chickamauga, the great battle which was fought between September 18 and 20, 1863, Forrest commanded the cavalry forces on the right flank of Bragg's army. He fired the first shot as he led his men into contact with the Union forces in order to secure crossings over Chickamauga Creek, and he fired the last shot two days later as the beaten Yankees were fleeing northwestward toward Chattanooga. Otherwise, he had little opportunity to use his talents: he was merely a link in the chain of command, he carried out his missions with characteristic dash and efficiency, and he gave history a picture of a competent subordinate—the role to which he might have been doomed even if old Shadrach Forrest had remained in Virginia, after all.

Once the Yankees were driven off the battlefield at Chickamauga, however, Forrest organized a pursuit force and led it toward Chattanooga. In a skirmish with the Union rear guard, Forrest's horse was shot; Forrest plugged the wound with his finger until his men had cleared the Federal troops, then he removed it and let the animal die. By that time, Forrest had reached a point on Missionary Ridge from which he could observe the Union army inside Chattanooga. He scribbled a message to General Bragg which urged immediate pursuit of the beaten enemy. Bragg had other ideas, though, and Forrest was obliged to shift his forces to the northeast. As a result, the Union army inside Chattanooga had a chance to regroup, build fortifications, and check Bragg's futile attempts to force them out.

On September 28, Bragg sent a message relieving Forrest of his command. Forrest complied with the order, rode off to see Bragg, and cornered the commanding general of the Army of Tennessee in his own tent. Forrest, who had been silent as he rode to Bragg's command post with Dr. J. B. Cowan, was in a sour mood: Cowan noted that Forrest did not return the salute of a sentry, would not accept Bragg's hand, and got straight to the point. "I am not here to pass civilities or compliments with you," Forrest began, "but on other business." He recited a series of complaints against Bragg.

Then he concluded: "I have stood your meanness as long as I intend to. You have played the part of a damned scoundrel, and are a coward, and if you were any part of a man I would slap your jaws and force you to resent it. You may as well not issue any more orders to me, for I will not obey them, and I will hold you personally responsible for any further indignities you endeavor to inflict upon me. You have threatened to arrest me for not obeying your orders promptly. I dare you to do it, and I say to you that if you ever again try to interfere with me or cross my path it will be at the peril of your life."

That said, Forrest walked out of Bragg's tent.

Dr. Cowan remarked that Forrest had asked for much trouble. "He'll never say a word about it," Forrest replied. Forrest might have resigned, but he refused to do so lest anyone think he was trying to evade punishment. Bragg took no action, but in time to come he would get his revenge.

Back in August, while Rosecrans was pressing Bragg backward, Forrest had written Adjutant General Samuel Cooper in Richmond to suggest that he be given authority to raise and equip troops in northern Mississippi and western Tennessee and to operate as an independent commander for the purpose of denying the use of the Mississippi River to Union forces. Forrest's proposal reached President Jefferson Davis, but Davis wanted Bragg's comments. "I know no officer to whom I would sooner assign the duty," Bragg replied, "but it would deprive this army [the Army of Tennessee] of one of its greatest elements of strength to remove General Forrest."

Bragg, at the time, was right: he needed Forrest. He would

refuse Forrest's suggestions for aggressive action to defeat Rosecrans' columns one at a time, and later he would ignore Forrest's plea for instant pursuit of the Union army Bragg could not realize he had beaten at Chickamauga. But though he did not know what to do with Forrest, Bragg meant to keep him— and he held him until mid-October, even though he had summarily relieved Forrest of his command and even though in late September President Davis had approved Forrest's plan for closing the Mississippi to Federal navigation.

By this point in the war, however, the tide had turned. While Forrest had been covering Bragg's retreat in early July, Grant had taken Vicksburg and General Robert E. Lee had gambled and lost at Gettysburg. Bragg's victory—partial though it was— had boosted Confederate morale, however, and Jeff Davis meant to hold everywhere until he lost everywhere.

— 10 —

General Nathan Bedford Forrest began his new assignment, which he had staked out for himself, in November, 1863, with only 279 men and four pieces of artillery. One regiment was ordered to join him, but when it arrived it added only about 150 soldiers to his command—and many of the newcomers were unarmed.

In December, Forrest pressed into west Tennessee, and once he was on his home ground, his recruiting efforts produced excellent results. As before, however, he was obliged to equip them with Union-made rifles. His success along this line was not great even though Union commanders sent detachment after detachment to capture him, but when he moved southward he was able to take along 100 enemy wagons, 200 head of cattle, and 3000 recruits; moreover, he had ripped out railroad tracks, cut telegraph wires, and driven the Federal authorities into a frenzy.

Sherman, who had long since learned to respect Forrest, decided to move eastward from Vicksburg in January, 1864. The initial goal of his offensive was Meridian, but he may have considered Mobile, Alabama, as his final destination. In any event, he directed a 7000-man Union cavalry force under General W. S.

Smith to drive from Memphis to join him at Meridian. From Sherman's messages, it seems clear that he meant for Smith to eliminate Forrest on the way to Meridian and then assist him in his campaign through Selma to Mobile.

While Sherman applied the scorched-earth policy to central Mississippi, Sooy Smith took his time in moving into the northern part of that state. In part, Smith's delay was due to horses which needed to be shod and other necessary factors—but wherever his men probed southward, Forrest had men ready to oppose him. Skirmish followed skirmish until Sooy Smith, awed by the number of men Forrest seemed to have, decided that he could not break through to Meridian and withdrew. Sherman, dismayed at Smith's failure and apprehensive lest Forrest turn and strike him in an exposed position—he had already burned out his line of retreat—let his Meridian expedition go into history as merely a raid and turned back to Vicksburg.

Forrest had no intention of letting Sooy Smith get back to Memphis intact. He maintained relentless pressure against Smith's rear guard until the Union general was forced to stand and fight at Okolona, Mississippi, on February 22. Okolona was a typical Forrest battle—beginning with the Union forces drawn up ready to advance, a quick appraisal of the situation by Forrest, a few stirring words from him to the troops, and then his command to "Charge!" He was outnumbered and he knew it, but he led his men forward anyway. At exactly the right time a detachment of Forrest's men rode in from another skirmish, and the general sent them around the Yankee flank. When confusion broke the Union line, Forrest shot forward for the kill. Something of a stampede followed as the Federal troops broke and ran. Forrest sent his men after them, stopped for a time to mourn the death in battle of his youngest brother, Jeffery, and then renewed the pursuit with savage fury. Two horses had been shot out from under him that day and a third had been wounded—but still Forrest urged his men onward. Only remnants of Smith's command survived.

Forrest threw back Sooy Smith's invasion of Mississippi with only 2500 men, many of whom had never been in battle before. Audacity was his great ally, and it had served him well: he had all but destroyed a force nearly three times as large as his own, and he had quenched Sherman's dream of slashing through Alabama to Mobile.

In mid-March, 1864, Forrest took his command into west Tennessee once again. So potent was the Forrest name that one of his subordinates was able to obtain the surrender of 500 men merely by stating that Forrest was not in the habit of giving terms to Union officers not of his own rank. Forrest drove as far northward as Paducah, Kentucky, on the Ohio River, and raided the place; gathered more recruits and armed them with captured Union equipment; and mentioned in the course of his preliminary report his intention to "attend to" a Union garrison stationed at Fort Pillow, about thirty miles above Memphis on the Mississippi.

Fort Pillow was situated on a bluff commanding a bend in the Mississippi, with ravines on either side of the stockade. It had been built much earlier by Confederates who meant to stop Union gunboats, but Federal forces had taken it and garrisoned it with nearly 600 troops. By the time Fort Pillow attracted Forrest's attention, it was protected by a series of three crescent-shaped trench systems which were designed to hold the Confederates back from the main position overlooking the river.

The commanding officer at Fort Pillow was Major L. F. Booth, but Booth had been instructed to rely on Major W. F. Bradford, a native of Tennessee, in any matters which presented problems of a special nature.

Forrest sent a detachment southward toward Memphis to create a diversion while he drew his forces nearer and nearer to Fort Pillow. On the morning of April 12, 1864, he launched an attack which quickly drove the Union troops from the first set of trenches. Next, he sent units out to occupy the ravines which flanked not only Fort Pillow but the only possible route the garrison could take in retreating to the river bank.

Now the fort itself was the only remaining objective, and Forrest put every available sharpshooter to work so that any Yankee who showed himself could be eliminated. While Forrest was riding around the battlefield, his horse was hit and fell: Forrest was badly bruised, but he found another mount and remained in the fight. Major Anderson begged him to continue on foot, for he was by that time an obvious target. Forrest replied that he was "just as apt to be hit one way as another," stayed up, and had two more horses shot from beneath him before the day ended.

By mid-afternoon, Forrest had his men poised for an assault on Fort Pillow. Under a flag of truce, he sent in a message demanding the surrender of the garrison. A Union gunboat in the Mississippi had been shelling the Confederates since the opening of the battle, but Forrest exempted it from his terms. Even so, the Union commander signaled the gunboat to cease firing while the truce was in effect.

While the Confederate white flag was being carried toward the fort, its bearers noticed a Union transport which was approaching the landing below Fort Pillow. The transport was filled with blue-clad soldiers, and there was no indication that the commander of the vessel meant to stop anywhere but at the landing. A message to that effect was sent back to Forrest.

In the meantime, someone inside Fort Pillow responded to Forrest's surrender demand by asking—in the name of Major Booth, who had been killed six hours earlier—for a delay of one hour "for consultation." Forrest rejected this proposal and responded with a note in which he allowed twenty minutes. While all this was going on, however, the Union transport moved steadily toward the landing below the fort.

Finally, another message was sent in the dead Union major's name to Forrest. "I will not surrender," it said.

Forrest ordered an assault against the garrison. Not a shot, he ordered, was to be fired until his men were inside the stockade: meanwhile, his artillery—loaded with canister—and his sharpshooters would provide cover for their advance. When everything was ready, he told his bugler to sound the charge. In an instant, 1200 Confederates let out their immortal yell and stormed into the fort.

During the truce, Union troops had taunted the Confederates, daring them to come and get them. This was extraordinary, and once Forrest's men were inside the stockade they saw the reason—barrels of whiskey were open, and dippers were not hard to find.

The power of the Confederate assault was irresistible, and the garrison's survivors fled down the bank toward the landing in the hope that either the transport—which bore the ironic name of *Olive Branch*—or the gunboat would pick them up. Instead, the panic-stricken Union soldiers were caught in a murderous cross fire from Forrest's men in the ravines which flanked the fort. Many surrendered when Forrest ordered a cease-fire after his men had yanked the United States flag from its mast.

In time to come, Forrest would be branded as the perpetrator of the "Fort Pillow Massacre." The viciousness of the fight made good propaganda in the North, beset as it was by draft riots and general disaffection with a war that Abraham Lincoln—who was up for reelection—did not seem to know how to win. Pro-Administration Union journalists branded Forrest as a blood-thirsty war criminal who had violated his own flag of truce, slaughtered men who were already beaten, ordered the burning of buildings in which Union wounded were known to be, and had the living buried with the dead. No one dared tell Forrest's side.

Actually, the burden of guilt for the tragedy of Fort Pillow rested on the unfortunate Union officer who allowed the *Olive Branch*—the troop-laden transport—to continue toward the landing even though a truce was in effect, or upon the Union officer who neglected to order the United States flag lowered when he gave the command to withdraw to the river bank. An important contributory factor was the curious state of mind of a commanding officer who would turn whiskey over to his troops and still expect them to behave according to the customs of war. They had continued their haphazard resistance to the water's edge, where many of them—still ignorant of what was going on—died needlessly. The battle won, Forrest ordered the Union captives to bury their own dead. Confederate soldiers had been withdrawn by that time and had no part in the mission. The charge that Union wounded had been burned alive was later proved to be wholly false, but by that time it made no difference.

The storming of Fort Pillow was, in fact, no more than a reminder from Nathan Bedford Forrest that when he struck a Union detachment, he meant business. There was nothing new about this. He had been warning wavering Union commanders that he would put the garrison to the sword since Sacramento, and many of them had wisely given in. Something was terribly wrong with the command system at Fort Pillow on the day of the alleged "massacre," but that—Forrest believed—was the Union's problem. He had intended no massacre, and indeed there had been none: the fact that there were enough survivors to bury the dead indicated as much. If the Union garrison had been led by experienced soldiers instead of men who would not even deal with Forrest except in the name of a gallant officer who was dead, who made no effort to stop the *Olive Branch,* who would fail to keep whiskey from troops, and who did not even know how to signal their surrender, Forrest's strike against Fort Pillow would have given Federal journalists little or nothing to deplore.

— 11 —

Forrest's raid into western Tennessee and Kentucky in the early spring of 1864 drove Grant and Sherman into rage bordering on panic. Sherman went so far as to offer a major general's commission to the commander who could kill "that devil Forrest," and he added: "It must be done, if it costs ten thousand lives and breaks the Treasury."

Sherman found a willing candidate in General S. D. Sturgis, who led more than 8000 troops, 22 cannon, and a supply train of 250 wagons and ambulances out of Memphis on June 1, 1864, to catch "that devil Forrest." Sturgis' orders were to burn as he conquered; he was as well equipped to carry out his mission as any Union commander had ever been.

Sturgis drove into northeastern Mississippi without difficulty, but as he neared a place called Brice's Crossroads he became apprehensive: most of the reports he was able to obtain were unreliable, but all of them suggested that Forrest was either on his flank or not far ahead. Accordingly, Sturgis slowed his advance.

Forrest, whose scouts had been performing magnificently as usual, gave him a clear indication of the location and mood of the Federal commander. He knew that he would be vastly outnumbered, but that was nothing new: he had often used the old Indian trick of parading the same men around and around to create the impression that he had the superior force, and he could do it again. His orders were clear: he would whip Sturgis' cavalry first, then he would deal with the tired infantrymen who responded to the call for help. "It is going to be as hot as hell," Forrest predicted, and he was right.

On the morning of June 10, 1864, Forrest's men reached Brice's Crossroads first. Sturgis' cavalrymen rode into the clearing, as Forrest had predicted, and opened the battle. Forrest was fighting at a one-to-two disadvantage, but his only fear was that the Union force would charge first. To forestall such a calamity, he ordered a spoiling attack which held the Federals back until additional Confederate troops arrived.

Finally, the moment for a maximum effort came. Forrest led his men into the center of the Union cavalry line, broke through, and drove the Yankees back. By noon, the first phase of the battle—as he had imagined it—was over.

Sturgis arrived along with the forwardmost elements of his infantry, and before long he had rebuilt a line on which he believed he could make a stand. If he was confident of victory, he had good reason to be: he had over 8000 troops and 22 cannon drawn up into a tight crescent, with a large force behind him in reserve. Widely dispersed around him were less than 3500 Confederates and only 12 guns.

Forrest made up in skill for what he lacked in numerical strength. While he pressed Sturgis' western flank with a heavy attack, one of his detachments struck the Union army in the rear. Inevitably, confusion broke out among the Yankees, and Forrest gave the signal for a general assault. Soon Forrest was sending flanking forces out to complete the destruction: artillerymen even pushed their guns forward by hand in order to stay in the battle. Sturgis ran, taking a personal escort with him.

The relentless pursuit continued all that night and throughout the next day. It ended only when Forrest, utterly exhausted, fell from his horse.

Sturgis not only missed getting his second star; he left a third of his men, most of his cannon, and all of his wagons and supplies behind him when he finally got away from the man he had been ordered to destroy. "I will have the matter of Sturgis critically examined," Sherman wired his Secretary of War, "and if he should be at fault he shall have no mercy at my hands. . . . Forrest is the devil, and I think he has got some of our troops under cower."

Sherman concluded that message by saying that "There will never be peace in Tennessee until Forrest is dead!" To underscore that statement, he sent another force under Generals A. J. Smith and Joseph A. Mower out to get Forrest.

Near Tupelo, Mississippi, on July 14, 1864, the Union task force was met by Confederate defenders commanded not by Forrest but by General Stephen D. Lee. Forrest was junior to Lee, but he was also ill: nearly two weeks earlier he had asked to be relieved. Lee, with Forrest's help, checked the Federal advance in the course of fighting a battle that was in itself indecisive. The Yankees, however, retreated to Memphis.

While the Union troops were falling back, Forrest led a pursuit. Near Old Town Creek on July 15 he was shot in the foot, and a rumor spread among his men that he had been killed. Forrest, in great pain, mounted his horse and rode from unit to unit to demonstrate that he was very much alive. Once that point had been made, he adopted the use of a buggy.

Generals A. J. Smith and Mower were sent back to complete the task Sherman had set for them. By mid-August, their troops were well inside Mississippi and driving ahead against light opposition.

Forrest directed one of his subordinates to hold the attention of the Federal attackers, disengaged the main portion of his troops without arousing any suspicion on the Union side of the line, and hooked around to the west. Heavy rains had filled the creeks, and Forrest was stopped by one that was at the point of overflowing. No boats were available. Delay seemed inevitable.

Muscadine and other grape vines were not far away, and Forrest sent men out to cut them. Before long, he had built a bridge —suspended on the grapevine cables his soldiers had strung— over which his command could pass. A few miles to the west, a similar bridge had to be built. Even so, Forrest was determined to press onward to wherever it was he meant to be.

Finally, on the morning of August 21, 1864, Forrest gave the order for a lightning raid into the center of Memphis, only a few miles to the west. His scouts had told him the locations of the local Union garrison, the quarters of three important Yankee generals, and supply centers.

Forrest planned the raid with great care, but the execution was far from perfect. Even so, he astonished his enemies with his audacity, killed or captured about 400 Union soldiers, took

300 horses and mules out with him, and forced a Union general to flee from his quarters without his clothes. As Forrest had intended, the strategic effect of his Memphis raid was felt in Mississippi: Smith and Mower turned back.

— 12 —

Since early May, 1864, Sherman had been driving General Joe Johnston's Army of Tennessee southeastward from Dalton, Georgia, toward Atlanta. Johnston had given up territory slowly, and he had forced Sherman to pay a terrible price for each mile; Johnston's brilliant defensive action was not appreciated in Richmond, however, and in mid-July he was relieved and replaced by General John B. Hood. By that time, Sherman stood before Atlanta. Behind him was a long and highly vulnerable supply line.

In early September, Forrest sent President Davis a suggestion which the Confederate Commander-in-Chief promptly approved: that Forrest be sent on a raid through northern Alabama into central Tennessee for the purpose of cutting Sherman's lines of communication. Forrest departed at once, bluffed a Union commander at Athens, Alabama, into surrendering by allowing the enemy officer to inspect the Confederate forces (which were being shifted from point to point as the tour went on), and destroyed a column of Yankee reinforcements which arrived only minutes after Forrest's monumental bluff had produced the desired effect.

From Athens, Forrest shot northward to within thirty-five miles of Nashville, cutting telegraph wires, tearing up miles of railroad track, and burning trestles as he marched. Blockhouse after blockhouse along the rail line fell as Forrest swept along.

When Forrest reached the Tennessee River on his way southward, enemy activity around his crossing site was heavy. For a time it seemed that he might have to leave a thousand of his men on the north bank. Not far away there was a long island in the river, and Forrest managed to get the stranded troops ferried over to it in time to save them. Forrest made a final inspection of the north bank, found four stragglers, and sent them along: he was the last Confederate to leave.

While Forrest was helping to pole the last boat from the north bank to the island, he became angered when he saw a lieutenant refuse to take his turn at the work: an officer, the young man maintained, should not have to perform that kind of duty when there were privates available. Forrest held his pole in one hand, slapped the lieutenant so hard the young officer fell overboard, then reached out his pole to bring the man in. The lieutenant needed no more guidance: he poled for the rest of the way.

Several days later, when Federal patrols were less active, Forrest brought the men on the island across to his main body on the south bank and continued his withdrawal. His raid convinced Sherman that he had better not rely on the railroads "now that Hood, Forrest, and Wheeler, and the whole batch of devils are turned loose. . . ."

By mid-October, 1864, Sherman had established a huge supply base at Johnsonville, west of Nashville on the Tennessee River. Forrest told his commanders to "fetch" their troops and follow him on still another raid.

This time, Forrest's men encountered Union gunboats and transports. On October 29 they captured the *Mazeppa* and quickly stripped it of supplies. Later, they seized the *Venus* and a gunboat called the *Undine:* Forrest put detachments on board and sent them up the river toward Johnsonville to assist him in his strike against the Union supply depot. Forrest's experiment in naval warfare was only a partial success, but it gave Federal authorities as far away as Washington something new to worry about.

Forrest decided to destroy the Union supplies at Johnsonville rather than to take the place by storm. His artillery performed brilliantly: in a matter of minutes, the entire warehouse area and the Federal ships tied at the landing were in flames. Upon his return to safety, Forrest could report the destruction of four gunboats, fourteen transports, twenty barges, and nearly $7,000,-000 worth of Federal property. He had salvaged 9000 pairs of badly needed shoes and a thousand blankets. His losses were two men killed and nine wounded.

While Forrest had been raiding in northern Tennessee, Hood had brought his army up for a strike at Nashville: Sherman left the task of checking Hood to General George H. Thomas and

departed from Atlanta on his march to the sea. Hood ordered
Forrest to join him as soon as he returned from the Johnsonville expedition.

Once again, Forrest and his men were to fight gallantly as
part of a larger force—this time, a doomed one. Forrest commanded the rear guard of Hood's army during the retreat from
Nashville in late December and saved it from complete destruction by holding Thomas' spirited pursuers well back from the
main body of beaten Confederates.

By March, 1865, Federal columns were ready to slash through
Alabama—and only Forrest could be put in their way. He was
still fighting near Selma (where he was wounded again) in early
April when General Robert E. Lee surrendered to Grant at
Appomattox, Virginia, although by that late date he was able
only to throw raids against isolated Union detachments.

Federal authorities, believing a rumor to the effect that Forrest meant to take his command westward to continue the war,
sent out orders to prevent him from getting away. "If he attempts such a reckless and bloodthirsty adventure," Thomas
wired his subordinate commanders, "he will be treated hereafter as an outlaw, and the States of Mississippi and Alabama
will be so destroyed that they will not recover for fifty years."

Nothing could have been farther from Nathan Bedford Forrest's mind, to the dismay of many of the men who had followed
him for so long. He wrote a message to his men on May 9, 1865,
in which he said: "I have never on the field of battle sent you
where I was unwilling to go myself, nor would I now advise you
to a course which I felt myself unwilling to pursue. You have
been good soldiers, you can be good citizens. Obey the laws,
preserve your honor, and the government to which you have
surrendered can afford to be and will be magnanimous."

— 13 —

After the war, Forrest returned to what remained of his plantations below Memphis. His former slaves refused to leave him,
and with their help he soon restored the land and made enough
money to support a number of Confederate veterans who had
been ruined and who could not make a comeback. Forrest

worked diligently to clear himself of charges stemming from the alleged Fort Pillow massacre. Three years after being chosen the first Grand Wizard of the Ku Klux Klan, he ordered the Klan to disband because they misused their power, and he resigned his position. Later he convinced a committee of the United States Congress that he was no longer a power in the Klan's activities. He died at Memphis on October 29, 1877, at the age of fifty-six.

Jefferson Davis, riding in a carriage to Forrest's funeral, remarked to the Governor of Tennessee, "I saw it all after it was too late." By this he meant that official Richmond had consistently looked upon Forrest as nothing more than a bold raider—which he certainly was—and did not appreciate his astonishing grasp of strategy until the Confederacy was doomed.

For the accomplished soldiers and statesmen in Richmond to have overlooked Forrest was not surprising. Most of them had never met him, and it was easy for them to believe that he was an ignorant backwoodsman and not much more.

Even today, Forrest is best remembered—when he is remembered at all—for having said, "Git thar fustest with the mostest" —something that corrupts a legend that is already obscure enough. Actually, Forrest once sat down with General John Morgan, the leader of Morgan's Raiders in Kentucky, and the two cavalrymen pelted each other with questions about engagements and ways of fighting: both men were naturally modest, and the answers seldom amounted to much because each general rushed on to ask the other about something else. In reply to Morgan, Forrest stated that many of his victories were due to the fact that he usually got there first with the most men. This was nothing more than a short way of attending to one matter before he could put another question to Morgan; but it was remembered—with dialect that did Forrest no credit—more vividly than the man who uttered it.

As a matter of fact, Forrest won by arriving first and by making splendid use of the men he had with him: he almost never had "the mostest." His genius was the ability to make a thousand troops fight like ten times that number, to make a quick appraisal of the situation, to make maximum use of his fertile imagination, and to provide the personal leadership which is always essential to success in battle.

A warrior's worth is sometimes measured by what his enemies thought of him. After the war, Sherman told one of Forrest's lieutenants: "I think Forrest was the most remarkable man our Civil War produced on either side. . . . He had never read a military book in his life, knew nothing about tactics, could not even drill a company, but he had a genius for strategy which was original, and to me incomprehensible. There was no theory or art of war by which I could calculate with any degree of certainty what Forrest was up to. He seemed always to know what I was doing or intended to do, while I am free to confess I could never tell or form any satisfactory idea of what he was trying to accomplish."

Joe Johnston, when asked for the name of the greatest soldier of the war, replied without hesitation: "Forrest."

British General Garnet Joseph Wolseley, who never met Forrest, caught the essence of the man's greatness in describing "nature's soldier." "His military career teaches us," Lord Wolseley wrote, "that the genius which makes men great soldiers is not to be measured by any competitive examination in the science or art of war. 'In war,' Napoleon said, 'men are nothing; a man is everything.' It will be difficult to find a stronger corroboration of this maxim than is to be found in the history of General Forrest's operations."

4

James Ewell Brown Stuart

The Knight of the Golden Spurs
1833—1864

"HOW I miss you this beautiful Sabbath morning," Major General James E. B. Stuart wrote his wife, Flora, in April, 1863, "and yet before yonder sun reaches the zenith, our blades may be gleaming brightly on the warpath. . . . I am going to church, but I go equipped for the field. . . ."

So Jeb Stuart revealed himself—a dedicated man of war who was devoted to his wife and his God, a romantic who could see poetry in bloody action. He was wonderfully uncomplicated: only thirty, but a seasoned commander, fond of music and gaiety and the laughter of women, thirsty for glory to the point of being rash in gaining it, utterly pious, utterly absorbed in the cause he served. His legs were too long for his tall body—he always looked better on a horse—but the animal had to be a stout one, for its rider had a fondness for long marches at top speed. A full beard covered his face, a beard that concealed strong but kindly features, a beard that glowed red in the sun, a beard he stroked whenever he worried. "Beauty" Stuart they called him at West Point, and "Beauty" Stuart he remains— hero of countless dashing cavalry clashes, a cavalier who lived and fought as though he expected to be the subject of legends which would long outlive him.

"I go equipped for the field," Jeb Stuart wrote Flora that April in the midst of the Civil War, but he might have made that statement at any time during his adult life.

Jeb Stuart was born at his family's home, Laurel Hill, in

southwestern Virginia in February, 1833. His generation was the fifth in the Stuart line to be Virginian, but he was the seventh child and youngest son of a father whose law practice and public service had not provided enough money for young Jeb to expect much of a start in life.

The man who had recently defeated Stuart's father in a Congressional election appointed Jeb to West Point in 1850. "I am green as a gourd vine," young Stuart wrote his family from Washington on his way northward. But Jeb soon caught on to the Military Academy's routine, and he had little trouble in the classroom. His conduct was spirited—with demerits marking his progress—but he was spotted as a leader by his classmates and by the superintendent, Colonel Robert E. Lee.

"As regards my entering the army," Jeb Stuart wrote in 1854, just after his graduation, "I have but one aim, to do some service to my country in return for what she has done for me."

There is a legend that Stuart let his class standing slip during his final year at West Point so that he would not be ranked into the elite Corps of Engineers, a branch in which he imagined he would be "entirely unexposed to actual fighting, and . . . [kept] in inglorious ease at some delightful station on the Atlantic." He had been drawn to the dash and color of the mounted service during practice charges at West Point, and he was overjoyed when he received his orders to join the Mounted Rifles in west Texas to put down a Comanche uprising. Lieutenant Stuart grew a beard, learned the ways of the army, and established a reputation as a solid, reliable soldier.

Jefferson Davis, a West Pointer who had served with distinction in the Mexican War of 1846–47 and who was now Secretary of War, saw that a new kind of combat force was needed on the western frontier: the Mounted Rifles were not enough. Accordingly, in early 1855 he created the first two regiments of United States Cavalry. To one of them, the 1st, he assigned Lieutenant J. E. B. Stuart.

The officers Davis placed in the new regiments were carefully picked men—Lee, Joseph E. Johnston, George B. McClellan, George H. Thomas. Stuart, who was far junior to them, was given the duties of regimental quartermaster and commissary— tasks which were hardly in line with his idea of what a cavalry officer's life should be. Dull though the work may have seemed, though, Stuart was in a key position—and before long, he was one of the few men in the Army who knew anything at all about the complex problems of supplying, mounting, and feeding a cavalry force.

Young Stuart had always had an eye for a pretty girl, preferably those with Southern origins, and at Fort Leavenworth, Kansas, in 1855 he found the one he wanted—Flora Cooke, the daughter of Colonel Philip St. George Cooke, commander of the 2d Dragoons. Although Flora had been educated in Detroit, the Cookes were an old Virginia family. Moreover, Colonel Cooke was well aware that Lieutenant Stuart had the makings of a splendid soldier. After a number of horseback rides on late afternoons, Flora won Jeb—or vice versa. An Indian raid delayed the wedding and the death of Stuart's father restrained its gaiety, but they were married in mid-November, 1855, and settled into spartan quarters at Fort Leavenworth.

The controversy over extending slavery to the Western states was something Stuart had ignored, but abolitionist activity led by John Brown disturbed the peace and drew in the 1st Cavalry. Stuart rode with a detachment that forced Brown to release a proslavery Missouri militia force he had captured. The leader of the men Stuart's column rescued was a Virginian named Henry Clay Pate: Stuart would meet him again.

In the summer of 1856, while Flora was awaiting the birth of their first child, Stuart took part in a battle against 300 Cheyenne warriors. During a hand-to-hand fight, Stuart was shot in the chest—but with his saber he managed to cut down the Cheyenne brave who had shot him. Dr. Charles Brewer, the regimental surgeon, saw that the wound was not serious, but he sent Stuart to the rear. "We have a pretty view up the creek for about two miles," he wrote Flora. "My Prayer Book—which I must say has not been neglected—and my Army Regulations are my only books. A few sheets of *Harpers Weekly* are treasures indeed."

Indian troubles on the frontier finally subsided, and old John Brown shifted his efforts to free the slaves to the Eastern states. Stuart was now able to be a family man, and he spent most of his time with his wife and their daughter, who was also named Flora. In odd moments, he invented a simple device for hitching horses and a better means of hanging a saber from a cavalryman's belt.

During a long leave in 1859 he took his Floras eastward to Virginia to visit relatives. While he was there, he attended an Episcopal convention at Richmond and later went up to Washington to urge the adoption of his inventions as standard equipment for the U. S. Cavalry.

While Stuart was waiting to see someone at the War Department about his inventions one day, he was asked to carry a message over to Colonel Robert E. Lee, who was also on leave at his home in nearby Arlington, Virginia. John Brown had raided Harpers Ferry, Stuart was directed to tell Colonel Lee, and Lee was designated to lead a force of United States Marines to the place to capture Brown and restore order.

Stuart rode to Arlington at once and delivered the message. At Stuart's earnest request, and remembering the young man from West Point days, Colonel Lee allowed him to go along on the mission as his aide.

— 2 —

Earlier, old John Brown had settled on a farm in Maryland which was to be his base for a grand movement he had planned for freeing the slaves. In mid-October, 1859, he opened his campaign by raiding the little town of Harpers Ferry, captured its leading citizens, and seized the brick building in which the village's fire engines were kept. Militiamen from nearby counties in Maryland and Virginia were ordered in to rescue the hostages—which included Colonel Lewis Washington, George Washington's great-grandnephew—but the citizen-soldiers' effort turned out to be a botched affair. President Franklin Pierce was forced to declare martial law and to send in professionals to take care of the fiery abolitionist who considered himself the agent of the wrath of God.

Colonel Lee and Lieutenant Stuart rode to Harpers Ferry in a locomotive. Neither of them bore arms. Someone later remarked that they resembled two businessmen passing through on their way to an important meeting. In a sense, they were.

When the locomotive reached Harpers Ferry, Lee quickly

made an appraisal of the situation. He deployed the Marines around the engine house, but he decided to give John Brown one final chance. Lee arranged a truce and ordered Stuart to carry an ultimatum to Brown: surrender at once, Lee demanded, or face the consequences. Stuart and Lee agreed upon a signal—if Brown refused, Stuart would wave his hat—and the young man went forward.

Old John Brown met Stuart at the door of the engine house. Stuart delivered Lee's message. From inside the building came the sound of Colonel Washington's voice. "Never mind us!" the hostage shouted. "Fire!"

Brown turned to Stuart and said that he "would as leave die by a bullet as on the gallows."

"Is that your final answer, Captain?" Stuart asked. Brown said that it was. Stuart stepped aside and waved his hat.

When Colonel Lee saw Stuart's signal, he ordered the Marines forward. The troops surged toward the engine house, broke through the door with a battering ram, and worked their way inside despite heavy fire from Brown and his men. Stuart charged with the Marines. He got inside in time to help capture the fiery old abolitionist, and he took Brown's bowie knife along with him as a souvenir.

Stuart was present a few hours later when Lee and Virginia officials questioned Brown. Lee decided that someone should go up to Brown's farm in Maryland to clean out the raiders' base, and he selected Jeb Stuart. When Stuart returned, he brought with him a wagonload of homemade pikes, pitiful weapons for a serious insurrectionist to have considered useful, but damning evidence all the same.

Their work done, Lee and Stuart caught a train for Washington a few days afterward. By the time John Brown had been tried, found guilty, and hanged, both men were back at their duty stations in the West.

Not long after Stuart and his family returned to Kansas, Flora gave birth to a son. They named him Philip St. George Cooke Stuart, after Flora's father.

As the Union began to fall apart early in 1861, Jeb Stuart moved quickly to file his application for duty with the forces of his native Virginia. He ignored his promotion to captain, resigned from the service of the United States, and reached

Richmond in early May. His rush to be of service to the Confederate States of America was dismaying to his father-in-law, Colonel Cooke, who elected to remain with the Union. For Stuart, though, there was no choice: like Lee, he could not draw his sword against Virginia. And like Lee, he was never to draw it except in Virginia's defense.

— 3 —

Most of the young men of Virginia who answered the call to arms had—like Stuart—been superb horsemen from earliest childhood. It was natural for them to be organized as cavalry, but the Confederate War Department was slow in grasping that fact. Experienced cavalrymen such as Lee and Joe Johnston were put into positions of high command and charged with the duty of building a conventional army—meaning infantry and artillery. Even Stuart was commissioned first as a colonel of infantry.

While Stuart was serving under Thomas Jonathan Jackson's command near Harpers Ferry in the summer of 1861, however, he was permitted to organize a cavalry force. Turner Ashby, also serving under Jackson, and older than Stuart both in age and in the Confederate service, protested: Jackson split the two and let them form their own units. Later, when Joe Johnston assumed command and withdrew the unit to Winchester, Stuart whipped his outfit into shape with West Point efficiency which soured many a trooper.

During a skirmish with Union forces one day in July, Stuart conducted a class in tactics under enemy fire. With Union infantry advancing and artillery rounds passing overhead, he said: "Now, I want to talk to you, men. You are brave fellows and patriotic, too, but you're ignorant of this kind of work, and I'm teaching you. I want you to observe that a good man on a good horse can never be caught. Another thing: Cavalry can *trot* away from anything, and a gallop is unbecoming to a soldier, unless he is going toward the enemy. Remember that. We gallop toward the enemy, and trot away, always."

Union General Robert Patterson was charged with the duty of keeping Johnston's Confederate forces around Winchester pinned in place while General Irvin McDowell's Federals rolled over General Pierre G. T. Beauregard's men who were guarding Manassas Junction, between Winchester and Washington. As McDowell's offensive took form, the War Department in Richmond ordered Joe Johnston to move his troops to Manassas. To keep Patterson from knowing anything about the move—and from launching an attack to disrupt it—Johnston sent Jeb Stuart northward to screen the shift and hold Patterson where he was.

Stuart gave Patterson the impression that a mighty Confederate army was about to attack him. In Washington, old General Winfield Scott knew more about what was going on than Patterson, in the field, did; but it made no difference, for by the time Stuart broke off his skirmishes with Patterson's men, Joe Johnston had joined Beauregard at Manassas and it was too late for Patterson to do anything but fume.

To Beauregard's great dismay, the Battle of Manassas did not follow his carefully wrought plans. He meant to strike McDowell from the south, but instead McDowell struck *him* from the north. Stuart's cavalry was in the path of the Union advance, and for a time it was up to him and General Jackson—who stood that day like a stone wall—to stem the Yankee assaults. Stuart's men charged into the New York Zouaves and threw them back in panic. Soon, General Jubal Early brought his troops into the line Stuart and Jackson had held. United States Congressmen who had come out along with other members of Washington society to watch the defeat of the Rebels had to make haste in getting out of the way as Stuart and Early drove the defeated and demoralized Federal troops eastward.

Stuart drove the fleeing Yankees for twelve miles that afternoon, and later he was ordered to man an outpost line which was within sight of Washington. No one knew it at the time, but McDowell was in no mood to test the Confederates again. Meanwhile, Stuart kept watch.

Back at Stuart's headquarters, there was a mixed air—part hard work, for he had men in the saddle every day, and part sheer fun. From another outfit Stuart took Sam Sweeney, a banjo-playing minstrel, and around him he built something of a traveling show. He made the acquaintance of the leading families in the neighborhood, charmed their ladies, and led many a ball. All the while, however, he was riding the lines himself. In September, he led a numerically inferior task force against a determined Union probe and sent it running toward Washington without losing a man or a horse—and won his promotion to brigadier general at the age of twenty-eight. One of his troopers wrote home to describe his commander: "Stuart sleeps every evening on Munson's Hill without even a blanket under or over him. He's very young . . . but he seems a most capable soldier, never resting, always vigilant."

Brigadier General Philip St. George Cooke was put in to oppose Stuart, and something of a family crisis ensued. Stuart instructed his Flora to change their son's name to James Ewell Brown Stuart, Jr., and chided her in letters when she forgot to refer to the boy as Jimmie.

Winter came, Stuart fought an indecisive action at Dranesville which inspired him to develop artillery that would be capable of keeping up with his cavalry, and he acquired John Pelham to command it. At his headquarters he played with his two setters, Nip and Tuck; wrote Flora; engaged in snowball fights with his men; and kept an eye out for Yankees.

By early spring, 1862, the Confederate nation—which had grown complacent after what had seemed to be an easy victory at Manassas back in July, 1861—was jolted into action when Union General George B. McClellan landed a huge army on the peninsula formed by the York and James rivers southeast of Richmond. Johnston shifted his forces southward to meet this serious new threat, leaving Stuart behind to screen his withdrawal and to burn the supplies that could not be carried out.

While higher commanders discussed ways and means of dealing with McClellan, Stuart took his cavalry down the peninsula to the vicinity of Yorktown. When Johnston finally pulled back, Stuart conducted a series of skirmishes that kept the Yankees from being able to interfere with the retrograde movement.

Toward the end of May, a huge German soldier carrying a large sword and bearing the name of Lieutenant Heros von Borcke of the Guards in Berlin reported to General Stuart just as the Battle of Seven Pines was about to begin. Stuart invited Von Borcke to ride with him, and the German eagerly accepted. Although the cavalry had been given no direct assignment that day, Von Borcke noted that Stuart managed to get "in the thickest of the fray." Stuart rallied broken ranks of infantry and led them forward again, encouraged others to hold, and provided Johnston with as much information as he could gather.

General Joseph Johnston was seriously wounded at Seven Pines, and General Robert E. Lee was appointed to succeed him as commander of the Army of Northern Virginia. Johnston's attack had stemmed McClellan's advance; but with the glow of Yankee campfires visible from Richmond in the eastern skies at night, a stalemate was intolerable. Lee called in his subordinate commanders, heard their recommendations patiently, and reserved decision.

Stuart sent John Mosby, a scout, around the northern flank of McClellan's army in early June. Mosby returned with a detailed report which Stuart quickly forwarded to Lee. Shortly thereafter, Stuart had orders from Lee to leave enough cavalry to protect the main army and to take the rest on a raid deep in McClellan's rear. "Remember that one of the chief objects of your expedition," Lee cautioned, "is to gain intelligence for the guidance of future movements," and he made it clear that Stuart was to avoid any contact which would prevent his getting back to Confederate lines.

Quietly, without telling anyone about the mission, Stuart ordered 1200 of his men to prepare three days' rations and get their equipment ready for hard work. The troops moved out well before daylight on June 11. "How long will you be gone?" someone asked Stuart.

"It may be for years, and it may be forever," he replied with a laugh.

Stuart went northward from Richmond to beyond Ashland, turned eastward, and camped for the night. The next morning, near Hanover Court House, he slipped through McClellan's pickets—who thought the presence of a few Rebels was nothing serious—and reached Old Church, ten miles or so behind the Yankee lines, before he ran into strong opposition. Stuart quickly ordered a charge and cleared a Union regiment out of its camp.

By this time, Stuart had obtained the intelligence data Lee needed. He could either turn back along the road he had used that morning or keep riding eastward and southward through the rear areas of the Union army. Stuart decided to take the long way around. "The hope of striking a serious blow at a boasting and insolent foe, which would make him tremble in his shoes," Stuart wrote, "made more agreeable the alternative I chose."

General Cooke, Stuart's father-in-law, commanded the Union cavalry forces which were charged with the duty of maintaining security in the zone through which the Confederates were rampaging. Cooke was slow to react, and when he did send out a pursuit unit he selected an infantry outfit. Mostly, Union troops found only the traces—smoking wagons, looted supply dumps—of where Stuart had long since passed.

The next day Stuart cut the telegraph wires and tore up the tracks of the York River Railroad, McClellan's main supply route, as he rode southward. Two transports were tied to a dock on the Pamunkey River: when Stuart's men left, the boats and the wagon trains they carried were in flames. Near the White House, a Lee plantation which was now McClellan's chief supply base, the raiders burned a long wagon train and freight cars filled with hay and forage. Von Borcke, who had tried in vain to capture a speeding train merely by firing his revolver at the engine, was given a bottle of champagne that had come from a wagon bound for General McClellan himself. "Never in my life have I enjoyed a bottle of wine so much," the German said later.

The ride continued that night, although Stuart paused around midnight to let stragglers catch up. While the main body rested, they were the unwelcome guests of Union army sutlers and ate figs, canned meat, and many delicacies that were unknown to Confederate commissaries. Finally, the march resumed. By moonlight, scouts who were native to the peninsula led the way across unguarded fords and down back roads.

At dawn, Stuart's column had reached the Chickahominy River. Rooney Lee, the army commander's son, swam across to test the current and returned with the news that another way of crossing would have to be found. Stuart tugged at his beard for a moment. Federal pursuers, he knew, were only a few miles behind. Stuart sent a messenger to General Lee to report his position and to ask for a diversion to be created on the Charles City Road to improve his chances of getting back through the Union lines; then he moved down the swollen Chickahominy to the ruins of an old bridge. Troopers brought in lumber from nearby barns and rebuilt the bridge, the command crossed, and the rear guard burned the structure just as the first Federal soldiers appeared. Stuart pushed on another five miles before he called a halt.

Richmond was still thirty-five miles to the west, and Stuart was anxious to get the information he had gathered to General Lee. He rode all night, slipped past Federal patrols, and got into Richmond on the morning of June 15. After he had reported to Lee, he rode back out to meet his troops and lead them to their camp.

It had been quite a ride—from Thursday morning until Saturday noon, past one major Union outfit after another, across many creeks and a swollen river, 200 miles of fighting, burning, pushing on. Only one man had failed to return, and he was dead, shot in one of the first engagements.

Lee was generous in his praise, but he was more grateful than he was at liberty to express: for the first time, he knew that the counterattack he had been planning stood an excellent chance of succeeding. He had already told Stuart that he was thinking of bringing General Stonewall Jackson's troops to Richmond from the Shenandoah Valley, where they had just conducted a brilliant diversion that had vexed even President Abraham Lincoln. Now Lee told Stuart to guide Jackson from Ashland into an attack against the northern flank of McClellan's line.

Stonewall Jackson was late in getting to Ashland, and even after Stuart met him he lost more time. Stuart was astonished at Jackson's strange lethargy, and before long Stuart was twisting his beard: Lee, he knew, was counting on Jackson to envelop the northern end of the Yankee army, and unless Stonewall hurried the entire plan would go awry.

Finally, Jackson struck—but his attack was feeble, and it came too late in the day to accomplish anything. To the south, other Confederates heard the firing and plunged ahead against determined Union resistance; they were cut to pieces, and the only gains they made were hardly worth the cost.

To Stuart's dismay, Jackson was still failing to perform as Lee had expected even after McClellan began pulling his forces back—but there was nothing Stuart could do about the situation, and he must have been glad to get orders to take his cavalry eastward to cut McClellan's lines of communication with his York River base near the White House. Stuart soon discovered what Lee had suspected: McClellan had shifted his supply line to the James River. Even so, Stuart captured and burned the matériel the Union quartermasters had been unable to carry out.

For a time Lee was uncertain as to the direction of McClellan's retreat. The Union army seemed to be backing southward toward the James, but there was always the chance that McClellan would decide to move southeastward along the peninsula toward Yorktown, instead. To check this possibility, Lee sent Stuart around to the east on another ride around the Yankee force. Stuart reported no indications of an enemy movement down the peninsula. By the time he had rejoined Jackson on the eastern flank of Lee's army, the last of the Seven Days Battles—Malvern Hill—had already been fought.

The next morning, Stuart led a column eastward in order to restore contact with the retreating enemy. At Evelington Heights, overlooking Shirley Plantation and McClellan's huge camp, John Pelham put his guns into action and fired into the masses of Union soldiers and wagons below. Stuart put his men into position to hold the Heights: reinforcements, he was told, were on the way. General James Longstreet, the leader of the Confederate troops Lee had sent, took the wrong road. Meanwhile, Stuart had to fight off one determined Union assault after another. Finally, his men ran out of ammunition. He withdrew, bitterly disappointed. Stuart was eager to renew the battle the following morning; he even showed Stonewall Jackson several possible routes of attack. Lee, however, ruled against the venture.

Stuart, still miffed over the loss of Evelington Heights, rested for a day or two. On the night of July 6, he took a couple of regiments and Pelham's guns down to the James River, waited until some Yankee transports steamed along, and ordered the artillery to open fire. Shells tore through the vessels: one sank, and the river was filled with screaming men. Stuart led the party home at a trot. Behind them, a Federal gunboat was pouring its fire at the spot where Pelham's guns had been.

The performance of Stuart's cavalry during the Seven Days Battles came in for some criticism—most of which was unjustified. He had performed his most valuable service before the offensive began, and at Evelington Heights as it was ending; in between, he had acted as Lee directed—skirting the eastern flank, reporting what he could. For Stuart's men to have fought as dismounted troops in pitched battles such as Gaines' Mill or Malvern Hill would have made little difference and would have amounted to a grave misuse of their capabilities—mobility and shock action.

Blame for Lee's failure to win a battle of annihilation during the Seven Days was more properly directed at others, and Stuart paid little attention to those who said he ought to have done more. Still, the experience gave him a certain seasoning: the laughter and the gaiety would remain, Sweeney would still break into a song at Stuart's signal, and there would be harmless flirtations with pretty girls—but the big cavalryman was more serious about what was required of him now, and the glory he craved seemed a long way off.

It did not seem so one day in late July when Stuart was spotted in Richmond, surrounded by young women, his horse bedecked with flowers the girls had brought. As Stuart was reciting poetry to his admirers, a column of infantry marched by: the men laughed and hooted and mimicked the adoring females. "Excuse me, ladies," the abashed Stuart said, and hurriedly rode away, trailing flowers as he fled.

— 4 —

President Abraham Lincoln, still determined to put Union troops in Richmond, sent General John Pope southward through Manassas toward Gordonsville in early August. Gradually, McClellan's forces east of Richmond were loaded on transports for shipment northward—Lincoln's idea being to add them to Pope's army as soon as he could.

Lee sent Stonewall Jackson over to Gordonsville to check Pope's advance, but he still kept an eye on the concentration of Federal combat power east of the Confederate capital. Like Stuart, Lee had learned a great deal from the Seven Days Battles: as a result, he tended to rely on three commanders whose performance during that campaign had been less than spectacular: Jackson, Longstreet, and Jeb Stuart. Lee was a keen judge of men, he knew value even when it was not apparent, and he was now in a position to use the Army of Northern Virginia as he saw fit.

Jeb Stuart emerged from the Seven Days as a major general. Even better, his cavalry corps was augmented: he now commanded three brigades of seasoned troopers. From this time onward, however, Stuart was obliged to remain in closer proximity to Lee and to coordinate the operations of his detachments. Fortunately, Stuart had excellent subordinate leaders—Wade Hampton, Beverly Robertson, and Fitzhugh Lee, the commanding general's nephew.

The effect of Stuart's changed status was that he could no longer be at the hottest part of every skirmish that was to take place. His cavalry units worked hardest while the rest of Lee's army was resting or moving: there were fords to be guarded, enemy movements to be watched, and raids to be carried out, and no man could hope to add his personal touch to the successful conduct of each isolated mission. It was in Stuart's nature to try, though, and he wore out many a horse in the attempt.

As Pope's offensive took shape, Lee decided to trap the Union army in the triangle formed by the junction of the Rapidan River with the Rappahannock. He issued orders for an envelopment that would sweep eastward and then northward, and a copy of his detailed directive for the operation was given to Captain Norman Fitzhugh of Stuart's staff to carry to Fitz Lee, above Richmond, whose cavalry unit was vital to the success of the undertaking. Captain Fitzhugh was captured, however, and Lee's order was forwarded with all possible speed to John Pope.

As Stuart and the rest of his staff were riding eastward to join Fitz Lee, Stuart called a halt for the night and stretched out on the front porch of a farmhouse. He knew nothing of Fitzhugh's capture, and assumed that Fitz Lee's men would be riding in at any time. Suddenly, a Yankee patrol appeared. Stuart and his companions managed to get to their horses and outrun the pursuers, but he had to leave his famous plumed hat behind. For days afterward, infantrymen yelled, "Hey, Jeb, where's your hat?"

The capture of Lee's order and other misfortunes forced the cancellation of the sweeping offensive the commanding general had planned. Pope withdrew beyond the Rappahannock to escape the trap Lee had hoped to spring, but he was still dangerous, and Lee was determined to find some way of crushing him before reinforcements from McClellan's army could reach him.

By August 22, 1862, Lee had approved a scheme for cutting Pope's lines of communication. Stuart took 1500 men and two guns and rode around to the west, swept through Warrenton, paused there long enough to learn that a certain young lady in that town had bet a bottle of wine with a particular Yankee captain that he would not be in Richmond in thirty days, and pushed on. As night came, a terrific thunderstorm broke. Just as Stuart was about to order a halt, a Negro came up to the cavalry leader with astonishing news: General Pope's headquarters area was not far away, and he could guide the Confederates to it.

Stuart quickly organized a force for the raid. The strike came just as the Yankee officers were settling down to a lavish dinner; one Confederate soldier even slipped in and joined them without attracting their attention. Stuart and his men tore through the camp, burning tents, taking supplies, and capturing—among other things—all of General Pope's belongings, including his uniforms and overcoat.

The next morning, as the raiders were passing through Warrenton with a long line of Union prisoners behind them, Stuart presented the Yankee captain to the young lady who owed him a bottle of wine. The captive took it off to prison in Richmond, bewildered at the strange way in which Jeb Stuart made war.

Pope's coat finally reached Richmond where Governor John Letcher put it on display. Stuart wrote Pope a mocking message in which he proposed an exchange of the coat for his hat, but Pope was not amused.

Now the campaign took on a wholly serious turn. Lee decided to send Jackson around the western flank of Pope's army, and Stuart was ordered to provide a cavalry screen for the audacious movement. Stuart performed, and before long his men and some of Jackson's troops were gleefully tearing into Pope's main supply depot at Manassas Junction.

Lee and Longstreet followed the path Stuart and Jackson had opened, and by August 29 the entire Army of Northern Virginia was in John Pope's rear. This brought on the Battle of Second Manassas (or Second Bull Run) and led to one of Lee's most illustrious victories: for the second time in less than a year, Union troops were running in panic into the defenses of Washington. In less than sixty days, Lee had reversed the entire strategic situation—moving the threat of capture from Richmond to Lincoln's own citadel.

The momentum of the Army of Northern Virginia's spectacular advance had to be maintained, and Lee sent his men northward into Maryland behind the cavalry screen Jeb Stuart provided. At many points, the Confederates were greeted as liberators—and at one of them, Frederick, Stuart received a royal welcome: he was invited to dine at the Cockey home, met a young lady to whom he gave the title of the New York Rebel, and ordered Sweeney to get a band from a nearby unit so that a ball might be held in a deserted building in Urbana, not far away.

The celebration was a gala one in every respect, with dashing cavalry officers escorting the loveliest local girls, flowers everywhere, and music filling the hall. Toward midnight, a Confederate soldier dashed in to report the presence of "lots of Yankees," and the men excused themselves to ride off into the night to face the enemy intruders. After a few spirited skirmishes, the Confederates rode back to the ball. Sweeney struck up the band, and the gaiety resumed as though nothing had happened.

Something had, however: wounded men from the recent fight were brought into the hallway of the building, and one girl screamed when she saw a litter carried past the doorway. Before long, the dainty girls were acting as nurses—including Stuart's favorite, the "New York Rebel."

There were to be other light moments during the Maryland campaign—there had to be around Stuart, for he would not let the hard duty of the war bruise his love of life—but mostly it was a matter of putting out screens, gathering information, and joining infantry in hot fights to keep McClellan from getting too far westward too quickly. Ordinarily, that would not have been a problem: McClellan was famous for his excessive caution. But this time, he moved—thanks to a captured order from

Lee that was sent to him. As a result, McClellan and Lee met at Sharpsburg and fought a bloody battle in which Stuart held the northern flank of the Army of Northern Virginia while Jackson and Longstreet threw back one Union assault after another. Stuart covered Lee's withdrawal into Virginia as the great adventure came to a dismal end.

Stuart's cavalrymen moved into the pleasant country around Martinsburg and enjoyed the comforts of the fall of the year 1862. The Bower, a plantation near the town, became Stuart's headquarters—and something of a social center, as well, for as soon as the Major General Commanding had finished his work for the day he ordered Sweeney to get cracking. Love took its toll of the bachelors on Stuart's staff, and reports of some enthusiastic kissing got back to Flora—but it was all harmless fun, Stuart assured her, and it probably was. Fond of pretty girls as Stuart was, he kept his Flora first in his affections.

In early October, Lee interrupted the gaiety at the Bower by ordering Stuart to take 1800 men on a bold raid to cut the railroad bridge near Chambersburg, Pennsylvania, and to capture civilian hostages who might be used in exchange for prominent Virginians the Yankees had captured and were holding. Stuart took his heavy column northward at once, brushed Union opposition aside, and reached Chambersburg in lightning time. The bridge was made of steel and could not be destroyed, much to Stuart's dismay, but he was able to burn the Union supply depot and equip his men with shoes and clothing and horses which they needed very badly.

In effect, Stuart was duplicating the ride around McClellan's army which had astonished observers on both sides back in June, for he decided to keep circling rather than to go back to Virginia by the route he had taken on his way northward. His men had not been able to cut all of the telegraph lines, however, and McClellan—who was still in command of the Federal forces—prepared a trap that was certain to catch Stuart as he tried to ride southward to safety.

Stuart worked his way around the Union concentrations with care, adding horses to his growing remount pool, capturing mayors and postmasters as he rode. Danger was increasing by the hour, and Stuart ordered an all-night march to the Potomac.

Some of the troopers fell asleep in their saddles as the long column moved southward.

"How would you like to see the 'New York Rebel' tonight?" Stuart asked a member of his staff. The officer was delighted by the idea. With about ten men and a few other officers, Stuart rode over to the Cockey house and knocked on the door. "Who's there?" someone called from an upstairs window. "General Stuart and his staff," he replied. The girls dressed hurriedly and came down. For an hour it was like old times—Sweeney and his banjo, gay talk, laughter.

Stuart and the men with him had to ride hard to catch the main column before sunrise. Although the raiders took a back road toward the Potomac, Union General Alfred Pleasonton had a small cavalry detachment at the river to meet them. Stuart attacked Pleasonton while Fitz Lee shot forward to secure the crossing site at White's Ford. While the weary troopers crossed into Virginia, Stuart worried about the safety of his rear guard: finally it managed to disengage, and Pleasonton's men were too tired from tracking down the Confederates to offer much of a pursuit. By mid-morning, Stuart's command was able to stop at Leesburg to get some rest. Stuart and his staff pressed on westward to the Bower, and once again Sam Sweeney and his banjo furnished the music for one of those impromptu parties his commander enjoyed so much.

There was much to celebrate. Stuart had taken 1800 troopers all the way around McClellan's army for the second time ("Three times," President Lincoln remarked, thinking of McClellan, "and out"). They had covered more than 130 miles in three days: the last 80 in only twenty-four hours. Lee had the Union hostages he needed to exchange for captive Virginians. Stuart's men could replace their worn-out horses for Pennsylvania-bred animals. But there was one failure to record: the railroad bridge at Chambersburg still stood.

A lady in Baltimore sent Stuart a pair of golden spurs, a gift that delighted him. Flora was at the Bower just then and buckled them on her dashing husband.

— 5 —

In late October, 1862, a strong Union force crossed into northern Virginia and brought Stuart's idyllic stay at the Bower to an end. The Confederate cavalry rode out to maintain contact with the new invasion force, and November was marked by one serious skirmish after another.

During those fights, Stuart received a letter from his brother-in-law, Dr. Charles Brewer, in Lynchburg, informing him that little Flora was gravely ill and urging him to come at once. "I received [the news] on the field of battle," Stuart wrote his wife. "I was at no loss to decide that it was my duty to you and to Flora to remain here. I am entrusted with the conduct of affairs, the issue of which will affect you, her, and the mothers and children of our whole country much more seriously than we can believe." A few days later, little Flora died.

McClellan moved his Army of the Potomac down to Warrenton, separating Jackson in the Shenandoah Valley from Longstreet's corps near Culpeper Court House. Stuart, with Jackson in the mountains of western Virginia, found the Union cavalry far more aggressive than it had ever been. The weather, too, seemed to favor the Yankees. The Confederates won few skirmishes, and Stuart lost his sense of humor for a time.

One day, while Stuart and his aide, Heros von Borcke, were taking part in a fight against the 5th New York Cavalry near the Rappahannock River, Von Borcke said something about the danger of their position. "If it's likely to be too hot for you, retire. I'll stay," Stuart snapped.

"My duty is with you," Von Borcke replied, but the German got behind a tree. Enemy rifle fire poured in, chipping the bark and narrowly missing Von Borcke. Stuart suddenly reached up and found that half of his moustache had been cut away by a Yankee round.

Lincoln replaced McClellan with General Ambrose Burnside on November 7, and the huge Federal army soon moved eastward toward Fredericksburg. Lee put Longstreet on the high ground overlooking the town, and later he brought Jackson and Stuart over from the Valley to occupy the low hills which extend southward from Marye's Heights.

Fredericksburg was to be a defensive battle as far as Lee was concerned, and he refused to allow Jackson and Stuart to attack when Burnside's men crossed the Rappahannock, took the town, and moved against Longstreet's corps on Marye's Heights. Stuart allowed John Pelham to take two cannon from the Horse Artillery forward, however, and "the gallant Pelham" tore the advancing Yankee lines to pieces with his flanking fire. When one gun was knocked out of action, Pelham doubled the rate of fire of his remaining piece. Men fell all around him, but still Pelham poured round after round into the Union flank. At one point 32 Federal guns concentrated their fire on the lone Napoleon gun—which Pelham had captured at Seven Pines—but not even Stuart's orders to withdraw could stop him: "Tell General Stuart I can hold my ground," Pelham replied to Von Borcke's message.

Finally, when Pelham's last round had been fired, he hitched the horses to the gun and headed back to Jackson's line. Lee, who had watched the young artilleryman's spectacular performance through his field glasses, remarked: "It is glorious to see such courage in one so young."

Fredericksburg was not to be a cavalry fight, but a few days after it ended (in crushing defeat for Burnside), Lee sent Stuart on another raid into Union-held territory. Stuart took 1800 men, circled around to the west on Christmas Day, and drove almost as far northward as Alexandria. A Federal telegraph operator was captured at one point, and Stuart had one of his men tap out a message to General Montgomery Meigs, the Union army's quartermaster general: "Quality of the mules furnished me very poor. Interferes seriously with movement of captured wagons. J. E. B. Stuart."

Apart from the poke at Meigs, Stuart's Christmas raid accomplished little. He estimated that the skirmishes up north had cost the Union about 200 lives, his men had cut telegraph wires, and some wagons had been captured—but he brought back no important information.

The winter of 1862–63 was a hard one, and Stuart was worried by the decline he saw in the fighting effectiveness of his command. Diseases took out men and horses, and the ranks of dismounted troopers—called Company Q—swelled alarmingly.

The quality of Federal cavalry, meanwhile, was steadily improving.

During an attempt to block a strong Union cavalry raid between Kelly's Ford and Culpeper on March 17, 1863, Stuart discovered to his dismay how much his enemy's horsemen had grown in fighting power. At the outset, Stuart was confident that Fitz Lee's men could clear the Yankees with little difficulty; but before long, Stuart was standing alone, waving his hat, and yelling: "Confound it, men, come back!"

Young Pelham, about to be promoted to lieutenant colonel and very much in love with a girl in Culpeper, was with Stuart that day although he was technically on leave. He had gone to great pains to get away to see Miss Bessie Shackelford while there was a lull in the fighting, but he had returned when he heard about the Yankee cavalry thrust. Pelham helped get the guns into action to stem the Union assault, but he was shot down. When Stuart heard the news, he broke into tears.

While Stuart and his men drove back the Federal cavalry, Pelham was taken to the Shackelford home in Culpeper. Doctors tried to save his life, and his beloved Bessie helped by heating water and bringing brandy, but "the gallant Pelham" died. Stuart wrote Flora: "I want Jimmie to be just like him."

— 6 —

Now General Joseph Hooker commanded the Army of the Potomac, and good fighting weather was at hand. Union cavalry probes increased in number and intensity in April, 1863, and by early May "Fighting Joe" was ready to cross the Rappahannock and the Rapidan for another "On to Richmond" offensive.

Lee was hardly pleased by that prospect, for Longstreet and most of his corps were in southern Virginia gathering food and forage, and a strong Federal force still faced him at Fredericksburg. Once Hooker's army had reached the Wilderness and Chancellorsville, about ten miles west of Fredericksburg, though, Lee responded in a way that astonished Hooker: he moved out to face the strong invasion force, leaving only light detachments behind to watch the Yankees at Fredericksburg.

While Lee and Stonewall Jackson were sitting by a campfire

in a clearing on the evening of May 1, 1863, Jeb Stuart rode up with the news that Joe Hooker's southern flank was "in the air"—unprotected by any natural obstacle or fortifications. Jackson astounded Lee by proposing that he be allowed to take his whole corps around Hooker's army and strike it from the rear.

That night, Stuart found a guide, the Reverend B. T. Lacy, who knew the roads in that country. He brought Lacy to the headquarters clearing. Early the next morning, with Stuart's cavalry providing a screen, Jackson led his men on a grueling twelve-mile march around Hooker's army while Lee held the Union force in place facing Chancellorsville with only a few thin divisions.

Jackson's attack came late in the afternoon, but it had the desired effect: Hooker's men broke in panic. The underbrush was too thick for the cavalrymen to be of much use, so Jackson sent Stuart northward to seize Ely's Ford and seal off a possible Federal escape route. En route, Stuart's men charged through one startled Yankee camp after another. He was at the point of attacking a major Union bivouac area when a courier rode up. "You'll have to come, General," the man said. "General Jackson's shot."

Stuart reached Jackson's headquarters at midnight and learned that he was now in command of the corps. He had no clear idea of what Jackson had meant to do next, and the wounded general was in no condition to say more than "Tell General Stuart that he must do what he thinks best." Lee's orders were only to press the enemy "so that we may unite the two wings of the army." Accordingly, Stuart issued orders for an attack eastward along the main road toward Chancellorsville: his main effort would be made on the southern end of his line so that the junction with Lee's forces could be made at the earliest moment.

All during the night of May 2 the sound of axes could be heard in the woods as Hooker's men braced for the next day's fighting. Reconnaissance reports indicated that the Union positions were very strong. Positions for Confederate artillery were few in number and poor in quality.

At dawn, though, Stuart was ready. "Remember Jackson!" he shouted as he led the Second Corps forward in an attack which was almost perfectly coordinated—a rare sight in the Confederate armies. But a stirring watchword was not enough: to the tune of "Old Dan Tucker," Stuart sang "Old Joe Hooker, won't you come out the Wilderness . . . ," and the men joined in.

By mid-morning, Stuart had led one infantry unit after another in assaults on the Yankee lines. His horse was shot from beneath him, but he remounted at once to continue the charge. Soon he had taken Hazel Grove, and Lee's men appeared on his right: the Confederate army was united once more, and Old Joe Hooker was trying his best to get his troops out of the Wilderness.

Just as Lee and Stuart were preparing to drive Hooker into the river, alarming word came from Fredericksburg: the Union force there had broken out and was moving westward toward Chancellorsville. Lee peeled off several divisions to meet this new threat, checked it, and returned his attention to Hooker too late—for Hooker had taken his army northward.

On May 10, Jackson died. Amid the grief at his passing, though, there was the problem of naming a successor as commander of the Second Corps. Although Stuart had led the unit with distinction on May 3 during the great Confederate assault, some criticized him for being too careless of his own safety and too hasty in throwing his troops into bloody assaults. Indirectly, those comments were compliments—or so Stuart chose to interpret them. Jackson, everyone knew, was irreplaceable. Lee pondered the matter for a while, and finally decided to split the unit into two corps under Generals Richard Ewell and A. P. Hill.

Stuart had no cause to feel slighted, for he had been told that Jackson, on his deathbed, had said that Stuart should have the command. "I would rather know that Jackson had said that," Stuart remarked, "than to have had the appointment." The determining factor was probably Lee's need for Stuart as his cavalry commander: Stuart, too, could not be replaced.

Somehow, a rumor to the effect that Heros von Borcke had been killed at Chancellorsville spread throughout both warring nations. The German's body, Governor Letcher requested, should be sent to Richmond for a state funeral. "Can't spare the body of Von Borcke," Stuart wired back. "It is in pursuit of Stoneman." And so it was: Union General Horace Stoneman's cavalry was still active south of the Rapidan, and Von Borcke was helping Stuart drive the Yankees homeward.

In early June, Stuart gave a ball and a grand review "inspiring enough to make even an old woman feel fightish," as an observer described it. His men were in comfortable positions around Brandy Station, not far from Culpeper. With Sam Sweeney's music softening the air at parties every night and Stuart riding amid admiring ladies nearly every day, waving his plumed hat, living life to the full, it was hard to believe that the war was not yet won.

Alfred Pleasonton, the Union cavalry commander who had failed to trap Stuart during the Chambersburg raid, decided to strike Stuart's happy resting place at Brandy Station. On June 9, he attacked with a heavy task force of 10,000 men. Stuart, badly shaken by the surprise attack, was hard pressed from the beginning. Only after he had put enough forces on Fleetwood Hill to stem the Yankee onslaught could any cohesion in his defense be obtained, and even then it was bloody work. A timely charge by Wade Hampton's men saved the situation just as General Lee, on his magnificent war horse, Traveller, was riding in with his staff. Lee arrived in time to see his son, Rooney, being carried off wounded.

Stuart held the battleground as a gesture of defiance. The Union cavalry, satisfied, rode northward.

"General S. loves the admiration of his class of lady friends too much to be a commanding general," an irate woman wrote President Davis. Someone on the President's staff sent the note to Stuart with a warning to "cease your attentions to the ladies or make them more general." There was more criticism, some of which charged "negligence and bad management."

But neither Lee nor Stuart lost his poise. The gaiety was behind the cavalrymen, anyway: the second invasion of the North was about to begin.

— 7 —

General Lee's plan was to move the Army of Northern Virginia northward through the Shenandoah Valley. Stuart's orders were to screen the march from Yankee cavalry patrols which struck at the gaps in the Blue Ridge in the hope of disrupting Lee's advance. Many of those cavalry skirmishes were serious, and one resulted in the loss of Heros von Borcke.

Stuart was in one of his stubborn moods that day, and he brushed off the German's warning that the Union attackers greatly outnumbered the Confederate cavalrymen who were fighting desperately to hold the Yankees back. A Federal sharpshooter cut the gold braid on Von Borcke's trousers. "Those Yankees," he said, "are giving it to me rather hotly on your account." Suddenly, a bullet struck his neck.

Von Borcke was evacuated. No one thought he would live through the night. Stuart came, and Von Borcke felt tears falling on his cheek. "Poor Von," the general said, "you took this wound for me." The big German rallied, and later he was almost captured when a Union patrol searched the house in which he had been hidden. Rumors had it that Stuart, not Von Borcke, had been wounded.

Stuart, saddened that Von Borcke was out of action but hopeful that he would survive, managed to maintain his screen even though Pleasonton pressed hard. Lee was ready to cross the Potomac, and he sent orders for Stuart to provide cavalry for Ewell's advance into Pennsylvania. At almost the same time, Lee approved Stuart's proposal for a raid against Joe Hooker's communications. Lee's order said: "If General Hooker's army remains inactive, you can leave two brigades to watch him, and withdraw with the three others. . . . You will, however, be able to judge whether you can pass around their army without hindrance, doing them all the damage you can, and cross the river east of the mountains. In either case, after crossing the river, you must move on and feel the right of Ewell's troops."

The river Lee referred to was the Potomac; the mountains were the continuation of the Bull Run chain which run through Maryland toward Gettysburg. Ewell's right, which Stuart was to "feel," was to be near York, Pennsylvania. In effect, Lee was authorizing Stuart to join the Army of Northern Virginia by riding east of Hooker's army, across the Union line of communication with Washington. An important—and often overlooked—element in Lee's order was the directive that Stuart should take only three of his five brigades on the raid; that left two, under capable leadership, which Lee could still use.

Stuart moved out—sending a message to Flora in which he said: "Don't be telegraphing General Lee's staff or anybody else. If I am hurt you will hear of it very soon"—and took his men across the Potomac at Rowser's Ford, only about ten miles from Washington. He drove through Rockville, Maryland, and captured 125 Union wagons on June 28.

For Stuart to be rampaging east of the Yankee army, tearing up the tracks of the Baltimore & Ohio Railroad and giving the residents of Washington and Baltimore a good scare, was actually of little help to Lee, for no messages reached him from Stuart. Instead, a scout brought Lee the fateful news that Hooker had been replaced by General George G. Meade as commander of the Army of the Potomac and that Meade was rushing northward. Lee quickly ordered Ewell back from York and began the consolidation of his army at Cashtown, Pennsylvania, only a few miles west of Gettysburg.

Meanwhile, Stuart pushed through Westminster, Maryland, toward Hanover and York in Pennsylvania. Federal troops pursued him, and the long wagon train and the Yankee prisoners in the midst of his column impeded his progress. Soon he learned that Ewell had left York. Stuart marched westward to Carlisle, where the Union commander replied to Stuart's surrender ultimatum by saying: "Shell away!" Stuart did, burning the depot and large quantities of supplies which had been stored there.

That day, Lee had engaged Meade's army at Gettysburg. He sent orders northward to Stuart recalling him, and Stuart turned toward Gettysburg at once. He arrived on the afternoon of July 2, while the men of Longstreet's corps were trying to wrest control of the Round Tops from the determined Union defenders.

"General Stuart," Lee said, "where have you been? I have not heard a word from you for days, and you are the eyes and ears of my army."

Stuart reported that he had brought 125 wagons and many prisoners. "Yes, General," Lee replied, "but they are only an impediment to me now." Then Lee's rage passed. "We will not discuss this matter longer," he said. "Help me fight these people."

Stuart did what he could. On the third day of the critical battle, while General George Pickett's men were making their futile but immortal charge, Stuart tried to attack the northern flank of Meade's army. He was beaten back after repeated attempts to break through.

While Lee's army, seventeen miles of misery, retreated in the rain on July 5, Stuart provided as much of a screen as he could muster. His men were worn out from the long ride to York, and many of the Union cavalry probes were more than they could contain. Even so, he shielded Lee's wagons and columns until the Army of Northern Virginia was back in safe country.

For a time, Jeb Stuart was so subdued that he would hardly eat. As the army moved past Martinsburg, though, his spirits revived. He made a detour to visit the Bower, but he could not tarry: there was no time for a ball, and the good times were all in the past.

— 8 —

Meade was slow in launching an offensive of his own, but in mid-September, 1863, it came. Stuart was the first to meet it, but he was forced to fall back, to fight off strong cavalry attacks, to buy time in which General Lee could get his army in hand. At one point, Stuart was surrounded: he had guns placed so that they could fire in all directions. Mostly, Meade's post-Gettysburg campaign was a series of cavalry skirmishes. It ended prematurely, in part because Stuart had created the impression that Lee was stronger than he really was.

While Meade retreated northward, Stuart staged a raid through the old Manassas fighting ground and brought on a fight that was afterward called the Buckland Races. Judson Kilpatrick, a rising young Union cavalryman, led a force westward one day in October, 1863, toward Stuart's men at Buckland Mills, just east of Warrenton. Fitz Lee was at Auburn, to the south, but he moved northward when he heard the sound of gunfire. Fitz Lee suggested that Stuart pull back: Kilpatrick would surely follow, and then Lee would hit the Yankees in the rear. The idea appealed to Stuart, and the trap was set.

Kilpatrick charged after Stuart, and Fitz Lee moved in as soon as the Yankee column had passed. Stuart's men blunted the Union advance and turned it back while Fitz Lee hammered from the rear. Then the race began—on Kilpatrick's part, to get eastward to safety; on Stuart's part, to annihilate him. Stuart won the day, but that was about all. He could not have known it at the time, but he had enjoyed his last triumph over Union cavalry.

In early October, Flora Stuart gave birth to a girl—named, appropriately, Virginia Pelham Stuart. The war during the winter of 1863–64 required little of the baby's father, and he was able to spend many days and nights with his family in Richmond where he was welcomed as a hero. Stuart saw action when Kilpatrick and Colonel Ulric Dahlgren staged a raid on Richmond in February, 1864. The Union probe ended in failure in early March with Dahlgren dead and Kilpatrick in flight down the peninsula toward Union-held Fortress Monroe and safety.

By May, the Union had a new general-in-chief—Ulysses S. Grant, a man from the West who had never been defeated. Grant sent Meade's Army of the Potomac southward, and Lee met it in the Wilderness.

Stuart's men saw little action in the Wilderness, where Lee delivered a series of punishing blows against a Union army that now had a leader who would not be beaten. Grant had lost 18,000 men in the Wilderness, but he was determined to press on to Spotsylvania. Stuart got there first and held the key positions until Lee's forces came up to relieve him. Lee would not win that battle, either, but at least Stuart's prompt action and gallantry in holding the ground had given him a fighting chance, which was all that Lee ever asked.

A new Union cavalry commander, General Philip Sheridan, had won Grant's admiration by arguing that Federal cavalry ought to be concentrated for the purpose of destroying Stuart and tearing up Lee's lines of communication with Richmond. "Go ahead," Grant ordered.

Sheridan started southward with 12,000 men. They moved slowly, for they meant to win and they saw no need for haste. Stuart organized a pursuit force and shot southward. He had a special reason for moving out quickly: Flora and the children were at the village of Beaver Dam, directly in Sheridan's path.

When the Union cavalrymen reached Beaver Dam, they were too busy burning Confederate supplies—a million rations of bacon, 500,000 loaves of bread—and tearing up the Virginia Central tracks and destroying trains to bother with Jeb Stuart's family. The fires led Stuart to the ruined town, but by the time he arrived the Yankees had moved on toward Richmond.

Stuart paused at Beaver Dam only long enough to have a few words with Flora and give her a kiss. He did not even dismount. There was work to be done, and he was running late.

A stand, Stuart decided, could be made at Yellow Tavern, an abandoned inn only six miles north of Richmond. At first, the battle went to his satisfaction: the 5th Virginia, under the command of Colonel Henry Clay Pate, was holding. Stuart had known Pate since 1856 out in Kansas when there had been some trouble involving a fanatic named John Brown; in the years between, however, Pate and Stuart had not been friends. In the midst of battle, Stuart found Pate, held out his hand, and suggested that they forget the past. Pate agreed. When Stuart asked Pate how long he could hold, Pate replied: "Until I die." Minutes later, Pate was killed while leading a charge.

Sheridan's troops swarmed through the area, and finally one of his men got a shot at a big officer: Stuart. Confederates pulled their general back to safety, and before long someone found an ambulance. "Go back!" Stuart shouted to the anxious men around him. "Go back! Do your duty as I've done mine. I would rather die than be whipped."

The ambulance driver had a hard time getting Stuart through the rough country without overturning the flimsy wagon. When he was clear of the boulders and the Yankees, the driver halted the mules so that the doctor could examine Stuart.

"How do I look in the face?" Stuart asked, mindful of the death pallor he had seen all too often during the past three years. "You are looking all right, General," he was told. The doctor offered him some whiskey. "No," Stuart said, "I've never tasted it in my life. I promised my mother that when I was a baby."

Hours later, Stuart was carried into the Richmond home of Dr. Charles Brewer, his brother-in-law, the same man who had treated his only previous wound in Kansas a long time ago. The doctors did what they could, but the Yankee's bullet had passed through Stuart's liver. Brewer left to summon Von Borcke, who had tried to reach the fighting at Yellow Tavern earlier: after a brief visit, Von Borcke left to send a message to Flora, who was still at Beaver Dam.

While Flora hurried southward toward Richmond, first by locomotive and then by wagon, a terrific thunderstorm raged. Later, Stuart heard cannon. "What's that?" he asked. Someone told him that his men were still fighting Sheridan. "God grant that they may be successful," he said, "but I must be prepared for another world."

President Davis came, stayed a minute or two, and left. Stuart asked for Flora. An Episcopal rector came, and Stuart joined in as the men in the room sang "Rock of Ages, cleft for me. . . ." Von Borcke sat on the edge of the bed, holding Stuart's hand.

Then, to Dr. Brewer, Stuart said, "I am going fast now. God's will be done."

James Ewell Brown Stuart, Lieutenant General, Army of Northern Virginia, Confederate States of America, died shortly before eight o'clock on May 12, 1864. Flora arrived three hours too late; she mourned him for the rest of her life.

— 9 —

And so the Knight of the Golden Spurs passed not only into history but into the legends that warmed the hearts of Southern men and women for a hundred years to come. What he failed to accomplish, his gallantry covered—and beyond that, the stirring spectacle of the rider with the plumed hat appealed to the romantic heart, wherever it beat.

There is this about Stuart: he was absolutely sincere. "I have but one aim—to do some service to my country in return for what she has done for me," he said when he was graduated from West Point. Ultimately, like many other Virginians and other sons of the South, he was destined to put his homeland first and fight the flag he had once defended. For Virginia he served in Kansas and at Harpers Ferry as well as inside her borders, and for Virginia and the Confederacy he died.

Many of Stuart's actions were hardly models. His first ride around McClellan's army before the Seven Days Battles may have convinced the Union commander to shift his supply base from the York to the James River, and that decision may have saved the Federal forces to fight on many another field. Similarly, his Chambersburg raid in October, 1862, may have led to the horrible slaughter at Fredericksburg, two months later, in that his bold action spurred Lincoln into ordering that offensive. Finally, Stuart's absence when Lee needed him most, at Gettysburg, is hard to justify.

Still, there was Stuart the man—the Knight of the Golden Spurs, idol of Southern womanhood, and inspiration of their warriors. Fond of frivolity though he certainly was, he knew how to fight—and he knew how to die. That counted, and it remained to remind his countrymen of the importance of valor and heartbreak and sacrifice long after the cause was lost.

5

Thomas Jonathan Jackson

The Bellicose Deacon

1824–1863

FROM the earliest days of the American adventure, Virginia has been rich in historic experience. Some of the earliest English colonists settled along her beaches; good climate and broad lands made her rich as plantations grew in productivity; gentlemen of advanced learning and deep wisdom made their homes there, and in time they would provide the intellectual and political leadership for a bold experiment in human freedom. By 1860, few states could match Virginia on any count: but by 1865, only five years later, Virginia would be in ruins.

It was Virginia's fate to become the iron gate to the Confederate States of America, to resist the repeated Federal attempts to win the Civil War by capturing her, to be the site of some of the most vicious fighting Americans have ever known. Her location was of key strategic importance. Added to that was the fact that the seat of the Confederate government was at Richmond, only a hundred-odd miles from Washington. Even topography destined Virginia for destruction, for her coastline and the corridors through her mountains gave the Union at least four clear avenues of approach to her heartland.

Given the inevitability of invasion, Virginia responded with characteristic vigor in 1861 when the Union mobilized to win the war by crushing her. For a time, Governor John Letcher proved to be an able administrator of a state geared to peace but ready to spring to the defense of all that she was: he called the Virginians to war, and they came forward in numbers which proved to be greater than the state could accept or equip. When the Confederate government assumed Letcher's burden later in that year, he gave the new nation the men who were soon to prove matchless in battle—Robert E. Lee, Joseph E. Johnston, and a strange and mercurial professor from the Virginia Military Institute, Thomas J. Jackson, along with tens of thousands of other warriors who would be killed at the height of their valor and be lost to history.

There was something about Virginia, a mystique, which served her gloriously during her four years of torture. This is a curious phenomenon, for the state is as varied in its topography and mixture of peoples as Texas or California or Tennessee. In the east, along Virginia's coast on the tidewater, wealth and culture developed at an early date. In time, the country around and to the west of Richmond flourished too. In the Piedmont, however, life was always hard; getting ahead was a constant challenge, and only the more rugged individuals survived and met that challenge.

The Civil War drew Virginians from all three geographical belts, as though there were no mountains or flatlands or anything in between to make one man of the Old Dominion different from any other. Local pride was never lost as long as one man from a region remained alive, but always there was that deep and ennobling force—the love of Virginia—to inspire them to extraordinary heroism in the countless skirmishes and memorable battles they fought to save their heritage.

One such inspired man was Thomas Jonathan Jackson, born in January, 1824, in Clarksburg, Virginia, in that portion of the state which would later become West Virginia. The people of the region just west of the Alleghenies were thrifty, hard-working folk who respected men of character and worshiped a stern God who exacted a maximum sense of duty from men so that they might match His mountains. Jackson's father met that severe test, but only in part: he was a gifted lawyer and a valued member of the community, but he had been lacking in investment judgment and was to leave his widow virtually in poverty with two little boys and a baby girl to raise when he died in 1826.

Julia Jackson refused charity and kept her home together by her own efforts. She sewed for other women, taught school, and got by. Later, she remarried—but her health failed, and the children had to be sent to relatives. She died in late 1831. Young Tom and his sister, Laura, were left with only their grandmother and an uncle, Cummings Jackson, to raise them.

Life at Uncle Cummings' was pleasant for the children for as long as Grandma Jackson lived, for she ran the house and took good care of them. When she died, Cummings Jackson—a bachelor—had doubts as to the fitness of the example he was setting: he was a spirited man who was little inclined to mend his ways. He found other homes for the orphans, but young Tom refused to accept the change. Before long, Tom ran away and returned to Uncle Cummings.

For Tom Jackson to have selected his own foster parent was not much of a surprise, for Cummings Jackson had already noticed a stubborn streak in the boy. Somehow, an idea of the difference between right and wrong had made a deep impression in young Tom's mind. When his sense of justice was upset, there was no controlling him.

If Cummings Jackson was sinful, and some maintained that he was, his influence on his adopted son was wholly beneficial. The years Tom Jackson spent with his uncle were to be the happiest ones he would ever know.

Young Tom found plenty of work at his uncle's sawmill, and the outdoor life helped him to overcome a stomach disorder which plagued him. Still, he was shy: he was distant, retiring, slow in making friends. At school he was a hard worker, and he had to be—he wanted to learn, but nothing came naturally to him. At sixteen, though, he became a teacher and struggled through two terms by managing to keep a lesson or two ahead of his students.

Jackson's exposure to learning left him with a craving to get more, preferably as a minister. The Bible fascinated him, but his lack of formal education and his terror of public speaking caused him to set that course of action aside. Instead, he became a constable, charged with the task of collecting debts. While Jackson held this position, he earned a reputation as a man who meant to keep his oath of office even though he was only seventeen and still woefully shy. Duty was something he understood implicitly; if other men did not, that was their problem.

There was an appointment to the United States Military

Academy at West Point available from Jackson's district, but he failed to win it because of his lack of background in mathematics. The successful candidate soon absented himself from the Academy without bothering to obtain leave, however, and Jackson got a second chance. He went to Washington, presented his letters of recommendation to his Congressman, and won the appointment. On June 20, 1842, he was sworn in as a cadet.

West Point was a severe challenge to Jackson, but it was different only in degree. As before, he had to work much harder than anyone else in order to get by: to excel was out of the question. Even so, he made good progress. Someone observed that if the course had lasted one year longer, Jackson would have been first in his class.

Jackson maintained his aloofness at West Point. The only nickname he won was "The General," and it had its roots in Andrew Jackson's popularity and backwoods origin rather than in any indications of Thomas Jackson's military promise. The maxims which "The General" wrote in his notebook, however, were the kind that any ambitious young soldier might well adopt:

> You may be whatever you resolve to be.
> Through life let your principal object be the discharge of duty.
> Resolve to perform what you ought; perform without fail what you resolve.

— 2 —

At graduation, in June, 1846, Jackson was commissioned in the artillery and ordered to join a unit in New York that was destined for service in the Mexican War. At first, the war seemed to be one movement after another with only long stretches of monotony sandwiched in between. Early in 1847, however, General Winfield Scott put an invasion force ashore near Vera Cruz and opened his drive toward Mexico City. Chances for action came, and Jackson proved to be a dependable soldier—but glory, he learned, seldom goes to those who most deserve it. In a letter to his sister, Laura, he said: "If an officer wishes to distinguish himself he must remain long in service until he obtains rank; then he receives praise not only for his efforts, but for the efforts of the officers and men under him."

During the long march up the valley toward the Mexican capital, Jackson used the scraps of his free time to learn Spanish. Garrison duty, however, bored him. "I throw myself into the hands of an all wise God and hope that it may yet be for the better," he wrote Laura. "It may have been one of His means of diminishing my excessive ambition."

By August, 1847, Scott's army was nearing Mexico City and Jackson's guns were finally put into action. During the Battle of Chapultepec, heavy gunfire from the Mexican defenders killed, wounded, or routed the men in Jackson's battery, but with the aid of a sergeant he kept one gun firing despite the best efforts of the enemy to knock him out. He was ordered to withdraw, but still he held his position, firing round after round into the Mexican fortifications.

There was the essential Jackson, the stubborn boy—though a seasoned soldier—who saw his duty in the bright Mexican sun and did it, regardless of all danger or threat of failure. The cannon he served had been transported all the way from somewhere in the United States to Vera Cruz; it had been lugged up the valley over a distance of more than 200 miles; it was there at Chapultepec to be used, and he used it. Like that cannon, he had been forged into a fighting man: he had no choice but to be what he was.

Jackson's performance that day won him glory and temporary promotion to the rank of brevet major—but his sudden fame embarrassed him. It all happened too quickly, perhaps: and he had always been shy. He had been wholly sincere when he had written Laura that an offcer "must remain long in service" before he achieves rank and recognition. The Bible had told him what the fate of an overly proud man must be, and he respected that warning to the point of becoming even more reticent than before.

Once the fighting had ended and the tensions in Mexico City had eased, Jackson made a number of friends among prominent Mexican families. He was a welcome guest, for his manners were impeccable and his knowledge of Spanish indicated a genuine interest in the country his nation's Army had just conquered. For a time, he even considered making his home there

—a senorita may have had something to do with that notion—
but duty intruded.

Jackson was ordered back to New York and assigned to an
artillery battery responsible for guarding a harbor no known
enemy was likely to try to enter. Behind him, in Mexico, he left
scenes he would never forget—the beauty of the place, the easy
days in the company of gracious and friendly people, the thrill
of battle, the wonder of accomplishment. To go at all must have
been something of a wrench; but Jackson, always alert to what
duty required, complied with his orders.

The man who reached New York in August, 1848, was hardly
the same person who had left there only two years before. Jackson had seen war. He had learned what the terms "strategy"
and "tactics" really meant. He had gained an appreciation of
the importance to an army of sound logistic support. He had
discovered, to his distress, perhaps, that he was considered to
be a superior soldier. And his curiosity regarding religion,
which had always been a vague but powerful force in his life,
had been stimulated tremendously.

Jackson's return to New York dismayed him. His health,
which had been excellent in Mexico, deteriorated. Dull routine
at his post bored him. Such romance as he may have known
south of the border was far behind him now. He spent his
idle hours in trying to find remedies for his physical maladies
or in the study of religious prospects for saving his soul. Even
when he went into the city on leave, it was either as a patient
wracked with pain or as an awestruck outsider utterly incapable
of finding amusement or relaxation or any other comfort there.

This was tragic. Here was Jackson, in the prime of his life,
a hero of a tough and exacting war, turning his thoughts in-
ward and dwelling amid his miseries, or upward out of concern
for the spiritual health of a soul which seemed to be in danger
of damnation only to its owner.

Jackson's religious fervor was his own business, but he elected
to use it in Laura's behalf, as well. By this time she was married
and the mother of a boy who adored his uncle, but that made
little difference to brother Tom who had seemingly given up
on the present world and looked forward only to a family re-
union in the next. "Oh! Sister," he wrote her in 1849, "drop

your *Infidel Books.* Come lead a happy life, and die a happy death."

— 3 —

In the fall of 1850, Tom Jackson was ordered to join an artillery unit in Florida where the Seminole Indians had been getting out of hand. He was the right kind of man for the assignment—a combat veteran—but on the first few scouting missions he conducted, no Indians turned up where his commander thought they would be. Even worse, Jackson did not seem able to find a prominent lake around which the Seminoles were said to be operating.

Ambitions clashed: the post commander wanted results, but Jackson—duty-bound to follow the commander's misplaced orders—could not produce them, through no fault of his own. The battle of wills, once joined, became a series of efforts on the part of two good men to destroy each other. Jackson discovered that his commander had been slightly indiscreet in escorting his family's maid back to her quarters, and he lodged serious charges against the officer. In retaliation, Jackson's superior raised complaints alleging that his subordinate was disloyal, at best. The paper war raged for a long time. Higher authorities, wise in the ways of garrison life, refused to consider either side of the dispute. They knew—as Jackson apparently did not—that a man often has to get along by going along.

That there had been some wrongdoing was clear. Jackson, however, had made a mountain out of the proverbial molehill. He gave his superiors the impression that he was something of an avenging angel, charged with the perfectionist mission of righting all wrongs. They dismissed his charges, hoping that both parties to the controversy would learn something from it.

Toward the end of that turbulent interlude in Florida, Jackson heard that a vacancy existed on the faculty of the Virginia Military Institute. He filed his application, waited anxiously week after week while other candidates were screened and found wanting, and considered himself a man delivered from perdition itself when word reached him that he was to become the professor of natural and experimental philosophy and artillery tactics. Although he would no longer be in the Army, he would carry the highest temporary rank he had ever earned—major—with him.

Lexington, Virginia, located as it is with high ground all around it, was reminiscent of the hilly country in which Jackson had grown up. The people of the town received him graciously even if the V.M.I. Corps of Cadets did not: the major was a modest unassuming man, but it was true that he seemed a bit odd—his feet were too big; he wore outsize artillery boots; he walked with a peculiar stride; he had no sense of humor.

Jackson soon settled into the academic routine. He usually was only one lesson ahead of his students in each of his subjects except artillery tactics, and the cadets were quick to spot his inadequacies; at times, to vex him, they moved a lesson ahead of "Old Hick." Earnest man that he was, he could only show them how he had mastered the assignment at hand. When the cadets' searching questions led him beyond the material he had prepared himself to cover, he was lost. Even so, Jackson attempted to write a textbook for the subject he understood least —optics.

As before, Jackson was strict. Any cadet who crossed him could expect a deluge of demerits—and some were even subjected to trial by court-martial for offenses many other professors might have overlooked or laughed off. "Tom Fool" Jackson was not popular, and there would come a time when certain alumni would try to have him dismissed. Jackson hardly seemed to notice. He merely continued to serve as effectively as he knew how.

The people of Lexington were far more tolerant of Jackson's eccentricities than the V.M.I. cadets. True, it was slightly disconcerting to see a guest sitting bolt upright on the edge of his chair during a formal call. The man was incapable of handling small talk, and any part of a conversation that was frivolous clearly baffled him: each statement had to be probed and clarified, even if it was utterly idle. But the major was interesting and unfailingly polite, and his neighbors accepted his shyness and stiffness with tolerance and grace.

Gradually, Jackson made a few close friends in the town. Major Daniel Harvey Hill was an instructor at Washington College in Lexington, and Jackson found a special welcome in his home: they had first met in Texas on their way to the Mexican War in 1846, and Hill had recommended Jackson for the post at V.M.I. Mrs. Hill's sisters were also frequent visitors. Jackson lost some of his reserve around them, and they found him charming. D. H. Hill and Jackson also shared a deep interest in religion, and it was through Hill that he became interested in the Presbyterian Church.

Similarly, Jackson became a welcome guest at the home of the Reverend George Junkin, who was president of Washington College. Dr. Junkin's daughters, Maggie and Elinor, could engage in the serious kind of conversation Jackson liked best—and before long, Jackson confessed to Hill that Ellie Junkin was causing him to have feelings he could not analyze. Hill laughed at his deeply embarrassed friend. "You are in love; that's what's the matter!" he said.

The courtship was an awkward one, partly because Jackson had no idea of how to win a young woman's heart. During a misunderstanding, Jackson renewed his attentions to Mrs. Hill's sisters—then, to the astonishment of everyone in Lexington who knew Jackson, he and Ellie were married by Dr. Junkin on August 4, 1853.

The Jacksons took Maggie along on their wedding trip. At the Plains of Abraham near Quebec, where British General James Wolfe had defeated the Marquis Louis Joseph de Montcalm during the French and Indian War in 1759, Jackson studied the scene with a soldier's eye. Later, when Jackson accepted an invitation to witness the Sunday drill of a Highland regiment, the ladies chided hin for violating a higher command: "Remember the Sabbath, and keep it holy." Jackson risked the sin, attended the exercise, and discussed the matter with the Reverend Dr. William S. White when he returned to Lexington. To have put professional interest ahead of the scripture's clear injunction, Jackson decided, had been wrong.

Jackson's health, which had troubled him constantly except for the period of his service in Mexico, improved at once through Ellie's care. He was more relaxed, and he even learned to laugh. Otherwise, there was little change in his routine. He continued to put long hours into study and prayer, and the V.M.I. cadets found him as inept and inflexible as ever.

Suddenly, Jackson's happy new life fell apart. In October, 1854, Ellie died in childbirth. He found his only comfort in religion. "The future is with God," he wrote to Maggie Junkin, Ellie's sister. "And who would have it otherwise, certainly not I. Though the future of this life appears . . . dark; yet I feel assured that it will be illuminated by the Sun of Righteousness." He visited Ellie's grave daily, growing more morose with each sad trip. Maggie grew concerned over the despairing tone of Jackson's letters and came home. Her father shared her alarm; Jackson "was growing heavenward faster than I ever knew any person to do," he wrote.

Jackson turned his attention to church work, and in 1855 he established a Sunday school for the Negro children of Lexington. He had no quarrel with the institution of slavery, and he even owned several household servants; but he felt that regardless of their condition on earth, Negroes were children of his God whose souls were in need of salvation.

In the summer of 1856, Jackson went to Europe. When he returned, refreshed and relaxed by the change of scenery, he renewed his friendship with D. H. Hill's sister-in-law, Miss Mary Anna Morrison, the daughter of a Presbyterian clergyman. On July 16, 1857, they were married.

Health problems again plagued Jackson, and the tragic loss of a baby daughter almost crushed him. With Anna, he visited one mineral spring after another in search of a cure. A heavy load of church activities kept his mind occupied, and there was always the next day's lesson to prepare.

In late November, 1859, Major Jackson was ordered to accompany the V.M.I. Corps of Cadets to Charlestown to witness the hanging of John Brown. He watched the fiery old man die a hideous death without flinching, and he prayed for Brown's soul when the final moment came. From that time onward, Jackson wanted to believe that the dispute between the North and the South could be settled amicably. He suggested to the Reverend Dr. White that religious people everywhere be mobilized to pray for peace, and on January 4, 1861, such an effort was made.

The prospect of war, however, was never very far from Jackson's mind. If it came, he meant to be ready. He recommended that Virginia acquire a new rifled artillery piece known as the Parrott gun, and in a V.M.I. assembly one day he said: "The time for war has not yet come, but it will come, and that soon;

and when it does come, my advice is to draw the sword and throw away the scabbard."

— 4 —

When war did come it seemed at first that Jackson might miss it. Once he had helped move the Corps of V.M.I. Cadets to Richmond in April, 1861, no one seemed to have much for him to do. He was assigned to the Engineering Corps, but no advance in rank came with it, and he hardly considered himself suited for duty of that kind. Governor Letcher quickly set matters straight. He commissioned Jackson as a colonel in the state forces and assigned him to the most sensitive trouble spot on the situation map: Harpers Ferry.

Colonel Jackson took charge of the militia units which had been concentrated at the junction of the Shenandoah and Potomac rivers and instituted a vigorous training program. Cavalrymen such as Turner Ashby and James E. B. Stuart joined him. Progress was slow, for many of the volunteers considered Jackson's discipline to be unduly harsh: he saw clearly what the future would demand of them, but they could not share his vision.

While Jackson was coping with massive supply problems, General Joseph E. Johnston arrived and assumed command. Jackson could not believe that the change amounted to a rebuke, but he was aware that General Robert E. Lee in Richmond had expressed his concern over some of Jackson's actions. Johnston removed Jackson's doubts by placing him in charge of a brigade of the Virginians he had trained for battle.

Johnston considered Harpers Ferry to be indefensible, and he soon got authority to move his command back to Winchester, about thirty miles to the southwest. Jackson conducted a few raids on the Baltimore & Ohio Railroad's lines north of Winchester, but Johnston refused to allow him to cross into western Maryland: Jackson might be right, Johnston conceded, in thinking that an important victory could be won over Union forces north of the Potomac, but there was still a chance that Maryland could be persuaded to join the Confederacy, and military action inside her border might blight that hope.

One morning in early July, 1861, a courier from Colonel Jeb Stuart's cavalry brought Jackson the news that a Union force was only a few miles away. Jackson's men moved out at once and made contact with the enemy near Falling Waters. At first, his brigade seemed to have the Federal troops on the run—but the threat of a flanking movement caused Jackson to shift his plan of battle to that of a rear guard action. The skirmish settled nothing, but—as the British say—it "blooded" Jackson's brigade. He had handled the skirmish expertly, and his losses were light. Shortly after that skirmish, he was promoted to brigadier general.

Well to the east of Winchester, near the Confederate strong point at Manassas Junction, a major Union invasion force was building strength daily. General Pierre G. T. Beauregard was pleading with Richmond to send him more men, and Johnston's troops were about the only ones that could be sent. In mid-July, the order to move eastward reached Johnston. Jackson's First Brigade, his best unit, was to lead the way.

At Piedmont, Jackson's men boarded trains which had been assembled there to take them on to Manassas. For the first time in the Civil War, the railroad was to be used for strategic purposes—and the men of Jackson's brigade were to be the first to enjoy it.

On the morning of July 21, 1861, when Beauregard launched an attack against the southern flank of the Union forces, Jackson was in reserve. As the day's fighting developed, Beauregard and Johnston learned that the Federal commander, General Irvin McDowell, was also determined to attack—and that McDowell's weight was striking the weak northern end of the Confederate line.

Orders came to Jackson to move northward to meet the Union assault. He took a position on Henry House Hill, and he held it against repeated Yankee charges. The onetime professor of artillery tactics put theory into gallant action that morning by placing his guns where they could do maximum harm to the enemy, but he also infused a will to stand fast among his infantrymen. Other units on his flanks broke, but Jackson's men stood.

General Barnard E. Bee's brigade fell back, and Bee rode up to Jackson. "General," he said, "they are beating us back."

Jackson replied: "Sir, we'll give them the bayonet."

Bee caught Jackson's fighting spirit and rallied his men. He pointed to Jackson's troops on the brow of the hill and cried: "There is Jackson standing like a stone wall. Let us determine to die here, and we will conquer. Follow me!"

General Bee did die there, but Beauregard rode up and built a line of battle along the position Jackson had held. Another Union charge surged into his lines, and once more the Confederates repelled it. Suddenly, General Edmund Kirby Smith's men arrived. Beauregard ordered a counterattack, and the Yankees fled in panic. To Jackson's disgust, his men became disorganized soon after the pursuit began. He ordered them to halt, knowing that this was only the beginning.

A shell fragment had broken the middle finger of his left hand. His horse, Little Sorrel, had caught another splinter. His coat had been nicked. But a great victory had been won, and Jackson was content.

News of the Battle of Manassas (Bull Run) spread throughout a jubilant Confederacy, and "Stonewall" Jackson was mentioned prominently. The people of Lexington, however, got only garbled reports of what had happened. Finally, the Reverend Dr. White got a letter from the town's hero. "Now we shall know all the facts," he told his eager parishioners.

"My dear pastor," Jackson wrote, "In my tent last night, after a fatiguing day's service, I remembered that I had failed to send you my contribution for our colored Sunday-school. Enclosed you will find my check for that object, which please acknowledge at your earliest convenience, and oblige yours faithfully, T. J. Jackson."

— 5 —

Manassas was no easy victory for the Confederacy, but a jubilant people assumed that it was. Complacency set in: who needed a large and expensive army, they asked, when Beauregard and Stonewall Jackson had demonstrated that one Southerner could lick ten Yankees?

Even so, the citizens of western Virginia grew more and more uneasy as summer ripened into fall. Another Union army, they knew, was massing behind the Alleghenies; before long, they feared, Federal troops would come southeastward through the misty, rugged mountains and capture the Shenandoah Valley's rich harvest. They petitioned Richmond for some seasoned force to defend them. To their great delight, Secretary of War Judah P. Benjamin sent Major General Jackson.

Stonewall had mixed emotions when he learned of his new assignment. The change meant that he would have to leave his First Brigade at Manassas; the bond between the commander and the men was strong, and it saddened him to think of having to break it. Moreover, he would have to build a new fighting force once he got to Winchester. Still, he shared the concern of the people of the Valley: he was a Valley man himself.

In October, 1861, the day of parting came. At a final review in his honor, Jackson stood up in his stirrups and shouted one of his rare speeches: "In the army of the Shenandoah you were the First Brigade; in the army of the Potomac you were the First Brigade; in the second corps of this army you are the First Brigade; you are the First Brigade in the affections of your General; and I hope by your future deeds and bearing you will be handed down to posterity as the First Brigade in our second War of Independence. Farewell!"

The troops let out a tremendous yell as Stonewall Jackson turned Little Sorrel away. That cheer, he said, was "the sweetest music I ever heard."

Jackson had passed through the Shenandoah Valley many times. He knew the sharp ridges and deep valleys of the Alleghenies; the broad lowland that runs southwestward from the Potomac on the north through Winchester and Strasburg and Harrisonburg on toward Staunton and Lexington; the strange barrier known as the Massanutten that separates the forks of the Shenandoah River and runs parallel to the valley from Strasburg to Harrisonburg; and the Blue Ridge mountains that break the skyline to the east of the Massanutten and the Luray Valley. It is beautiful country, watered by creeks and streams which tumble out of the hills south of Staunton and Waynesboro and run on northeastward to the forks of the Shenandoah which flows on to Harpers Ferry and the Potomac. There were good roads along the valley floors, and trails wound through gaps in the Blue Ridge, the Massanutten, and the Alleghenies.

The region, Jackson realized at once, could not be held even with an army of a hundred thousand men: it was too vast, and the terrain was too complex. Besides, he would have only those militia units the people of the Valley had not already sent off to war. The best he could do, he saw, was to block the Union invasion attempt when and where it came.

Secretary Benjamin ordered General William W. Loring's Army of the Northwest to come down from the passes they were guarding in the Alleghenies to join Jackson at Winchester, and later he sent him his beloved First Brigade—to General Joe Johnston's great distress. Jackson quickly put his troops into a rugged training program which irritated the raw militiamen, but they soon learned—as the First Brigade already knew—that Stonewall tolerated no laxity in any particular. Slowly, amid much grumbling, his Army of the Valley became worthy of its name.

With winter coming on, Jackson suspected that the commander of the heavy Union concentrations north of the Potomac and west of the Alleghenies would expect him to suspend military operations for the season. For armies to go into winter quarters was almost habitual, and there was a great deal to be said for observing the custom in that forbidding region. Jackson, however, had no such intention. Like Napoleon, he believed that it was preferable for the men to remain active. Besides, he could best protect the Valley by attacking isolated Federal detachments and destroying them one at a time—thus preventing them from combining their strength and crushing him.

Audacious as Jackson's plan was, the authorities in Richmond approved it. In early and mid-December he took raiding forces out to strike the Chesapeake and Ohio Canal and the Baltimore & Ohio Railroad, but these were merely graduation exercises. While preparations for the campaign went on at Winchester, Jackson kept his intentions secret: the men would find out where he meant to take them when they got there, and that would be soon enough.

Anna Jackson came to Winchester for a brief visit around Christmastime, and she stayed behind with friends when Jackson led his army off to the northwest on the morning of New Year's Day, 1862. She had been pleased to find that her husband's health had improved tremendously: his old symptoms were gone, and she had never seen him happier—or busier.

The day was deceptively warm, and as the men marched up through the foothills of the Alleghenies some of them threw away their overcoats. But before long, the wind turned bitter cold, and snow and sleet lashed them. Even Jackson was caught by the sudden change in the weather. Someone had given him a bottle of whiskey, and he astonished his staff by taking a long drink before passing it around. Jackson soon complained of being hot, and he unbuttoned his coat. Moreover, he grew talkative. This was most unusual, the men on his staff agreed: the general had often said that he was fond of whiskey, but they had never seen him enjoy it.

But this was a new Jackson. No longer was he obsessed with his maladies. Ambition, the force that had always frightened him because it was so strong, had ceased to trouble him: he was a major general in command of an army that was moving forward to contact, and no man could ask for a better opportunity to be of service.

Jackson's mellow mood did not last very long, for the march seemed to be deteriorating into a fiasco. The wagons had not been able to keep up with the troops on the winding mountain trails. The men were miserable and hungry. The weather grew steadily worse. "Press on!" Jackson shouted, but the command could not be heeded by soldiers who were tired and chilled and unable to keep their footing on the glare ice that covered the road.

On the fourth day of the campaign, Jackson reached Bath—roughly forty miles north of Winchester—and attacked the Union garrison. Everything went wrong. After prolonged skirmishing, however, the Federal troops withdrew. Jackson ordered a pursuit, but nothing came of it.

Several days later, Jackson turned his men toward Romney. As before, the march was a nightmare: snow and sleet fell, horses and men slipped continually, rations ran out. At night there was no shelter, and each day seemed worse than the one before it.

On January 14, the Union garrison at Romney saw Jackson's weary, frozen troops approaching. Curiously, they decided to abandon the town and even a large amount of supplies without putting up a fight. While Jackson's men got some rest, he planned a march that would carry him even deeper into western Virginia—but that campaign never took place, for his soldiers were simply too tired to go on. Reluctantly, Jackson gave up his hopes for a vigorous winter offensive. He left General Loring's forces at Romney and took the remainder of the Army of the Valley back to Winchester.

Jackson knew that he had little to lose by dispersing his units; at the same time, he felt that he should station them near enough to Winchester to effect a concentration rapidly if a Union invasion force broke through his thin screen. Accordingly, he scattered detachments along a rough perimeter with Winchester in the center. To protect that key point, he ordered the construction of fortifications on the northern side of the town.

General Loring's opinion of Jackson's generalship was never very high, but it plummeted after his forces were left behind to hold Romney. Loring's men had suffered miserably during the march, and morale was dangerously low. In addition, Loring considered Romney indefensible: in an out-of-channels message to Secretary of War Benjamin, he said so.

Benjamin immediately ordered Jackson to have Loring withdraw from Romney, and Jackson complied at once. In acknowledging the Secretary's telegram, however, Jackson said: "With such interference in my command I cannot expect to be of much service in the field, and accordingly respectfully request to be ordered to report for duty to the superintendent of the Virginia Military Institute at Lexington. . . . Should this application not be granted, I respectfully request that the President will accept my resignation from the Army."

Jackson forwarded his letter to Benjamin through General Joseph Johnston, as was proper. Johnston read Stonewall's words in utter astonishment. If anything, he was more enraged than Jackson at Benjamin's inept handling of Loring's complaint. As the officer commanding both Jackson and Loring, he should have been consulted; instead, he learned of the Secretary of War's order to evacuate Romney only when he saw Jackson's letter of resignation. "Is that not as great an official wrong to me as the order itself is to you?" Joe Johnston asked Jackson.

In Jackson's mind, however, the matter was already settled.

He had never been the kind of man who hesitated to act when he faced a situation in which the right could easily and clearly be distinguished from the wrong, and this was just such a case. Men could and would disagree with his decision; but that was their problem, not his.

Johnston, for example, reminded Jackson of the danger the Union's threat posed to the very survival of the Confederate people and appealed to Stonewall to ignore Benjamin's "official wrong" for the good of the cause. His effort was sincere, but it was doomed—not because he had overestimated Jackson's patriotism, but because he failed to appreciate the depth of Jackson's dismay.

The error was a natural one, for at the time no one really knew Stonewall well enough to be able to understand why he behaved as he did. Even today, when there are a number of searching and detailed biographies of Jackson, the task may be impossible. This much, however, seems clear: in order for him to perform, he required a set of rules which had been ordained by the kind of authority in which he could put his absolute trust.

When Jackson's father died, he gave his obedience to his Uncle Cummings and even ran away from another foster home so that the loyalty he had awarded could be maintained. He was not prepared for West Point, but he adapted himself to the Academy's requirements with zeal and—ultimately—remarkable success. When God won him, He won him completely. Any physician who put forth a remedy for Jackson's ailments could be sure of his compliance with the prescription. The old physical symptoms being gone, he had no further need of doctors, but Presbyterian ministers still held him in awe of their learning and piety.

Such a man was ideally suited for service in the Army, as Jackson's splendid conduct during the Mexican War demonstrated. To stand like a stone wall in battle at Manassas was gallant, but it was also what duty required. The rules were sound and well known. And it was in this kind of world that Jackson was certain that he could be an effective servant not only of his country but of his Lord God.

Jackson respected authority, but he was also ruthless in demanding respect for the authority which—according to the rules of the Army—he was due. He was no martinet who required proper uniform or spit and polish, but any subordinate commander who failed to measure up to his standards of obedience in matters directly related to combat operations could expect no mercy at his hands. He gave, in turn, his very best efforts to see that the men committed to his care were well equipped, well fed, and well led.

There was nothing about this new war, or about Jackson's conduct of command, which suggested that the rules in which he had put his complete faith no longer applied. Jackson gave loyalty and received it, and everything seemed to be functioning effectively. When he had called for assistance, Secretary Benjamin had done his best to provide it. When the War Department had asked for information, he had supplied it.

Suddenly, by interfering with his performance of the duties assigned him, the Secretary of War shattered the whole framework in which Jackson had found his only basis for effective operation. An authority had destroyed Authority.

Jackson, bereft of all that was important to him except his trust in God and his love for Anna and his hope of making V.M.I. cadets better educated soldiers, resigned. To him, no other course of action was worthy of consideration.

Benjamin, however, had simply been human enough to panic when he had received Loring's complaints about the conditions at Romney and an unsubstantiated report of Federal activity in that area at roughly the same time. His response had been to order Jackson to withdraw Loring's command from what seemed to be the site of a disaster in the making. Time, the Secretary probably believed, was of the essence. If he could have issued the order to Loring directly, he might well have done so—but this was not possible, and he had done the next best thing by sending it to Jackson.

Still, Benjamin had broken the rules. His proper course of action would have been to order Jackson, *through Johnston,* to look into Loring's situation and to reexamine the desirability of holding Romney in the light of the intelligence he had received regarding Union threats to that outpost. He could have added the authorization to abandon Romney if either commander considered such a solution appropriate or necessary. No significant amount of time would have been lost in the transmission of such a message: as it turned out, much might have been saved.

Loring was in no real danger at Romney, and if his men were not comfortable there it is doubtful that they would have enjoyed a higher standard of living anywhere else along the battle line of the Confederacy. They had suffered during the marches to Bath and Romney because of Jackson's insistence that they "Press on!"—but so had the rest of Stonewall's command. If their misery had been greater than that endured without complaint by the First Brigade, it was possible that their leadership had not been as determined or their discipline as seasoned.

Jackson may have been guilty of showing some favoritism to the brigade which had stood with him like a stone wall back in July while Loring's men were as yet unblooded, but he had certainly not left Loring at Romney to be destroyed. If anything, he had spared Loring's relatively weak troops the rigors of still other hard marches. And if he had not trusted them, he would not have assigned them a place of key responsibility in his scheme for the defense of the entire Shenandoah Valley.

Moreover, Federal threats to Loring's outpost at Romney were to be expected. Jackson's audacity in launching a winter campaign could not be left unchallenged. If Union patrols had not probed the area, Jackson *would* have been surprised. But he did not mean to be surprised in any sense: he was trying to get materials for the construction of a telegraph line to Romney, and in the meantime his couriers were keeping him in close communication with Loring.

Loring, of course, was the key man in the controversy. He violated the rules by communicating with Benjamin directly, but Jackson took no obvious notice of that act of insubordination. Benjamin then compounded the error by giving in to panic, breaking vastly more important rules in the course of trying to cope with an emergency which existed only in his own mind. As a result, President Jefferson Davis—a West Pointer and Mexican War regimental commander who knew what the rules were—was obliged to face a major crisis: the price of a clear-cut decision was the loss of Benjamin or Jackson, but he could not afford to lose either man.

Davis, who had been Secretary of War in the Administration of President Franklin Pierce some years earlier, was inclined to carry out his role as Commander-in-Chief of Confederate forces with maximum vigor. Accordingly, he needed the kind of Secretary of War who would be useful but who would not interfere with Davis' own direction of operations. Benjamin did not quite fit that specification, and his improper handling of the Loring case was not his first error. Davis decided to shift Benjamin to the post of Secretary of State, a position in which his great talents could be retained and put to better use. Benjamin's replacement would have to be the kind of man who could be content with communicating the President's wishes and handling routine War Department administration.

Loring, obviously, could not continue to serve effectively under Jackson. It was an easy matter to transfer him to another theater of operations, and this was done. That left only the problem of Jackson's resignation, and with the causes for his indignation removed it was not difficult to persuade him to withdraw his letter for the good of the Confederate nation.

The adroit solution Davis worked out was soon to be of incalculable importance to the Confederate war effort, for with the return of good fighting weather in the spring of 1862 the Union mounted a determined offensive to crush the South. Jackson and his Army of the Valley were essential to the preservation of the embattled nation. Within the next few weeks they were to conduct one of military history's most brilliant campaigns.

— 6 —

In March, 1862, General George B. McClellan opened the Union's massive attempt to capture Richmond, the Confederate capital, by taking his Army of the Potomac by sea down to the long peninsula that extends southeastward from Richmond between the York and the James rivers. Other Federal forces had already started to move toward Richmond by way of Harpers Ferry and Winchester, so that Jackson's Army of the Valley could be cut off from Joe Johnston's men.

Johnston evacuated the old positions around Manassas and shifted his troops southward to block McClellan's advance up the peninsula. His orders to Jackson were to hold the Shenandoah Valley and to be prepared to join him if necessary, but

Jackson promptly pointed out that the geography of Virginia made one mission or the other impossible. Johnston then told Jackson to draw as much Federal strength over into the Valley as he could.

General Nathaniel Banks' Union troops approached Winchester in early March. Jackson ordered an evacuation of the town and called a council of war to discuss the Federal threat, but little came of the conference because his brigade commanders had already withdrawn their troops too far to the south to enable Jackson to propose a counterattack he had in mind. There was, however, one firm decision: there would be no more councils of war.

Jackson let the withdrawal continue through Strasburg to Mount Jackson, forty-odd miles southwest of Winchester in the western corridor of the Shenandoah Valley. He used the time he had gained to put his troops through another rugged training cycle and to improve the food and supply systems on which so much would soon depend. During those two quiet weeks, he also asked Major Jedediah Hotchkiss, his engineer, to prepare new maps of the Valley and to work out tables of mileage from point to point.

Colonel Turner Ashby's cavalry kept the enemy forces under constant surveillance while Jackson's main units were going through their commander's hardening process at Mount Jackson. On March 21, Ashby brought in the news that Banks had pulled the Union garrison at Strasburg back north to Winchester. Jackson interpreted this report to mean that Banks was about to send troops over to reinforce McClellan, and he saw that there was only one way to keep this from happening. He ordered his men to prepare for a hard march at once.

The performance of Jackson's troops during the advance to Strasburg and then to the vicinity of Winchester disappointed him. There was too much straggling and not enough speed. Still, he reached Kernstown, just south of Winchester, shortly after noon on March 23.

That day happened to be a Sunday, and Jackson's initial inclination was to postpone aggressive action until the next day lest he incur the Lord's displeasure. Ashby reported the enemy's strength at only a few regiments, but it was always possible that Banks would send back reinforcements. On any day but Sunday,

Jackson would have attacked at once—but could he risk a violation of the Sabbath? Earlier, he had not even dared to read a letter on the Lord's Day. Now, however, military circumstances suggested that he should fight.

With trust in the assumption that the Lord would forgive one sin for the sake of preventing a greater one, Jackson sent his men forward against the Yankee line. At first, all went to his satisfaction. Suddenly, however, he saw the First Brigade reeling backward. He rode up to rally them, but even he could not arrest their retreat: the Union defenders were far more numerous than Ashby had indicated, and the Confederates had run out of ammunition. "Go back and give them the bayonet," Jackson urged, but in vain.

Finally, Jackson was obliged to order a withdrawal. His chief surgeon, Dr. Hunter McGuire, expressed his concern about the Confederate casualties who were still lying where they had fallen. "Make yourself easy about that," Stonewall said grimly. "This army stays until the last wounded man is removed. Before I will leave them to the enemy I will lose many more men."

Jackson considered the Battle of Kernstown a defeat, but he was correct only in part. The vigor of his assault that Sunday had caused the Union officers to cancel their plans to reduce Federal strength in the Valley. While Jackson had lost in a tactical sense, then, he had won in strategic terms.

After Kernstown, with his men in camp once more at Mount Jackson, Jackson was more determined than ever to get his army in hand. He relieved General Richard B. Garnett of the command of the First Brigade and pressed charges against him. He issued strict orders for the conduct of marches. The Army of the Valley, he decided, would make up for its lack of size by being incredibly fast: it would be a shock force, literally a foot cavalry.

Hotchkiss' geography lessons helped Jackson to plan his next moves. The Valley's long corridors, the engineer pointed out, were ideal for Stonewall's purposes. He could lure the Yankees down one side of the Massanutten Mountain and then slide into a gap, thus setting a trap. Or, if Jackson chose, he could slip into the other corridor and use its roads in striking deep in his enemy's rear. There were a number of splendid opportunities open: it was merely a matter of having men who were capable of moving fast enough to take maximum advantage of them. While Jackson was toughening his army at Mount Jackson in early April, President Abraham Lincoln was still reacting to the Battle of Kernstown. General Irvin McDowell's Union corps had been scheduled to move to the peninsula to join McClellan's invasion force, but Lincoln decided to hold that important unit near Washington. In addition, he sent reinforcements which might otherwise have gone to McClellan over to General John C. Frémont's army west of the Alleghenies, on Jackson's flank. Banks was definitely to be kept in the Valley—at least, until Jackson was destroyed.

Banks had 15,000 men to throw against Jackson's 6000, but he was reluctant to advance against the Mount Jackson Confederate position because Jackson could ease eastward through the Luray Gap in the Massanutten at New Market, move northward through the eastern corridor past Front Royal, and cut his supply line. By mid-April, however, Banks decided to accept the gamble: he pressed Jackson past New Market all the way up to Harrisonburg. Jackson let the Yankees have the ground without much of a protest, for his mind was on something else.

Joe Johnston, alarmed by Banks' superiority in numbers, sent Jackson 8000 men under the command of General Richard Ewell. This welcome reinforcement arrived in the Blue Ridge mountains at Swift Run Gap just as Jackson was closing into Conrad's Store, a settlement about twelve miles east of Banks' forces at Harrisonburg.

As always, Jackson was keeping his thoughts to himself—but the officers on his staff knew that he was up to something. "He's in one of his crazy moods," one of them remarked. Clues were few, and they raised more questions than they answered. At Harrisonburg, during the withdrawal from Mount Jackson, he had sent only half of his wagons on to Conrad's Store; the rest had been sent to Staunton, but no one was told why. At Conrad's Store, General Edward Johnson—who commanded an outfit in the Alleghenies well to the west of Staunton—came to see Jackson. Still, Jackson's position at Conrad's Store blocked Banks from pressing southward to Staunton. Everything was in balance, and the men on Stonewall's staff were certain that their commander would not allow the equilibrium to last for very long.

They were right. Late in April, after a mysterious conference with Dick Ewell, Jackson moved his troops southward to the railroad. While the men climbed aboard trains that were obviously going to take them westward, Jackson ordered Turner Ashby to bedevil Banks' forces at Harrisonburg with vigorous skirmishes to screen the movement. Ewell's division remained at Swift Run Gap to watch Banks.

"As sure as I live," Major John Harman, Stonewall's quartermaster, said, "Jackson's a cracked man." So he seemed, and that impression gained in credibility as he yelled "Press on!" through the rain to wagon masters and the drivers of artillery teams who were bogging down in the mud. "Press on" where? And why? Jackson said nothing, except when he had to issue an order. Usually, all he said was, "Press on!"

— 7 —

Only Jackson really knew what he meant to do, but that did not keep men on both sides from guessing. Some rumors had him advancing toward Winchester. Others suggested that he was about to strike Banks at Harrisonburg. Banks was aware that Jackson had moved, but he was as baffled as anyone else. The citizens of Staunton were at their wits' end: they had seen much coming and going, and none of it gave them any reason to expect anything but their abandonment.

Actually, Jackson had foreseen the threat a Union force under General Robert H. Milroy posed to the vital east-west railroad which carried supplies from the Valley through Staunton to Richmond. With characteristic secrecy, he had sealed off the movement of his army so that he could combine his forces with "Allegheny" Johnson, beat Milroy, and then return for a strike at Banks. Ewell's arrival at Swift Run Gap to check Banks at Harrisonburg had made this possible. Still, there was some madness in the scheme: Napoleon had long since warned that a commander should never divide his forces in the face of an enemy, and "Tom Fool" Jackson had done precisely that.

Jackson and Allegheny Johnson collided with Milroy's troops near McDowell on May 8, 1862. Milroy attacked and was thrown back. Jackson ordered a pursuit, but forest fires checked his advance well short of Franklin.

Much as Jackson may have wanted to protect the railroad and to save both Staunton and Allegheny Johnson's forces, he had his own interests in mind, as well: Jed Hotchkiss had shown him the routes Milroy's troops could take if they were ordered to move eastward through the mountains to reinforce Banks at Harrisonburg. When the pursuit had to be called off after the Battle of McDowell, Jackson ordered all of those roads blocked. That done, he turned his men eastward—but only after a pause for an army-wide service of thanksgiving to God.

Harrisonburg and General Banks' forces were his new objectives. He pressed his men on to Mount Solon, a community about eight miles southwest of Harrisonburg; paused there to observe a national day of prayer and thanksgiving; and held a conference with Dick Ewell, who had come over from Swift Run Gap in order to get untangled: too many men were giving him too many conflicting orders.

Ewell had good cause to be confused. Jackson, Ewell's immediate superior, had told him to stay at Swift Run Gap to prevent Banks from moving southward to menace Staunton and the railroad, and this he had done. General Robert E. Lee, who was responsible for directing Confederate operations outside the Richmond area, had noted that Banks was abandoning Harrisonburg and moving northeastward toward Strasburg and Winchester, and he had authorized Ewell to pursue the Yankees. Joe Johnston, who still considered himself in charge of Jackson's forces even though he was locked with McClellan in battle east of Richmond, informed Ewell that he expected him to remain ready to shift either to Fredericksburg or Richmond on short notice.

Jackson straightened Ewell out by giving him still another order: to move up the Luray Valley so that he could join him in an attack against Banks, wherever he could be made to stand and fight. By doing this, Jackson risked Johnston's displeasure —but he had Lee's approval. There had been a time, much earlier in the war, when Jackson had not thought much of Lee's generalship; now, though, a curious rapport was growing between them even though they had no personal contact.

Turner Ashby's cavalrymen had discovered that Banks' positions at Strasburg in the western corridor of the Valley were heavily fortified. Jackson responded to that report by slipping eastward through the gap in the Massanutten near New Market to Luray, where he joined forces with Dick Ewell for a rapid drive northward to Front Royal. Banks' troops at Strasburg were only ten miles west of Front Royal, and from Front Royal a march up to Winchester would be easy.

On the afternoon of May 23, Jackson's men drove the Union garrison out of Front Royal in a spirited fight. Stonewall ordered a pursuit, for he was disappointed at not having trapped the Federal defenders. He led it for a few miles toward Winchester, but he finally decided that enough had been done for one day and reluctantly ordered a halt.

Banks, over in Strasburg, was astonished—and so was President Lincoln. By everything that was right and holy, Jackson should have advanced along the western corridor from New Market to Strasburg; instead, he had routed the Union force which was supposed to guard Banks' eastern flank. Banks gave up his elaborate fortifications at Strasburg and shot northward to Winchester.

Jackson expected as much, but the plan he developed for stopping Banks left much to be desired. It was too complicated: he tried to block the Federal retreat everywhere, and he wound up by missing it almost everywhere. Turner Ashby and a brigade under the command of Colonel Richard Taylor caught Banks' wagons near Middletown, but most of the Yankees had already moved northward. The vigor of the Confederates' pursuit was also retarded by the pleasure of looting the Union supplies they had captured.

Although Jackson pressed his men northward all that night, Banks stayed well ahead of him. A few ambushes slowed Stonewall's advance, but he ignored them and rode on toward Winchester. A regimental commander begged him to grant an hour's rest. "Colonel," he replied, "I yield to no man in sympathy for the gallant men under my command; but I am obliged to sweat them tonight, that I may save their blood tomorrow."

Once again, Jackson was obliged to fight a battle before Winchester on a Sunday. This time he did not hesitate: he sent his troops forward. And this time, despite strong Union opposition, his men cleared the town of the enemy. The jubilant citizens of Winchester greeted Stonewall's men with baskets of food, but Jackson felt that celebration was premature and sent cavalry after Banks. Most of the Federal army escaped.

Even so, there was much to be thankful for—and Jackson, who now saw that the Lord was not unalterably opposed to battles on Sunday, proclaimed the next day as a time for the expression of gratitude. While the men knelt in prayer, panic rocked the capital of their enemies: Banks had been diligent in passing on every rumor he picked up, and most of them had exaggerated Jackson's strength tremendously. Lincoln had been on the point of letting Irvin McDowell take his corps southward to join McClellan in the final offensive to capture Richmond. Now he turned them westward to crush Jackson.

What Lincoln had in mind was a gigantic pincer movement which would trap Stonewall while he was still in the Winchester area. General John C. Frémont, west of the Alleghenies, was ordered to move eastward. McDowell was told to dash westward. The junction point would be somewhere south of Winchester.

McClellan needed McDowell's forces desperately, especially since their route of advance would require Joe Johnston to weaken his lines east of Richmond to meet the new threat from the north. McDowell was all for joining McClellan, for he had serious doubts as to his ability to reach the Valley in time to stop Jackson and he could do more, he respectfully advised the President, if he could be permitted to consider Richmond his objective. Lincoln told McDowell to go west, and westward he went. Jackson, and not Lincoln or McClellan, was dictating Union strategy.

Nothing could have given more pleasure to Joe Johnston and his men east of Richmond. For weeks, Yankees had been setting their watches by the capital's church bells. "Old Joe" was anxious to throw the invaders back, but he had been hesitant to order an offensive as long as McDowell had been a threat. With Jackson pulling McDowell deeper and deeper into the Valley, however, Johnston could lash out at McClellan.

Jackson, meanwhile, was making sure that the enormous stockpiles of Union supplies his troops had captured at Winchester and Martinsburg were shipped to the rear. His patrols were along the Potomac, and he even had forces moving into position to take Harpers Ferry. He was aware of the Lincoln-directed effort to trap him, but he meant for it to fail. So great was his confidence that he sent a trusted and influential friend, Colonel Alex R. Boteler, to Richmond to plead for reinforcements: with 40,000 men, Jackson believed, he could invade the North and panic Lincoln into lifting the siege of Richmond.

By May 27, Jackson had withdrawn his men from the banks of the Potomac and was moving southward to attend to Lincoln's latest effort to eliminate his troublesome army from the war. Now the hard training and strict march discipline Jackson had imposed paid off, for the foot cavalry's salvation depended upon the speed with which the troops cleared Strasburg—a point Jackson held open until his old First Brigade, which had been acting as his rear guard, caught up and passed through.

Jackson moved along the western corridor of the Valley toward Mount Jackson, but his mind was well ahead of the vanguard of his army. He got a briefing from Jed Hotchkiss on the terrain around Port Republic, a little town south of the Massanutten near Harrisonburg and Conrad's Store, and he liked what he heard: from Port Republic he would be in a position to strike at Union forces in either compartment. The weather also favored Jackson's plan. Heavy rains had caused the streams to overflow, and he destroyed the bridges he did not need.

By this time, Joe Johnston had launched a counterattack east of Richmond which was possible only because Jackson had drawn McDowell to the Valley. In the first day's fighting Johnston had been seriously wounded, and Lee assumed command. The drive accomplished little in terms of ground gained, but it made an impression on General McClellan: his timetable for the capture of Richmond had been upset, and Lee now had a few days in which to get the Army of Northern Virginia ready to drive the invaders away from the capital.

Jackson closed into the Port Republic area and waited for his enemies to make their moves. Ashby's cavalry screened the area, but the cost was high: in a skirmish with a Union outpost, Ashby was killed while leading a charge.

The Massanutten, Jed Hotchkiss pointed out, was worth several divisions to Jackson because it separated the Union army under Frémont in the western valley from McDowell's forces in the eastern corridor. The Federal commanders could not combine their strength and crush Jackson as long as the branches of the Shenandoah were out of their banks, for the bridge at Port Republic—the only one left standing—was in Confederate hands. Jackson, however, could use that bridge in launching attacks against either enemy army.

Ewell's troops faced Frémont's outposts a few miles northwest of Port Republic. On June 7, Jackson decided that it would be better to assault Frémont first: his artillery batteries at Port Republic could probably keep the Union division under the command of General James Shields, which threatened the town from the east, from causing him any trouble. Ewell moved out, but Frémont was in no mood for a fight. Jackson called off the attack.

The next day was a Sunday, and Stonewall had hoped that it would be a day of rest: his enemies, however, had other ideas. Shields broke the Sabbath morning calm by throwing a determined raid against Port Republic, and for a time it seemed that his troops would capture the town's key bridge. Jackson needed reinforcements from Dick Ewell, but Frémont had suddenly turned belligerent and was pressing Ewell at the little village of Cross Keys. While the men in Port Republic fought off Shields' attackers, Ewell repulsed Frémont's charges with such vigor that one of his regiments drove the Yankees back for more than a mile. Ewell wanted to press on, but Jackson was inclined to be more cautious. Meanwhile, Shields pulled back from Port Republic.

That night, Jackson decided that Shields' division had to be eliminated. It was the smaller of the two Union forces, and their position was within easy reach of his troops. He directed Ewell to leave only one brigade to hold Frémont and to bring the rest of his men through Port Republic to the line of departure east of town at earliest dawn. With luck, or—as Jackson put it—the blessing of Providence, a quick victory over Shields would enable him to turn his troops westward against Frémont well before noon.

The attack against Shields moved out on time, but Union resistance checked Jackson's advance from the beginning. As the morning wore on, it was apparent that the position Shields held could not be taken by frontal assault. Jackson tried a flanking maneuver, and it worked: by eleven o'clock that morning, Shields was pulling back.

That left Frémont, but Jackson was content. He ordered his men to march into Brown's Gap, a saddle high in the Blue Ridge a few miles to the southeast: neither Frémont nor Shields could bother him there, and his presence on their flank would keep them from venturing south of Port Republic. Moreover, if General Lee needed the Army of the Valley at Richmond, Jackson would be ready to move.

Even then, it was not apparent that the Valley Campaign was over. In late May, while his forces had been on the Potomac above Winchester, Jackson had suggested an advance into Maryland and Pennsylvania and had sent Colonel Boteler to Richmond to plead for reinforcements. Lincoln's clumsily executed pincer movement made the proposal academic while Jackson was in the upper valley at Port Republic, but the idea was remembered when Confederate cavalrymen brought in reports that Frémont and Shields were retreating northward. Lee sent fourteen regiments to him, and President Davis approved Stonewall's invasion plan.

While Jackson's men rested near Port Republic, couriers carried a series of messages from Richmond to Stonewall's headquarters and back again. In one of them, Lee outlined his plan for a massive counterattack against McClellan in which Jackson's troops would deliver the critical assault; Stonewall liked it, and gladly set aside his earlier proposal for a strike at Pennsylvania.

Jackson turned his thoughts to the east, but he shared them with no one. "Leave your enfeebled troops to watch the country," Lee had said. He could do that easily: in fact, the rest of his instructions—to move to Ashland by road and rail, to be prepared to sweep from the north across the rear of the Union army, and to join Lee for a conference as soon as possible—presented no great difficulties. Lee's plan was sound by every test. Moreover, it contained the kind of audacity Stonewall relished.

After Jackson had preserved the secrecy of the operation in his usual way—by saying almost nothing, and by behaving in such a contradictory fashion that even his closest staff officers were bewildered—the movement began. Jackson rode ahead of the vanguard and seemed to disappear for several days; actually, he had gone to Lee's headquarters near Richmond to assist in working out the final details of the new offensive.

— 8 —

The last stage of Jackson's journey eastward was a hard one, but by mid-afternoon on June 23, 1862, he had completed it. For fourteen hours he had been in the saddle, and he had covered more than fifty miles. Weary as he was, he reported to General Lee. Gracious as always, Lee offered him a choice of refreshments: Jackson accepted a glass of buttermilk.

Lee assembled the rest of his commanders—Generals James Longstreet, A. P. Hill, and Jackson's good friend and brother-in-law, D. H. Hill. Longstreet was not impressed by Jackson: the Army of the Valley, Longstreet believed, was a second-rate outfit. The other officers at the conference, however, were in awe of the tired man who had just conducted a lightning campaign which had diverted more than 60,000 Union troops from George McClellan's invasion force at the very time "Little Mac" had needed them most.

In an even, methodical manner, Lee presented his plan to the leaders. He envisioned a huge envelopment of McClellan's northern flank, with Jackson's troops making the first move. Once Jackson had swept past the end of the Union battle line east of Ashland and had broken into McClellan's rear area, Lee expected his enemy to withdraw from positions covering the crossings of the Chickahominy River and Beaver Dam Creek, thus enabling first A. P. Hill and then D. H. Hill to commit their forces to the turning movement. Later, Lee could feed his other units into the offensive.

Everything depended upon Jackson. Under his leadership, the Army of the Valley had earned a reputation for being able to cover maximum distances in a minimum of time without loss of combat effectiveness. Moreover, Lee was mindful of the shock and surprise that could be gained by putting Jackson into the battle at a point which had not been covered by Confederate forces earlier—a point which was also the nearest one Jackson's men could reach within the next few days.

That conference was held on the afternoon of June 23. Jackson said that his army could be east of Ashland on the line of departure for the offensive by the next night and that they could go forward on the twenty-fifth. Longstreet objected: another twenty-four hours ought to be provided, he thought, because of the possibility of Union cavalry raids or Yankee roadblocks. Jackson agreed. His men, he said, would be ready to attack at dawn on Thursday, June 26.

Jackson climbed back into the saddle and rode northward all that night through a driving rainstorm. By sunrise, he was at Beaver Dam, about twenty-six miles northwest of Ashland. The head of his column was there, but march discipline had fallen apart in his absence and for all he knew the line of men stretched all the way back to Brown's Gap. Fatigue caught up with him; before he rested, though, he told his staff officers to have the rest of his unit close in behind the vanguard which he had halted at Beaver Dam.

The staff officers did what they could, but the results were poor. If Stonewall rode up and said "Press on!" men obeyed. For an aide or "yaller dawg" to appear and to utter the same command, however, invited—and got—only derisive replies from the troops, not response. There was not much the reviled staff officers could say in rebuttal. They had no idea of how important it was for the Army of the Valley to press on to Beaver Dam, much less to Ashland, for Jackson had told them nothing that indicated a need for haste or urgency.

On Wednesday, some progress was made—but not enough. Jackson rode along his column shouting "Press on!" and the men did get to within five miles or so of Ashland, but that still left them roughly eleven miles west of where they ought to have been if Lee's timetable for his offensive was to be observed.

Jackson was supposed to attack at three o'clock on the next morning, Thursday, June 26. At eight o'clock, his men started their march of eleven miles to the line of departure. The day was hot and humid. Yankee cavalry patrols skirmished along the flanks. Roads were poor, at best. Bridges had been washed out by recent rains, and precious time was lost while scouts found fords. Men who had never been east of the Blue Ridge, soldiers who had lived all their lives at altitudes in excess of 2,000 feet, were all but suffocated by the dense air of the coastal lowlands. "Press on!" Stonewall demanded, and the troops trudged eastward—slowly, too slowly.

Lee's entire drive was contingent on Jackson's success in striking the Union flank, getting behind its northern end, and demoralizing the Yankee troops facing A. P. Hill and D. H. Hill so that they could cross the streams in their path without having to take intolerable losses. Jackson was late, but he sent no progress reports to Lee to advise him of that critical fact. Lee was aware that Jackson was late, but he made no effort to find out why or what Jackson still considered attainable.

General Jeb Stuart's cavalrymen fought off Union probes during the afternoon, in accordance with their mission to screen Jackson's advance, and the sound of gunfire in the north gave A. P. Hill the impression that Jackson—though hopelessly late —was opening the offensive. That was to have been his signal to advance, and he observed it. He was mistaken. His men were cut to pieces as they attempted to cross Beaver Dam Creek, a line the enemy could not have tried to hold if Jackson had delivered his assault on time.

Where *was* Jackson? He was on the line of departure he should have reached almost a day before, going into bivouac for the night.

During the next day, Friday, Jackson sent his men forward to accomplish the mission they ought to have completed twenty-four hours earlier, before 1400 men of A. P. Hill's division had paid the highest toll the crossing of a mere creek can require. Union resistance was light, and Jackson made good progress. At Walnut Grove Church, Jackson paused to confer with A. P. Hill, who told him that a battle might be shaping up to the southeast near Gaines' Mill.

Suddenly, Lee rode up. He took Jackson aside, and for a long time the two men talked. No one ever learned what either man said. When they parted, Jackson had a new destination: Cold Harbor, a crossroads settlement to the southeast of Walnut Grove Church and east of Gaines' Mill. A guide came forward and led Jackson along the most direct route.

The sound of firing told Jackson that he was not heading in the direction Lee intended and that he was probably on the wrong road. He questioned the guide, who was bold enough to say that if Jackson had been more explicit earlier they *would*

have been on the correct road: Stonewall took the rebuke without comment, turned the column back to the junction, and
arrived at the Battle of Gaines' Mill too late to deliver the
flanking attack Lee had expected him to launch. Even so, his
units charged along with the rest of Lee's long line and took
their objectives—at very great cost.

On Saturday, Jackson spent most of the day supervising the
repair of Grapevine Bridge over the Chickahominy River—and
there were the dead to bury and wounded to evacuate. On Sunday, Grapevine Bridge was still not open. Meanwhile, Lee had
given the honor of conducting the critical attack to Longstreet:
what Jackson apparently could not accomplish from the northeast, perhaps Longstreet could attend to from the southwest.

By Monday morning, June 30, Jackson's men were finally
across the Grapevine Bridge and moving south of the Chickahominy. Orders had been given him much earlier to join forces
with General John Magruder. As Jackson was carrying them
out, General Lee rode up. Jackson should move due south to
White Oak Swamp and cross it, Lee directed.

Now the troops who had fought so brilliantly up beyond the
Blue Ridge during the Valley Campaign were to be subjected
to combat in one of the most dismal bogs in Virginia. Rotten
stumps stood in the mud lake, moss hung from tree limbs, and
mosquitoes swarmed in the foul air. It was—and is—the kind
of dense hell a man wants to pass through as quickly as possible,
but roadbeds and bridges were not easy to find.

White Oak Swamp was a Union asset that day, and the Federal units just to the south of it made full use of the miserable
barrier. Jackson, riding at the head of his troops, saw Yankee
artillery on the high ground beyond the swamp: he found a
position on which he could mass his own guns without attracting the enemy's attention, and before long the Union gunners
were reeling backward—stunned into senselessness by Professor
Jackson's sudden concentration of fire.

Jackson quickly led his cavalrymen across the swamp to engage the Union infantry. To his horror, more Federal guns—
concealed in the underbrush—opened fire and broke up his
attack. Stonewall withdrew.

By this time, Jackson was utterly exhausted. He had been
tired even before he had left Brown's Gap, more than a week

before—and in the days and nights that followed he got practically no rest, hardly ever ate a decent meal and missed most of the more usual kind, spent hour after hour in the saddle, fought skirmishes and battles, and kept pressing himself onward, ever onward, whether his men could keep up with him or not. That afternoon, however, his stamina left him. He took a nap, but it did no good: his body got up, but his mind remained asleep—or so it seemed to the men who came to him for the orders he could not give.

That night, as Jackson and his staff were eating, Jackson dozed off with a biscuit between his teeth. He snapped out of his stupor a moment later and said: "Now, gentlemen, let us at once to bed, and rise with the dawn, and see if tomorrow we cannot *do something!"*

While Jackson had been staring at the ground in a trance brought on by extreme fatigue that Monday, Longstreet had fought the Battle of Glendale (or Frayser's Farm) to the south of White Oak Swamp. It had been anything but a brilliant engagement, but at least Longstreet had done something: McClellan's army was now pocketed on Malvern Hill, only a mile or so from the James River.

A good night's sleep had restored some of Jackson's vigor, and Lee granted him the honor of leading the advance to contact with the Union forces. The march was a short one, and it was abruptly halted by Federal artillery fire from Malvern Hill. Jackson took up the line of battle. Other units arrived and extended the Confederate front to the west and southwest of him.

Malvern Hill was not to be taken that day, no matter how many gallant charges D. H. Hill and other commanders led into the murderous fire of the artillery McClellan had massed to stop them. Jackson rode into danger time and again, but in vain. Once, a Union shell exploded only a few yards away and knocked Jackson's horse to the ground, stunned but unhurt. Lee saw the incident and sent a staff officer to order him back to safety "at once."

Night ended the battle. Dick Ewell came to Jackson and said that he thought McClellan would launch a counterattack the next morning. Jackson disagreed. "McClellan will clear out in the morning," he replied—and he was right.

Rain fell throughout the next day, July 2, 1862. Lee called his commanders to a conference, and President Davis paid a surprise visit. No pursuit of McClellan was possible in such weather, Lee felt, and Davis concurred. Jackson's opinion was not sought, but it was to the contrary. To let McClellan get away, he felt, was madness: the rain and the mud were problems for him, too, and he had all but run out of maneuvering room. It was a time to strike. "Never take counsel of your fears," Jackson believed and often said. That day, however, he was obliged to remain silent and to accept orders to do nothing.

McClellan reached Harrison's Landing, a few miles east of Malvern Hill, despite the rain and the quagmires which hampered his withdrawal. Jeb Stuart found a position at Evelington Heights which overlooked the sprawling Federal camp, but Longstreet could not reach it in time to reinforce Stuart. The last chance to destroy the Army of the Potomac on the banks of the James passed. The Seven Days Battles, which Jackson's Valley Campaign had made possible, were over.

— 9 —

Richmond welcomed Stonewall Jackson as a hero, but he had his doubts about whether the acclaim was deserved. That was his nature—praise always made him feel uncomfortable, for he believed it was the Lord who should be honored, instead—but there was more: he had performed miserably during the Seven Days, and he knew it.

Lee gave Jackson no rebuke, but no commendation came from him, either. If Lee was displeased with a man, he simply dropped him. He did not drop Jackson.

That was important, for Jackson's concept of the chain of command was unique. God, and not President Jefferson Davis, was his actual Commander-in-Chief. Among men, Lee was surely God's deputy. "So great is my confidence in General Lee," Jackson told a friend, "that I am willing to follow him blindfolded." His old system of loyalties had been shattered back in the winter when Davis had worked out a solution of the Loring controversy that was clearly based on expedience;

but his rapport with Lee, which was more spiritual than any-thing else, was replacing it.

Even so, it was still much easier for Jackson to work out his problems with God—on his knees, deep in prayer for hours at a time—than it was for him to deal with his commanding gen-eral. Jackson knew that it would be dangerous for the Con-federate people to become as complacent after the Seven Days as they had been during the weeks following the victory at Manassas, a year earlier. Offensive action—and he may have had his old plan of invading Maryland and Pennsylvania in mind—ought to be launched, he believed, while the South's fighting spirit was still high. Lee was cool to the proposal Jackson offered. Jackson then quietly violated one of his own strict rules and asked an influential friend to carry his plea for action to the President—who rejected it.

Did this make Jackson a hypocrite? Perhaps. It also made him human.

General John Pope inadvertently solved Jackson's problem—and removed all possibility for the people of Virginia, at least, to become lethargic—by sending strong Union forces down through north-central Virginia toward Gordonsville in mid-July. Jackson was delighted to receive orders to take his men westward to block this new threat, for he was anxious to get clear of the humid, fever-infested lowlands and back to the high country he loved best—and from a less personal point of view, he saw in Pope's challenge an excellent stimulus which would check any tendency on the part of Confederates to consider the war won.

Stonewall moved into a blocking position near Gordonsville —which was a key railroad center—and waited. Finally, in early August, a Union corps under the command of Jackson's old Valley foe, General Nathaniel Banks, moved toward him. Jack-son clashed with Banks at Cedar Mountain on August 9, 1862, in a bloody and inconclusive battle that checked the Federal advance but left Jackson disappointed: his hope had been to defeat Pope by destroying one unit after another as each of them came within his reach, but Banks had been able to com-bine enough of them in time to frustrate Stonewall's will.

Moreover, the Battle of Cedar Mountain was not well managed by Jackson. He committed his forces in piecemeal fashion, and no one really knew what his plan of attack was. Only when he seemed to be presiding over a disaster did he gain control of himself and of his troops: he rode out to rally the left wing of his army, restored the crumbling battle line, and conducted first an assault and then a pursuit which he was wise enough to stop at the correct time and place. But by then too many men had died, and too many opportunities had been missed, for him to have taken much satisfaction from having stopped Banks.

Lee, however, was both proud of Jackson's audacity and grateful to him for developing the extent of the Union commitment to the new attempt to take Richmond. He had sent A. P. Hill to Jackson earlier; now he added James Longstreet's heavy divisions, and not long afterward he assumed command in person. It was fortunate that he did, for Stonewall was not on the best of terms with either A. P. Hill or Longstreet.

With the bulk of Pope's army concentrated around Cedar Mountain, and with McClellan's men moving by naval transports up Chesapeake Bay to Aquia Landing on the Potomac north of Fredericksburg and then westward to join Pope, Lee had to act quickly to eliminate Pope if anything was to be accomplished. He worked out an excellent plan to envelop Pope from the east, but it was aborted when one of Jeb Stuart's aides was captured with a copy of the operations order in his possession. Lee then decided to strike Pope from the west, and the campaign that would later be known as Second Manassas was on.

Lee outlined the new idea to Jackson on the afternoon of August 24. It was simple—to move his wing of the Army of Northern Virginia westward, then northward, then eastward, and to strike Pope's line of communication with Washington. Such a move would probably attract Pope's attention and cause him to draw strength to the northwest, away from the direction from which his reinforcements were expected. At the proper time, Lee would move northward and crush Pope.

It was an exciting plan. Jackson accepted it eagerly.

His troops moved out at dawn the next morning. On the night of August 26, Jackson's men went into camp on Pope's supply line at Bristoe Station; from there it was only a few miles northeastward to Manassas Junction, and his forces reached that rich Union supply depot the next morning. While the Confederate soldiers rampaged through the stockpiles of clothing, weapons, food, and liquor, Jackson was torn between his affection for his men and his aversion to looting and disorder: they had been deprived too long, he felt, but he could not abide gluttony. If anything, gluttony won: Jackson's only victory was the destruction of all the whiskey his surgeons could not use for medicinal purposes. Confederate quartermasters loaded all of the treasure they could move, Jackson's troops helped themselves to what was left, and the rest was burned.

Once the orgy was over, Jackson moved his troops to Stony Ridge just to the north of the Warrenton Pike near Groveton and not far to the west of the old battleground at Manassas where he had won his nickname. He put his men into a line of battle facing southward, with woods concealing their presence from enemy scouts. It was a time for waiting, not action: he was the anvil against which Lee's hammer would soon smash John Pope's army.

As it turned out, neither Pope nor Lee moved as Jackson had expected. Pope was slow to react to Jackson's audacious slashing of his line of communication, and Lee elected to bring Longstreet along Jackson's route rather than to press Pope from the south.

While Jackson waited, a strong Union column passed his concealed positions on the afternoon of August 28. Jackson relished opportunities to destroy Union detachments before they could concentrate against him, and he was sorely tempted to crush this one. To be sure of its size and capabilities, he rode out alone to within easy rifle range of the Yankee column and let it pass in review. To the vast relief of his horrified staff, he finally galloped back to his command post. "Bring up your men, gentlemen," he said. A few minutes later, with the chilling Rebel yell ringing in the late afternoon air, his forces charged.

The Union force put up an astonishingly effective defense and withdrew only after darkness had halted the fight. This was not one of Jackson's better battles, for it quickly degenerated from an ambush attack into a head-on collision. He launched it too late in the day to have a chance to win by maneuver, and success depended almost entirely on the valor of his men and the gallantry of the officers who led them. As a result, the number of unit commanders he lost that day was high. Dick Ewell lost a leg, and his name was merely the first by rank on a list that was all too long.

Even so, the fight at Groveton on August 28 drew Pope's attention as nothing else had. Earlier, the Union general had placed roughly half of his army at Gainesville, between Jackson and the forces Lee and Longstreet were bringing in from the west. After the raid on the Manassas supply depot, he shifted them eastward to demolish Jackson. In so doing, Pope opened the road Lee needed most—and Lee was quick to exploit the advantage. The fight at Stony Ridge, then, pulled Pope northward: the anvil had become a magnet.

Pope apparently forgot all about the threat Lee and Longstreet posed to his safety, for he was obsessed with the idea of destroying Jackson. While Pope threw a series of poorly coordinated attacks against Jackson's line on Stony Ridge on August 29, Longstreet brought his wing of the Army of Northern Virginia in from the west and put it facing southeast with its left flank tied in to Jackson's line.

Only Jackson's iron nerve—which he managed to breathe into his entire command—saved him, for Longstreet blocked several of Lee's suggestions that he attack and clear the field of Yankees. A. P. Hill's men held Jackson's left, the flank nearest Longstreet's troops, and Hill's men took the brunt of the Union assaults. When his men ran out of ammunition, they threw rocks or clubbed the Yankee attackers with their rifle stocks. Jackson was there. Desperate as the situation was, with another wave of Federal troops advancing, Jackson said: "General, your men have done nobly; if you are attacked again you will beat the enemy back." With the aid of reinforcements Jackson sent, Hill repulsed the enemy. When an aide brought this welcome news to Jackson, he said: "Tell him I knew he would do it."

Finally, after six tremendous Union assaults, the sun went down. Jackson still held Stony Ridge. That night, Dr. McGuire reported the casualties to Stonewall and concluded his grim recital by saying, "We have won this battle by the hardest kind of fighting."

That was true, but Jackson replied: "No, no, we have won it by the blessing of Almighty God."

Certain it was that the struggle was not made more victorious or less costly by the strange reluctance of James Longstreet to join the fight. Historians notice such things: Jackson gave no indication that he did.

For most of the next day, August 30, nothing much happened. Finally, late in the afternoon, Pope launched a massive attack against Jackson's lines. Once again, Jackson took all of the punishment: Longstreet's forces sat on the sidelines and watched wave after wave of blue-clad men sweep across their front. Jackson's ammunition ran low. Some units were all but wiped out. He called for reinforcements, but in vain: it would take too long to move his units, Longstreet replied.

With Jackson's men throwing stones and swinging their rifles at the heads of the Yankees who were bent on overrunning them, Longstreet finally gave his artillery batteries the order to open fire. Indirect though it was, fire from this new quarter stunned the Federal forces. Not long afterward, with demoralization rampant in the Union ranks, Longstreet sent his men forward in an attack.

Lee was delighted. He had sent an order to Longstreet to move out, but Longstreet had anticipated it. Jackson's men, too, surged out of their lines and pressed the Yankees. Pope's men were routed: panic was in the air.

— 10 —

Now Jackson's old dream of invading Maryland and carrying the war to the enemy came true. It had to, for Lee's Army of Northern Virginia could not be sustained by the depleted resources of its home ground; moreover, there was a fair chance that Maryland would secede from the Union and join the Confederacy if Lee could demonstrate that he was strong enough to protect her.

By early September, Jackson's veterans were on their way to the banks of the Potomac. Jackson pressed his men onward, as always. A. P. Hill, however, was not moving his men along as rapidly as Stonewall expected. Tempers flared, and Hill wound up in arrest, riding at the rear of his column. Despite that upsetting incident, Jackson got great satisfaction out of the day's work on September 4, for his troops were in Maryland.

Several days later, while Lee was driving toward Hagerstown, he called Jackson to his headquarters for a conference. Harpers Ferry, he pointed out, was still in Union hands. Since the enemy garrison was to the south of his route of advance, it posed something of a threat to the Confederate supply line. Lee wanted Jackson to eliminate it. Jackson was more than willing to oblige.

Harpers Ferry had been Jackson's first station in the war, and he knew its strengths and weaknesses as well as anyone on either side. He put his troops in commanding positions in minimum time, fired a brilliant artillery concentration which destroyed the Union guns, and won the surrender of the Federal commander on September 15. He left A. P. Hill to attend to the details and took the bulk of his forces back across the Potomac to Sharpsburg, Maryland, where Lee was concentrating his army for battle against a strong counteroffensive led by General George McClellan.

In Jackson's absence, the Maryland invasion had turned into a major crisis—not because Jackson was away, but because of bad luck: Lee's operations order had fallen into McClellan's hands, and for once Little Mac moved aggressively. Lee would do well to hold his position at Sharpsburg: nothing else, except inglorious retreat without a fight, was possible.

When Jackson reached Sharpsburg, Lee put his units on the northern end of the battle line; Longstreet commanded the southern portion. By sunrise on September 17, the battle had already taken on a furious character—and most of its force was being thrown against Jackson's thin lines. Stonewall's men threw back assault after assault, taking hideous losses but never giving up. By afternoon, the weight of the Federal attack shifted southward—McClellan was making the critical mistake of committing his units in piecemeal fashion—and Longstreet was pleading for reinforcements. Jackson sent as many men as he could.

Just as a strong attack led by Union General Ambrose E. Burnside was about to crush the southern wing of Longstreet's corps, A. P. Hill's men came up from Harpers Ferry. Lee fed them into the battle, and their charge broke Burnside's drive. The day ended with nothing much changed, except for the fact that thousands of dead and wounded men were lying in the rolling country between the two armies where corn had grown and cattle had grazed.

Lee waited for McClellan to attack the next day, but the will to fight had gone out of Little Mac. After that act of defiance, Lee crossed back into Virginia.

During the fall of 1862, Lee reorganized the Army of Northern Virginia and put on a formal basis the command scheme he had long been following. Longstreet and Jackson became corps commanders with the rank of lieutenant general. Of even greater importance to Jackson, however, was another title he accepted as a gift of God—that of father: Anna had given birth to a daughter in November.

Such pleasant developments were welcome, but they did not divert Jackson from his duty. It seemed that there would be no winter quarters for his troops this year, for Ambrose Burnside was bringing a huge Union army southward to Fredericksburg. Longstreet was already there, and Jackson was ordered to move his corps into the hills to the south of Marye's Heights.

Fredericksburg was not Jackson's kind of battle, but he fought it well. Burnside struck him first, made a minor penetration which Jackson quickly checked, and then turned his fury northward against Longstreet. Union losses at Fredericksburg were appalling. The tragedy was all the more disturbing to Jackson because there was to be no opportunity to take the offensive against Burnside. No army, Jackson knew, ever won a war by winning defensive battles. Costly as Fredericksburg had been to the Union, it was a Confederate victory only in the sense that it was not a Confederate defeat.

Jackson and his corps spent the rest of the dismal winter of 1862–63 south of Fredericksburg. Federal troops on the northern side of the Rappahannock River showed no inclination to fight, and Lee was able to send Longstreet and most of his First Corps down to southern Virginia to gather food and forage and to clear the area of Union detachments.

The season was a hard one, for the weather was generally poor and diseases raged through the ranks of Jackson's corps. By March, even General Lee's health had failed. While the surgeons did what they could in their way for the sick, Jackson sent out a call for clergymen of all faiths to bring their ministry to his men. The response was gratifying, and Presbyterian Jackson sent the chaplains out to save souls regardless of sectarian distinctions.

In April, Anna came to Guiney's Station with little Julia. Jackson's staff officers were amused at the sight of their battle-hardened commander playing with his five-month-old daughter, and they were honored guests at her christening. General Lee and other officers of the Army of Northern Virginia paid calls on Mrs. Jackson, and on those occasions Stonewall wore the fine new uniform coat Jeb Stuart had given him to replace the threadbare, faded one he had worn so long. It was a happy time for the Jacksons, and the men who loved him rejoiced to see the family together at last.

Toward the end of April, good fighting weather returned—and with it came orders to prepare for battle. Jackson sent Anna and Julia to safety in Richmond and gave his full attention to the ominous advance of General Joseph Hooker's revitalized Army of the Potomac toward the lush green thickets of the Wilderness region west of Fredericksburg.

Everything pointed to an easy victory for Hooker. He was new in his assignment, but he was seasoned enough to have won the nickname Fighting Joe. His army had more than 70,-000 men, not including the 40,000 under General John Sedgwick he had left east of Fredericksburg to hold Lee and Jackson in place: by contrast, Lee had only a little over 50,000 troops—and there was no hope of getting Longstreet back from southern Virginia in time to be of any help.

Once again, anvil and hammer strategy was to be attempted. This time, however, the Army of Northern Virginia was to be crushed between Sedgwick and Hooker. With Lee and Jackson destroyed, the road to Richmond would be wide open: even if Longstreet chose to fight, he would be outnumbered by at least three to one. Success could mean the end of the rebellion, and Joe Hooker meant to succeed.

Sedgwick put his men across the Rappahannock River and drew Lee's attention at Fredericksburg while Hooker's heavy columns crossed the Rapidan and closed into the tangled forests of the Wilderness. Lee and Jackson rode out to look over Sedgwick's positions on the morning of April 30. Jackson's inclination was to attack. "If you think it can be done," Lee said, "I will order it." But Jackson was not certain: he wanted to see more. Lee granted him time for a careful reconnaissance, and Jackson rode on.

Late in the afternoon, Jackson came into Lee's headquarters. An attack against Sedgwick, Stonewall reported, was not advisable. Lee knew that Jackson was certain about that: if there had been a chance for victory at Fredericksburg, his lieutenant would have found it.

Earlier, Lee had sent General Robert H. Anderson's division westward to block Joe Hooker in the Wilderness. That had been a natural response, a minimum commitment. But if Jackson could not attack at Fredericksburg, something might still be done in the west. Lee ordered Jackson to leave a reliable division to hold Sedgwick at Fredericksburg and to take the rest of his corps to join Anderson's force near Chancellorsville.

The sheer audacity of Lee's plan appealed to Jackson. With great skill, he withdrew his men while General Jubal Early's troops stretched out to cover the front they were leaving. Before sunrise on May 1, Jackson's command was pressing westward.

In Jackson's saddlebag was a copy of Napoleon's *Maxims*—one of which warned that a general should never separate his army in the face of an enemy. Lee had just violated it, and Jackson was delighted.

By noon, Jackson had put his men into the fight, feeding them in to the south of the line Anderson held. The Union forces were still in the dense forest: it was hard to tell just where they were. As skirmishers moved in through the green saplings, slowed by vines and underbrush, Yankee sharpshooters gave away their positions by firing—but no man could say for sure that he had encountered a line of battle, for the forest hid everything.

Jackson knew that it was imperative to keep the Union forces inside the trackless thicket—where their superiority in numbers and in artillery could be held to minimum effectiveness—but he was far from certain as to how this could best be done. The northern end of the Yankee line was Anderson's concern; Jackson's problem was to determine where the southern flank ended and to decide what could be done to roll it up.

Lee's gallant cavalry commander, Jeb Stuart, sent Jackson a message that afternoon that opened a wide range of possibilities. Stuart had found the Union army's southern flank, he reported, and he was keeping it under pressure. "I trust God will grant us a great victory," Jackson replied.

For a long time that afternoon, Jackson sat on his horse, Little Sorrel, on a hilltop while Federal artillery shelled the exposed position—but he saw nothing that would do him much good. Later, he and General Lee sat down in a clearing to discuss the next day's fighting. Even then danger was not far away: a Yankee sharpshooter was somewhere in the green hell, trying his best to knock out Confederate artillerymen who were serving a cannon near the road.

Somehow, Jackson had gained the impression that Hooker was already checked and that he would retreat northward across the Rapidan by the next morning. The ease with which Confederate skirmishers had pushed the Union lines back that afternoon may have given him that idea, but those encounters hardly amounted to a battle. Lee was convinced that Hooker meant to advance: he respected Jackson's judgment, but this time he could not accept it.

Still, an enemy was before them: the problem was how best to destroy him. While Lee and Jackson were discussing the possibilities, Jeb Stuart rode in with the exciting news that the Union southern flank was "in the air"—not tied to any natural obstacle which might have afforded a defense against attack.

Suddenly, the plan of the next day's work was clear. The opportunity to get around the exposed flank was there, and Jackson would make the most of it. While scouts went out to find roads and trails for Jackson's men to use, the two generals got some rest.

Jackson took off his sword, leaned it against a tree, and selected a place on which he could spread his saddle blanket. Major Alexander Pendleton, his chief of staff, offered him his overcoat for cover, but Jackson—not wanting to deprive his aide of the garment—refused. Sandie Pendleton detached the cape from the coat, and Jackson gratefully accepted it. But the night was chilly, and before long Jackson was wide awake. A head cold, he feared, was beginning: he would be better off by the campfire that was burning in the clearing. He placed the cape over Pendleton and made his way over to the low flame.

Not long afterward, the Reverend B. T. Lacy came over to

the campfire and sat down by Jackson. At other times, Jackson would probably have welcomed the opportunity to discuss the fine points of scriptural doctrine with the clergyman—but now they were both soldiers who faced a critical test, and Jackson led the conversation to the matter at hand. Lacy had lived in the area, and he knew the roads. Did Lacy know of a route which could be used to get around the Union flank? No, the chaplain replied, but there might be one. Jackson sent Lacy and his trusted geographer, Jed Hotchkiss, out to find it.

Jackson sat alone by the fire for a few minutes. Colonel A. L. Long of Lee's staff came up with a cup of hot coffee and joined him. Suddenly, Jackson's sword—which he had placed against a tree—fell to the ground. Long shuddered: it was an ill omen.

General Lee came to the campfire and sat down, and before long Lacy and Jed Hotchkiss returned: they had found the road Jackson needed. "General Jackson," Lee said, "what do you propose to do?"

Jackson's answer was simple. Pointing to the map, he said: "Go around here."

Lee inspected the trace Hotchkiss had drawn. "What do you propose to make this movement with?" Lee asked.

"With my whole corps," Jackson replied.

Lee was astonished. This meant that he would have to hold Hooker's forces back with only a third of his command: a Union penetration anywhere would mean disaster everywhere. For Jackson to make the flank march with so many men would take a number of hours, and while they were on the road communication would be haphazard, at best. There would be no real possibility of recalling any of Jackson's units. And there were no other Confederate divisions upon which he could call for the help he had to expect he would need.

But Lee knew Jackson. "Well," he said, "go on."

Lee had already violated Napoleon's warning—never divide your forces in the presence of your enemies—once: General Jubal Early was watching Sedgwick back at Fredericksburg. Now he was compounding his risk by splitting his army again.

Early on the morning of May 2, 1863, Jackson rode away to the south along the road Lacy and Hotchkiss had found. His entire corps fell in behind him. Lee's hopes, and the fate of the Army of Northern Virginia, went with them.

The march was a hard one, for the day was hot and the road was long. "Press forward," Jackson urged, and the men responded. They had followed him over many a rough trail: they would follow him anywhere. Although Stuart's cavalry was out to screen the movement, Jackson had to assume that Union observation posts had seen his men. When he came to the Brock Road, which could have taken him into the Federal rear, he turned away from his enemy—hoping to create the impression that Lee's forces were withdrawing—and led the column southward for about half a mile until he came to a road which took him westward and then northward parallel to the Brock Road.

Finally, Jackson had his men where he wanted them to be. The hour was late, and he could not dare to expect the Lord to hold the sun still in the sky as he had for Joshua. Even so, at a quarter past five, he said to General E. Rodes: "You can go forward."

With the demonic Rebel yell, Jackson's men—who had been marching for most of the long, hot day—charged forward, as their leader commanded. Union regiments, already settled for their evening meal, were startled and put to rout. On through the shocked Yankees the determined Confederates surged, driving back the Federal troops who had formed lines to resist them. Nothing could stop the gray-clad soldiers: their formations broke as they pushed the demoralized enemy deeper and deeper into the Wilderness, but still they heeded Jackson's words—"Press on! Press on!"

They stormed through one Federal line after another until darkness fell. Still Jackson was not satisfied: if the victory could be made complete, the Union might abandon the war and leave the Confederacy in peace. He gathered a small staff and rode ahead of the skirmish line to find a road to United States Ford over the Rappahannock River, Hooker's most attractive escape route. It was nine o'clock by then, and he would have to reorganize his forces before long. "General," an aide asked, "don't you think this is the wrong place for you?"

Jackson dismissed the question, saying: "The danger is all over—the enemy is routed! Go back and tell A. P. Hill to press right on!"

Jackson rode into enemy territory until he picked up the sound of Union axes cutting timber for use in building fortifications. Soon after he turned back, a Confederate outpost heard the pounding of hoofbeats. A Union patrol? In the darkness, no man could be certain. There was a volley. General A. P. Hill, knowing that Jackson was out there, somewhere, ordered the men to cease firing. A similar cry came from one of the men in Jackson's staff: "You are firing into our own men," he shouted.

"It's a lie!" a Confederate officer yelled. "Pour it into them, boys."

They did.

Little Sorrel, alarmed by the gunfire, carried the wounded general off into the woods. Jackson fought to regain control of the frightened horse, but branches cut into his face and a limb almost knocked him out of the saddle. Finally, someone grabbed the reins. Jackson's left arm was useless, and his right hand, too, was bleeding.

Staff officers eased Jackson down from the saddle. A. P. Hill came over and asked: "Is the wound painful?"

Jackson and Hill had hardly been on speaking terms for some months. Now, though, their quarrels were all forgotten. "Very painful," Jackson replied, "my arm is broken."

A. P. Hill gently removed Jackson's sword and belt, and he sent for a surgeon and whiskey. The gunfire had roused the Yankees, however, and Hill had to leave to attend to the trouble. A few moments afterward, he was hit across his boot tops by shrapnel and had to be carried away. Command of the Second Corps then passed to Jeb Stuart, the cavalryman who had never led infantrymen before in his life.

The men around Jackson took him back to the Confederate lines. Before anything more could be done about evacuating him, Federal artillery opened up and blasted the forest. To protect Jackson, four members of his staff stood up and formed a human screen to take any fragments which might be coming their commander's way.

When the artillery bombardment lifted, Jackson offered to try to walk westward to the corps hospital. After a while, though, Jackson's strength gave out. Someone found a litter, but men were needed to carry it, and most of the staff officers had gone to find a doctor and whiskey. Soldiers were asked to help take "a Confederate officer" to the rear, but they refused

—not knowing that the officer was their beloved Jackson. Finally, in desperation, a staff officer asked for help in evacuating *Stonewall*. That was enough: men took up the burden willingly.

One of the litter bearers stumbled, and the man they were carrying fell to the ground. For the first time, Jackson groaned. An aide asked: "Are you much hurt?"

Jackson, suppressing his pain, replied, "Don't trouble yourself about me."

When the litter bearers reached an ambulance wagon, they saw that it was full. An officer inside, whose wound was light, quickly gave up his place to Jackson, and the driver told his mules to "giddap."

Beside Jackson in the ambulance was Colonel Stephen Crutchfield, the Second Corps' chief of artillery, who had been seriously wounded in the leg. Jackson was worried about Crutchfield, and the colonel was concerned about his general: to keep both men resting as easily as possible, no man in the ambulance would tell either of them anything.

Both men needed whiskey, and the ambulance driver made a number of stops in the hope of getting some. The identity of the wounded men might have made a difference, but the driver was under orders to keep that a secret; in any event, no soldier seemed to have any "spirits" to give up. After a long and horribly bumpy ride, though, the ambulance pulled up in front of the home of the Reverend Melzi Chancellor. Whiskey was brought out, and with it came Dr. Hunter McGuire.

Jackson, McGuire saw, was in shock. Even so, the general answered all of the doctor's questions in a calm and courteous manner. "He controlled, by his iron will, all evidence of emotion; and more difficult than this even," McGuire said later, "he controlled that disposition to restlessness which many of us have observed upon the field of battle, attending great loss of blood."

More than two hours after Jackson had been hit, the ambulance reached the Second Corps hospital. The verdict of the doctors was that Jackson's left arm would have to be amputated. He was asked if this might be done. "Yes, certainly," he replied. "Do for me whatever you think best."

Some hours later, after the operation had been completed,

Sandie Pendleton rode in. General Stuart, Pendleton said, wondered what orders Jackson might have to give. "I don't know," Jackson replied. "I can't tell; say to General Stuart he must do what he thinks best." Pendleton was shocked to see his beloved leader unable to give instructions for battle; without the mighty Stonewall, how could the war be won?

The next day, May 3, ended with Stuart and Lee driving Hooker into a pocket against the Rappahannock—winning the battle Jackson had made possible. He spent the day resting. In the afternoon, a message came from Lee. It said: "General: I have just received your note, informing me that you have been wounded. I cannot express my regret at the occurrence. Could I have directed events, I should have chosen for the good of the country to be disabled in your stead. I congratulate you upon the victory, which is due to your skill and energy."

Jackson could barely remember informing Lee of what had happened. He replied, "General Lee is very kind, but he should give the praise to God."

They took Jackson southward and then eastward to Guiney's Station, south of Fredericksburg, in the hope that he might make a better recovery there. He stood the trip well—Jed Hotchkiss had selected the smoothest route possible—and he was welcomed by the Chandlers family who made a modest frame building available to him for his convalescence. For a day or so it seemed that he was making good progress toward recovery.

"Many would regard [these wounds] as a great misfortune," Jackson said to his aide, Lieutenant James Smith, "[but] I regard them as one of the blessings of my life."

Smith replied with something he had often heard Jackson say: "All things work together for good to those who love God."

Jackson nodded. "Yes," he said, "that's it."

Anna Jackson brought Julia from Richmond. The Reverend Mr. Lacy came in with a message from General Lee: "Give him my affectionate regards, and tell him to make haste and get well, and come back to me as soon as he can. He has lost his left arm; but I have lost my right arm."

On the morning of May 7, it was apparent that pneumonia had set in. That head cold Jackson had worried about days before in the clearing near Chancellorsville had turned into something more serious than the wounds he had suffered, and now the mood of optimism which had prevailed around his bedside vanished. By the morning of the tenth, a Sunday, it was clear that he would die. Anna Jackson was asked to tell him, for the doctor—her brother—knew that he wanted a few hours to prepare for the great journey. Anna spoke: in a few hours, she told him, he would be in heaven.

"Yes," he said, racked with fever, "I prefer it, I prefer it."

There was some talk of family matters; Jackson looked at his little daughter for the last time; delirium returned. In a moment of calm, Jackson said: "Very good, very good, it is all right." A doctor offered opium, but Jackson refused it. "It will only delay my departure, and do no good," he said. "I want to preserve my mind, if possible, to the last."

Outside, the mid-afternoon air was still. "Let us cross over the river," the tired warrior said, "and rest under the shade of the trees."

— 11 —

When Stonewall Jackson died, some said, the Confederate States of America died with him. There is some truth in that judgment, for nothing was ever quite the same again. Lee could not replace him; the only solution he found was to reorganize the Army of Northern Virginia into three corps, and one of the reasons for his failure at Gettysburg was his inability to manage three corps commanders, none of whom possessed the qualities of Jackson.

"Remember Jackson!" Jeb Stuart had cried as he led the assault that won the Battle of Chancellorsville. The men responded that day, and for the rest of their lives. Even now, Virginians in Confederate uniforms march over Jackson's old fighting country, telling curious tourists that they are "members of the Stonewall Brigade." There is pride in their voices, pride in the valor of their forefathers, pride in the glory of Virginia, and —most of all—pride in their identification with "Old Jack."

Even if it is true that the Confederacy died with Jackson, something of very great value has survived. Leader of a lost cause though he was, Stonewall remains as a reminder to Virginians and to all Americans of the power of a man to be what he chooses to be.

6

Robert E. Lee

Last Leader of the Lost Cause
1807–1870

AT any given moment, there are bound to be a large number of men who do not really belong to the time in which they live. Some would have been much more at home in the world as it was a generation or two earlier; others, fifty years or so *ahead* of their contemporaries, are doomed to live in perplexed frustration.

In many instances, an age draws its most important men from the ranks of such misfits—although the judgment as to who the truly great ones are must often be left to posterity. Perhaps there is something about being alienated from the mainstream that inspires a man to excel, or maybe his motivation is an involuntary response to challenges he faces but does not understand: the subject is a deep one, and not enough is known about it.

But there is this: Robert E. Lee was an eighteenth-century man who was destined to cope with nineteenth-century conditions, and he brought to that task a wisdom that is greatly needed today, a century after his death. He is something of an exception to the rule in that he was considered immeasurably great in his own age, but that is incidental. The important thing about Lee is that he may well have been one of those rare people who are great for all time.

To praise Lee is almost an automatic response, for he has come down to us as one of the finest men America has ever produced. Some observers have elected to stress his faults—which were many—but usually with a curious tone of apology for pointing out that the man was, after all, human. Other students of Lee have been lost in fascination: the more they have probed, the more respect for him they have gained.

As a result, there is an aura of majesty about Lee which makes him seem to have been—like his fellow Virginian, George Washington—more of a god than a man. Accordingly, it is easy to overlook some extremely harsh facts about his life.

Lee was born in poverty, a child his mother had not wanted. When he was only six, his father ran off to the West Indies in disgrace, never to return. He spent his early teens as a nurse for his invalid mother. A lurid scandal brought shame to his family's proud name just as he was finishing West Point with high honors. He was educated as an engineer, but he was obliged to live on a modest salary during a period in which less gifted members of his profession were becoming enormously wealthy men. Most of the jobs he was given bored him. When he was called to a command for which he was not prepared, in a war he dreaded, he proved to be a failure and was forced to surrender. In his last years, many of his countrymen damned him for not striking back at the viciousness of the conquerors who were ruining his homeland. He died without any indication that he had not lived in vain.

This negative picture of Lee—overstated and oversimplified though it may be—is at least as accurate as the usual glossier positive images, and it is vastly more interesting. It suggests that Lee's claim to greatness rests not so much on what has been said about him as it does on the nature of the struggles he had to endure and overcome in order to survive. It does not bring him down from his pedestal or raise us automatically to equality with him, but it conveys a fact about America that is worth remembering: that it is what a man is, and not merely what he accomplishes, that counts most.

— 2 —

By the fall of 1806, when Ann Hill Carter Lee was expecting the birth of her fifth child, her marriage was ruined. Her husband, Richard Henry Lee, who had won considerable glory and the nickname of "Light-Horse Harry" during the Revolutionary

War while serving as a cavalry commander under Generals George Washington and Nathanael Greene, had not proved to be as successful in peace as he had been in combat: bad investments had impaired his ability to care for his family, his political activities had made him an unpopular figure, and his lack of consideration for his wife had strained her tolerance severely. She had not wanted this new child, and the death of her beloved father during her pregnancy merely added to her despair.

At Stratford, a once beautiful Lee family plantation hall which was rapidly deteriorating under "Light-Horse Harry" Lee's lax management, Ann Hill Carter Lee gave birth to Robert Edward Lee on January 19, 1807. During the next few years, as her relationship with the father of her children became even more precarious, Ann Lee determined that her last-born son would be raised to resemble the grandfather he had never known—Charles Carter, the worthy contemporary of George Washington and other eminent Virginians who had made the United States possible. Under no circumstances would Robert be like his father, if there was anything his mother could do to prevent it.

There was good reason for Ann Lee's decision. "Light-Horse Harry" Lee's creditors put him in jail for debt when his newest son was only two. He tried to recoup at least a portion of his former glory by writing biographies of Washington and Greene, but the financial return was disappointing. Although he had been Governor of Virginia, a major general, and the man who would be best remembered for having praised Washington as "First in war, first in peace, and first in the hearts of his countrymen" at Washington's funeral, "Light-Horse Harry" simply could not cope with the ordinary business of living. In 1813, after Ann Lee had moved the family to a modest home in Alexandria, he fled the country. For the next five years he drifted from one island to another in the West Indies. He died in the act of trying to return home and was buried on Cumberland Island, off the coast of Georgia, in March, 1818.

Charles Carter, however, had been quite another kind of man. Virtue, he had believed, was not something to be revered but lived. He was a man of action who never hesitated to give his support—through deeds—to whatever needed to be done locally, within the state, or nationally. In all of his dealings with his fellowmen he was scrupulously honest, and he grew in wealth through hard work and careful management of available resources rather than through speculation or chicanery. Carter was an old-fashioned man in a time that relished sound values, and he won the respect of all who came in contact with him.

On this model, Ann Carter Lee raised young Robert. Their home in the little town of Alexandria was modest, and the boy had to watch his pennies when he went out to buy the family's groceries. After his older brothers went away—one to Harvard, the other to the navy as a midshipman—his mother's health failed and he had to take care of her. She told him of the old-time glory of the Lees and the Carters, and on a few visits to the great Carter family houses such as Shirley on the north bank of the James east of Richmond he saw what might have been his heritage—but for the most part, he grew up in an atmosphere of genteel poverty as what Southerners used to call a poor relation.

In school, Robert Lee quickly won the respect of his teachers because of his meticulous attention to proper handling of whatever kind of problem he was assigned to solve. Benjamin Hallowell had this to say about his pupil:

> Robert E. Lee entered my school in Alexandria, Virginia, in the winter of 1824–25. . . . He was a most exemplary student in every respect. He was never behind time at his studies; never failed in a single recitation; was perfectly observant of the rules and regulations of the Institution; was gentlemanly, unobtrusive, and respectful in all his deportment to teachers and fellow-students. His specialty was *finishing up*. He imparted a finish and a neatness, as he proceeded, to everything he undertook. One of the branches of mathematics he studied with me was conic sections, in which some of the diagrams are very complicated. He drew the diagrams on a slate; and although he well knew that the one he was drawing would have to be removed to make room for another, he drew each one with as much accuracy and finish, lettering and all, as if it was to be engraved and printed. . . .

Still, there was something of his father in young Lee that no amount of countertraining could eliminate. It would remain latent for a long time, as far as the world was to know, but in years to come it would emerge as a significant determinant of his conduct. For the present, his actions conformed neatly with his mother's wishes: one of Ann Carter Lee's earlier sons bore the name of Charles Carter Lee, but Robert was living up to it.

Given the necessity of getting by on a small inheritance, and with no husband to support her, Ann Lee had done well to put Charles through Harvard and to win an appointment as a midshipman in the navy for Smith. When Robert was ready for college, though, there was nothing she could do for him except to try to mobilize family influence to obtain his acceptance as a cadet at the United States Military Academy at West Point. In a letter of introduction which a relative, William Fitzhugh, provided when Robert Lee went to Washington to call on the Secretary of War, John C. Calhoun, Fitzhugh said that young Lee was "disposed to devote himself to the profession of arms." Perhaps he was: in any event, he had no choice.

— 3 —

On July 1, 1825, ninety-four young men arrived at West Point to be admitted as new cadets. They had come from twenty-five states, and their backgrounds were as varied as their appearance. Some of them had come to the Military Academy—rather than to any other institution—because they wanted to prepare themselves for a career in the army which would eventually bring them fame. Others knew that West Point offered the best education a would-be engineer could obtain in the United States. A few were there because their families believed that the discipline would do them good. For at least one new cadet—Lee—there seemed to be no other way in which he could obtain a higher education.

Lee was acutely conscious of the need for him to succeed. Cousin Fitzhugh, in his letter to Secretary of War Calhoun, had reminded that honorable gentleman that the United States owed a debt of gratitude to "Light-Horse Harry" Lee despite his later "misfortunes." In addition, he had praised Ann Carter Lee as "one of the finest women the State of Virginia has ever produced." The honor of the Lee and Carter families, then, went with him into the Military Academy.

Even in 1825, West Point was known to be an institution

which separated the men from the boys with ruthless rapidity. By September 1 of that year, Lee's class had grown to ninety-nine. Within the next four years, more than half of them would leave. Lee had been one of ten cadets from Virginia when he entered. At graduation, only two would be left—Lee and Joseph E. Johnston.

The academic and disciplinary systems at West Point were virtually unique among American colleges in that it was almost impossible for anyone to enter completely prepared to cope with the demands he would face. Lee's previous schooling had given him threshold competence, but not much more: the rest was strictly up to him.

Even a hundred years ago it was most unlikely that any cadet could endure four years of daily inspections without being reported for at least a few minor infractions of the regulations; but at graduation, Lee's record indicated that he had never been awarded a demerit. Academic subjects required long hours of diligent study, and at first Lee's standing was high but not spectacular. Before long, however, he was coaching other cadets.

On July 1, 1829, when the ordeal finally ended, Lee was the second man to receive his degree in a class of forty-six. He had been the top-ranking cadet militarily, and he was leaving behind him a record that would not be surpassed for many years.

Curiously, none of Lee's fellow cadets seem to have been envious of him. They did not consider him a drudge because he took the need for study seriously. When he was obliged to impose discipline on them, they took their punishment with good grace. It was as though they considered him to be a special kind of man. They might have resented his distinction, but apparently they did not. Instead, they respected him.

Still, Lee was not aloof. Joe Johnston remembered that "he was full of sympathy and kindness, genial and fond of gay conversation, even fun, while his correctness of demeanor and attention at all duties, personal and official, and a dignity as much a part of himself as the elegance of his person, gave him a superiority that everyone acknowledged in his heart."

Brevet Second Lieutenant Lee emerged from West Point with tragedy directly ahead of him. His father's son by a previous marriage, Henry, brought fresh disgrace to the family because of moral and financial ineptness which won him the nickname of "Black-Horse Harry" Lee. Added to this was Ann Carter Lee's critical condition. While Lieutenant Lee, on his gradua-tion leave, was once again nursing her, she died. As soon as he had settled her pitifully small estate, he left for his first assignment—bleak and desolate Cockspur Island, not far from Savannah, Georgia.

Cut off as he was from most family ties, Lee became friendly with congenial people wherever he happened to be. Before long, he was paying more than usual attention to Mary Custis, the only child of Washington's adopted son, George Washington Parke Custis, the master of Arlington plantation directly across the Potomac from the Capitol. Robert Lee and Mary Custis were married in mid-1831, and he took his bride to his new station, Fortress Monroe, Virginia.

Mary Custis Lee was too fond of the pleasures of Arlington to care much for the relative austerity of army life, and her visits to her girlhood home became longer and more frequent. The chief of engineers inadvertently solved a vexing marital prob-lem for Lee by assigning him to duty in his office in Washing-ton, only a six-mile horseback ride from Arlington. Children came along, and Lee settled into the role of father with ease and grace; only Mary Lee's precarious health disturbed an other-wise happy home life.

Lee's professional career, however, was no source of satisfac-tion to him. His duties were mostly clerical, and they bored him to the point of his wanting to resign. Other engineers were transforming the face of America in those years—for this was the era in which railroads were being pushed westward, waterways were being improved for navigation, and public works of all kinds were expanding. Lee, meanwhile, stayed at his desk and worried about what would happen to his family if he accepted the risk of becoming a civilian.

In 1836, Lieutenant Lee finally got a chance to apply his talents to a major engineering problem. The course of the Mis-sissippi River at St. Louis had changed, and the city's port facil-ities were being choked with silt. Lee's solution was to build a jetty which would deflect the current toward the St. Louis waterfront and clear away the mud islands which had formed there. Progress was too slow to suit the townspeople, and Lee was severely criticized. He went on with his work until Federal funds ran out and the project had to be abandoned, but he saved the city: the Mississippi got just enough of a nudge from Lee's unfinished deflecting wall to clear the channel to the docks.

Assignments to army engineering projects in North Carolina and Fort Hamilton in New York Harbor followed, and in 1844 Captain Lee was detailed as a member of a board headed by General Winfield Scott to examine the cadets at West Point. He was only in his mid-thirties, but he had the resigned manner of a much older man. Wherever he served, he was respected but never quite accepted. Some thought him too patrician; others, feeling inferior, were uneasy in his presence. Lee had his own code of conduct, which he followed without thinking much about it, but he did not attempt to impose it on anyone else. He was content to live and let live, but because of his instinctive adherence to the values of an earlier time he was condemned to be a lonely man.

— 4 —

Within a few weeks of the outbreak of war with Mexico in 1846, Lee was ordered to San Antonio, Texas, for duty with an expeditionary force commanded by Brigadier General John E. Wool. At first, Lee's assignments involved such prosaic tasks as obtaining shovels and picks and writing orders for the march into Mexico. Later, he became a scout for Wool and selected the routes of advance into the enemy country. Wool's men reached Saltillo without making contact with any significant opposition, and for a time it seemed that General Zachary Taylor's troops would win the war while Wool was marching all over northern Mexico trying to find an enemy to fight.

In the early part of 1847, however, General Scott ordered Lee to join the staff he was creating for the amphibious landing he intended to make at Vera Cruz. Scott sent his forces ashore on March 10, 1847, and Captain Lee waded in with them.

Scott quickly cut Vera Cruz off from the rest of Mexico and put the city under artillery bombardment. Naval guns were brought ashore, and Lee was delighted to find his brother, Smith Lee, in command of one of those batteries. For the first time in his life, Robert Lee was under enemy fire: he paid little attention to it, went on with his work, and left the rest to God.

Mexico City was Scott's strategic objective, and he moved westward after the fall of Vera Cruz along the same route Hernán Cortés' conquistadores had followed more than two hundred years before. Twenty miles or so to the east of Jalapa, Mexican General Antonio López de Santa Anna blocked the American advance at a hill known as Cerro Gordo. Lee, acting as a one-man intelligence force for Scott, found a trail along which the army commander could send a major portion of his troops around Santa Anna's flank. His report had the effect of determining Scott's plan of attack, and "Old Fuss and Feathers" showed his admiration and gratitude by promoting Lee to brevet major not long after his forces won the decisive victory the daring staff officer had made possible.

Lee continued his scouting activities as the march through the mountains toward Mexico City continued. By mid-August, Scott's army reached the southern approaches to the enemy capital. The Mexican defenders placed a great deal of reliance on the assumption that the Americans would be unable to cross a huge lava bed known as the Pedregal, but Lee found a pathway through it; later, he led divisions from Scott's force to attack positions. In the course of those operations, Lee had been the only one of eight engineer officers to get through the rugged Pedregal. He had gone without rest for over forty-eight hours; he had acted voluntarily, not on orders; and even after his task was finished, he was still up and ready for action.

The other engineer officers on Scott's staff, including Lieutenants Pierre G. T. Beauregard and George B. McClellan, were good men who had done their best—but there was something about Lee which kept him going long after they had lost their way and turned back. It was as though Lee was sustained by some peculiar confidence, or by the conviction that he was obliged to perform in a superior manner now that he had finally been given the opportunity. For Lee to have failed would have been no disgrace. But for Lee, failure was unthinkable.

Scott rewarded Lee for the Pedregal crossing with promotion to brevet lieutenant colonel, and he brought the younger man (who was nearing forty-one) closer to him by making Lee his chief aide. This gave Lee a matchless opportunity to watch

Scott function as an army commander, and he did not waste it: he was particularly impressed by Scott's close attention to terrain, a tendency to rely on subordinate commanders to perform as ordered, and audacity.

The climactic battle for Mexico City was to be the assault against the fortified hill of Chapultepec, and once again Lee worked around the clock to carry out the commanding general's orders. He put the artillery in place and guided troop units to their lines of departure, and one day turned into another without his notice.

When the attack opened, Colonel Joseph E. Johnston led his gray-clad skirmishers up the slopes. Lieutenant James Longstreet was shot while carrying a battle flag, and a young Virginian named George E. Pickett took it out of his hands. Not far behind them, Lieutenant Thomas J. Jackson was manning an artillery piece; the bodies of his men were stretched out on the ground a few yards away. Beauregard and McClellan, like Lee, were everywhere at once—shifting the direction of advance, leading men forward, shouting encouragement to those who lagged behind.

At some point during the battle, Lee was hit by a Mexican bullet, but he remained in the saddle and carried out every order Scott gave him. Finally, loss of blood and lack of sleep caught up with him: as he was riding forward in Scott's command group, he lost consciousness and fell to the ground.

Lee's wound was slight enough for him to return to duty the next day in time for Scott's victorious entry into Mexico City. Scott recognized Lee's gallantry at Chapultepec with promotion to brevet colonel, and other commanding officers added their praise of his conduct in their reports of the campaign. No man had won more respect during the entire war than Lee, and no other man there accepted it with such easy grace.

—— 5 ——

When Brevet Colonel Lee returned to Arlington in mid-1848, his children hardly knew him. His fame, he quickly realized, had been left behind in Mexico, never to follow him. He was an aging man, successful in a career that was no longer important, skilled in another one he dared not try to exploit at this late date. Life resumed its ordinary character: his task was merely to live it out, or so he thought.

After a tour of duty in Baltimore, Lee was ordered to West Point as superintendent of the Military Academy. His son, Custis Lee, was there as a cadet, and so was Smith Lee's son, Fitzhugh. Another veteran of the Mexican War, the Honorable Jefferson Davis of Mississippi, was Secretary of War and Lee's immediate superior. The three years of Lee's superintendency passed quickly, and in 1855 Secretary Davis selected him to be second in command of one of the new cavalry regiments that would be posted on the Western frontier.

Although Davis had meant Lee's new assignment to be a compliment, the graying lieutenant colonel soon found himself presiding over one court-martial board after another in desolate outposts scattered throughout west Texas. By this time, Mary Custis Lee's health would not permit her to leave Arlington—and most of the children were either beginning their own lives or were away at school. Despite the talk Lee heard of trouble between the North and the South, he considered himself an old man whose task it was to attend to his duties as they came to him until retirement age arrived. Lee's service with the Second Cavalry Regiment from 1855 until 1857 was probably the dullest, loneliest period of his entire life, and it was broken not by relief and reassignment to a more challenging command but by a family tragedy.

Mary Lee's father, George Washington Parke Custis, died in the fall of 1857 and left the problem of settling his estate to his son-in-law. Lee came back to Arlington, made an analysis of the situation, and got a leave of absence from the army so that he could meet his responsibilities as executor of Custis' will.

Ordinarily, such an obligation could have been met within a few months, but Custis' affairs turned out to be hopelessly complicated. Lee was obliged to take over the active management of Custis' properties so that enough money could be raised to clear the debts his father-in-law had failed to pay. Custis had directed that his slaves should be freed as soon as possible, and Lee—who had long since associated himself with those Virginians who opposed the institution of slavery—let them go as soon as he was certain that they could survive on their own.

The progress he made was not complete enough to satisfy rabid abolitionists in the North, however, and he was described in the columns of New York City newspapers as a man who not only refused to obey the terms of Washington's son's will but who had also stripped and flogged a Negro woman who had tried to run away.

Lee ignored the venomous and insane propaganda which had been directed against him in the North and worked patiently within the laws of Virginia and of bedrock humanity to do those things George Washington Parke Custis had left for him to accomplish. He had not sought this duty, but he would not be stampeded into expedient shortcuts while he carried it out. At the end, he was able to settle Custis' estate in a manner which was eminently fair not only to the memory of his improvident father-in-law but to the Lee children who were the inheritors of Custis' property, as well.

In October, 1859, during the period of Lee's leave of absence, a militant abolitionist who called himself Smith caused some trouble at Harpers Ferry, Virginia. Lee was not aware of the disturbance until Lieutenant James E. B. Stuart appeared at his door with a request from the War Department that Lee go to Harpers Ferry and assume command of the Virginia militia's efforts to put down what could easily become a widespread slave insurrection. Lee, remembering Stuart from the days when Lee had been superintendent at West Point and the spirited young man had been a cadet, quickly accepted the lieutenant's offer to accompany him as his aide. They left at once.

At Harpers Ferry, Lee, in civilian clothes, took charge of the situation and sent Jeb Stuart to the door of the fire engine house with a demand for Smith's surrender. Stuart recognized Smith—he was really John Brown, the fiery abolitionist who had moved eastward from Kansas where Stuart had known him as "Ossawatomie" Brown—and delivered Lee's ultimatum. Brown refused it, Stuart gave a signal, and a detachment of Marines under Lee's command opened the assault. When it was all over, John Brown was a prisoner, along with those of his followers who were still alive. The threat of a slave uprising, which had never been very great except in John Brown's warped mind, was over. Brown was tried and sentenced to be hanged. Lee was not present at the execution, but a detachment of cadets from the Virginia Military Institute at Lexington were there under the command of Major Thomas J. Jackson.

In February, 1860, Colonel Lee went westward once more to resume his duties as executive officer of the Second Cavalry. The desert was as hot as ever, the court-martials were just as interminable as he had remembered them to be, and retirement seemed a thousand years away. He was gray now, and at fifty-three—after more than thirty years of service in peace and war as a commissioned officer—the end of his career would come as a blessing. His old dream of buying Stratford and of restoring that once-great manor house to its proper grandeur had not died, but from the sandy expanse of west Texas' Llano Estacado it seemed terribly remote.

Lee was well aware of the disruptive currents which were destroying the unity of the nation he had served for so many years, but he took no part in the angry discussions that went on around him. His own mind, molded as it was in the values of George Washington, Thomas Jefferson, James Madison, and especially Charles Carter, would not permit him to believe that the bold experiment in human freedom which had been launched less than a hundred years before was doomed to fail so soon. In his letters, he made his own position clear: he considered the principle of union paramount, and he deplored the extremism, both in the North and in the South, that threatened the continuation of a good life for all men under the law.

Once again, Lee was obliged to be a man apart from the mainstream of the enthusiasm that fired the minds of the men among whom he served and lived. He could only hope and pray that the madness would be arrested before incalculable ruin resulted. He was in a desolate outpost in west Texas when the great decisions were made: he was to learn of them only long after their effects tore his world to pieces.

— 6 —

In early February, 1861, Colonel Lee was ordered to report to Washington. When he reached San Antonio on his journey eastward, he found the city in turmoil: mobs ran through the streets, the United States flag was nowhere to be seen, and sud-

denly he found himself to be a prisoner of war. Texas, along
with a number of other Southern states, had withdrawn from
the Union. United States Army property had been confiscated.
The city's disarmed Federal garrison was even then marching
out of Confederate territory.

Lee was appalled. "Has it come so soon as this?" he asked a
friend in San Antonio's plaza as the frenzied mob surged
through the streets. It *had* come: Lee was fortunate in being
able to get out of the city at all.

By the first of March, Lee was back at Arlington. Mrs. Lee,
crippled by arthritis, was in a wheelchair. Their home, within
plain sight of Washington, was directly in the path of invasion,
if it came to that. All that Lee held dear was in dire jeopardy,
and there was nothing he could do to stop the mass insanity
which gripped the nation.

Virginians, at least, had remained relatively calm, and Lee
drew some comfort from that fact. Despite the precipitate withdrawal of the Deep South from the Union and Federal firmness
with regard to the tiny United States Army garrison on Fort
Sumter in Charleston Harbor, the moderates in Virginia still
sought some kind of compromise that could ease the tensions.
Even newly elected President Abraham Lincoln's inaugural
address gave some basis for hope. For as long as he possibly
could, Lee remained loyal to the pro-Union traditions that had
been bred into him and which he had served throughout his
life.

Finally, the decision Lee had dreaded most had to be faced.
Confederate forces won the surrender of Fort Sumter; Virginia
was on the point of secession; and President Lincoln decided to
offer command of the United States' forces to Lee.

Francis Blair, a man from St. Louis who remembered the engineer who had tamed the mighty Mississippi River, was selected
to put Lincoln's question to Lee: Would he accept the assignment to command? The answer Lee gave was candid and courteous: He could take no part in an invasion of the Southern
states.

General Scott also asked that Lee call upon him, and Lee
obliged. There was no need for diplomatic sparring among
these two old soldiers; they knew each other too well for that.
Lee reported the gist of his conversation with Francis Blair.

"Lee," Scott said sadly, "you have just made the greatest mistake of your life; but I feared it would be so."

Colonel Lee rode back to Arlington. Behind him in the April afternoon's sunshine was the city that symbolized all that his father and the other patriotic Virginians who followed the incomparable leadership of Washington had fought to achieve. Behind him were all of the years of his manhood, spent unstintingly in the service of the United States. Behind him were all of the hopes he had had for an untroubled old age.

Ahead was Arlington, the scene of his marriage, the birthplace of his children, the heritage he had preserved for the crippled but still valiant woman who had grown old too soon. Ahead was the certainty of Virginia's secession, a Federal invasion, and immediate loss of the stately old house. Ahead was utter and inescapable ruin.

Lee paced the floor in his study long after most of the candles in the old house had been snuffed out for the night. Finally, he wrote his letter of resignation to General Scott. "Save in defense of my native State," he said, "I never again desire to draw my sword."

— 7 —

For Lee, the decision had turned not so much on political principles as on the location of his roots. Virginia had nourished generations of Lees and Carters, and he could not abandon the homeland of his spiritual heritage. When Governor John Letcher asked for his services, he had no choice but to give Virginia all that he was.

Lee left Arlington—for the last time—on the night of April 22, 1861. At Richmond, Letcher offered him the post of commander of Virginia's military and naval forces. Lee stated that he wished that an abler man could have been found, but he accepted the duty he had not sought.

Virginia—through its lawmakers—left no doubt in Lee's mind as to what she expected of him. "Sir," the president of a special convention said to him, "we have, by this unanimous vote, expressed our conviction that you are at this day, among the living citizens of Virginia, 'first in war.' We pray God most fervently that you may so conduct the operations committed to your charge, that it will soon be said of you, that you are 'first in peace,' and when that time comes you will have earned the still prouder distinction of being 'first in the hearts of your country-men.' " After a pause, the speaker continued: "Yesterday, your mother, Virginia, placed her sword in your hand upon the im-plied condition that we know you will keep to the letter and in spirit, that you will draw it only in her defense, and that you will fall with it in your hand rather than that the object for which it was placed there shall fail."

No call to service could have been more direct, more im-pressive, or more challenging. Lee's own disgraced father had written part of that speech; and in a sense, "Light-Horse Harry" —long since dead—was spurring him now.

For the rest of April, 1861, and the beginning of May, Vir-ginia's sword remained in its sheath while her statesmen made a final maximum effort to effect a reconciliation with the Lin-coln government. Lee had scant hope that their attempt would succeed. On May 13, he advised Mary Lee at Arlington to "make your plans for several years of war." She left at once. Shortly after Virginia's voters ratified the ordinance of secession on May 24, Federal troops crossed the Potomac. Arlington be-came the headquarters of the invasion forces.

As Virginia's senior soldier, Lee's first task was to organize the state's military resources to meet at least four imminent threats. West of the Alleghenies, a Federal column was moving south-ward; another Union army was gathering north of the Potomac near Harpers Ferry for a thrust into Virginia's granary, the Shenandoah Valley; a third Yankee force was on Virginia soil between Arlington and Manassas; and the enemy garrison at Fortress Monroe, on the long peninsula that stretches southeast-ward from Richmond, was being reinforced by sea. To meet these thrusts, Lee had only a few hastily recruited, poorly equipped, and barely trained militia units.

To complicate an already discouraging situation, Lee's offi-cial status was altered once Virginia entered the Confederacy. President Jefferson Davis left him in command of all Southern troops in Virginia, but Lee's authority did not include the right to direct combat operations. This meant that he could send forces into a threatened area to block a Union advance, but he could not exercise any degree of control over those units once they came under the command of the general in charge of that area.

During May, June, and early July, 1861, for example, Lee built up the forces at Manassas under General P. G. T. Beauregard and the army commanded by General Joseph E. Johnston at the northern end of the Shenandoah Valley. When those units combined to meet Union General Irvin McDowell's attack at Manassas on July 21, however, Lee was obliged to remain in Richmond and to learn of the outcome of the battle in the manner of a man on the street. "I wished to partake in the struggle," he wrote to Mrs. Lee, "and am mortified at my absence. But the President thought it more important that I should be here. I could not have done as well as has been done, but I could have helped, and taken part in the struggle for my home and neighborhood. So long as the work is done I care not by whom it is done."

Davis sent Lee into western Virginia in late July, 1861, to advise three unit commanders who had the common mission of blocking a Union advance led first by General George B. McClellan and later by General William S. Rosecrans. The effort Lee was directed to make was doomed from the outset, for he was not given authority to command: he was expected to achieve the desired results through persuasion alone. For the next three months, in wretched weather, with inadequate supplies, Lee did his best to coordinate the operations of the three inept generals (who hated each other and agreed only in resenting Lee). Although the campaign was a fiasco, the show of force Lee managed to put up succeeded in keeping the Union thrust from reaching the vital Virginia Central Railroad and held Federal activity in western Virginia in check for the time being.

Seldom in history has a man had to endure more frustration than Lee encountered during those three agonizing months in the mountains of western Virginia. The camps of the units he was expected to coordinate were so filthy that he often pitched his own tent in remote areas without any local security. The promises of the commanders with whom he was obliged to deal meant nothing. Since no one else was either prepared or willing to do any scouting, Lee rode out virtually alone time and again to gather the intelligence data he required—just as he had in Mexico, fourteen years earlier.

Lee's reputation suffered tremendously from the apparent failure of his first mission in the field as a Confederate officer. The publicity he had received back in April as Virginia's first soldier caused the people of the state he loved to expect him to bring off a miracle; instead, he came back to Richmond as the man who had lost all of Virginia's counties west of the Alleghenies (the present state of West Virginia) to the enemy without a fight worthy of the name.

Even so, there were a few compensations. Lee had seen the worst features of warfare—political bickering among ineffectual commanders, lack of sources of supply, the erosion in troop strength and morale that poor sanitation and general lack of discipline can cause, and the folly of trying to carry out a mission without adequate authority to correct even the most obvious deficiencies. This was a side of military service that Lee—coming as he had from the Regular United States Army—had never seen before, for it had its roots in the fact that the soldiers in western Virginia had been raw militiamen. For the rest of the war, he knew, his problem would be to deal with such troops—and his task, he realized, was to learn to work with that reality.

Lee emerged from that harrowing period of seasoning with a friend who would be with him to his life's end, a magnificent gray horse he saw for the first time in Greenbrier County, Virginia, where the animal had been bred. Lee was drawn to the iron-gray horse at first sight. Captain Joseph L. Broun—the owner—offered the mount to General Lee as a gift, but Lee could not allow himself to accept it. Broun then offered to sell the horse to Lee, but the general replied that he could not afford a fair price and would pay nothing less. Later, Lee bought the iron gray from Broun for $175—but he insisted on adding another $25 to compensate Broun for the falling purchasing power of Confederate currency. "You and I travel so well together," Lee said to the horse after he had used him for a few days, "I think I'll call you Traveller."

Another assignment as an adviser awaited Lee at Richmond when he returned at the end of October. This time, the threatened area was coastal South Carolina—and this time, Lee insisted on having command authority and got it. Not long after he arrived, he worked out a defense concept that made maximum use of available resources at a minimum number of key points. Armed with the power to order the execution of his plans, Lee quickly prepared the region to withstand Union attempts to invade the state from the sea. The militia forces who manned the fortifications caught some of his spirit: the will to fight he gave them was the kind that professional outfits might well have envied.

Still, Lee got no credit for his success in South Carolina. As far as the public knew, he had not done a thing to advance the cause: Joe Johnston, Pierre Beauregard, and Thomas J. "Stonewall" Jackson were the Confederacy's new heroes, and Robert E. Lee was tagged as a man who had been sold for much more than he was really worth.

The Confederate Congress, however, grew impatient with President Davis' reluctance to use Lee's talents and passed a bill which would have put Lee in charge of all military operations. Davis used his veto, for he could not accept the implied rebuke. The Congress then produced a compromise measure which left Davis' powers as Commander-in-Chief unimpaired and established Lee as the military official who would carry out the President's wishes. This legal maneuvering left Lee where he had been almost a year before—as a clerk in the War Department.

Lee understood Jefferson Davis completely, but the President could never quite accept the Virginian. The men were similar in some respects: both had been graduated from West Point, both had served in Mexico, and both knew the ways of the old Army—Davis as Secretary of War under President Franklin Pierce, Lee as a career soldier. The difference between them was not so much a matter of the natures of the roles they were now obliged to play, although that factor was highly significant, as it was a function of their backgrounds. Davis, from the rich Mississippi delta, was a wealthy cotton planter, a leader of the aggressive element in Southern politics; but he was a man whose values were acquired rather than natural, and he could not really be quite sure of them. As a result, he always felt uncomfortable in Lee's presence. Davis was never free from the compulsion to dominate. Lee dominated without trying, for he knew who he was, what he was, and what he ought to be—and for him, that was enough.

As Davis' military adviser, Lee acted as communicator of the President's wishes rather than the planner he ought to have been. When Davis grew uneasy about the Federal invasion force under General George B. McClellan that was pressing north-westward up the peninsula from Fortress Monroe toward Richmond, Lee directed Joe Johnston to abandon the lines around Manassas and to move into a blocking position near Yorktown a few miles up the peninsula from McClellan's lines.

Johnston's inclination was to pull back into the defenses of Richmond so that he could face McClellan on a battleground of his own selection. The terrain of the peninsula was such that Johnston's policy was not as passive as it sounded to Davis—who was against giving up any ground anywhere—but it was too timid to be popular, and Johnston was doomed to be listed in the President's book as a man who had rather retreat than fight.

While Davis and Johnston carried on their feud, Lee quietly shifted small detachments of troops northward to protect the sector Johnston had been ordered to leave defenseless. Lee also opened a correspondence with Stonewall Jackson, and he was delighted to learn that the enigmatic Virginia Military Institute professor was of one mind with him in the matter of striking the Union forces north and west of Richmond which could—if ordered—outflank Johnston's defenses and assist McClellan in taking the Confederate capital. Jackson and Lee barely knew each other, but that made no difference. With Lee helping as best he could from Richmond, Jackson launched a brilliant series of slashing attacks in the Shenandoah Valley that diverted more than 70,000 Union troops from McClellan.

The position Lee occupied between the President and General Johnston—who grew more antagonistic toward each other with each passing day—was hardly an enviable one. Lee acted as a buffer between the two men, and for his trouble he won only the hostility of both adversaries. His only comfort was the success Stonewall Jackson was winning in the Valley. Otherwise, his role was a dismal and vexing one.

Meanwhile, Johnston's withdrawal up the peninsula toward Richmond was throwing the capital into a panic. If Johnston had any plan for stopping McClellan, he was unwilling to divulge it to anyone. Davis sent his family to North Carolina for safety and called a Cabinet meeting to discuss the evacuation of the government from the city. "But Richmond *must* be defended!" General Lee insisted, and his spirit was enough to give his civilian superiors new courage.

Mrs. Lee had been at the White House, the old Custis plantation on the York River, east of Richmond. General McClellan's advance caught her behind Federal lines, but she was given an escort to the nearest point of contact with Confederate forces. This was an act of personal courtesy on the part of George McClellan, the man who had served with her husband on General Scott's staff in Mexico many years before.

With virtually all of the peninsula lost, Johnston moved into Richmond's defenses and prepared to face McClellan's final assault. From the beginning, Johnston had been subjected to vicious criticism for his unwillingness to stop the Union invasion at points more distant from the city's fortifications—and if Johnston had any arguments to offer in rebuttal, he had elected not to use them. Now it was all up to him: if he could defeat McClellan, he would be vindicated—but if he lost the critical battle of his otherwise timid campaign, he would be tagged by history as the man who lost the war.

Without letting either Lee or Davis know anything about his plans, Joe Johnston launched a counteroffensive on May 31. Lee rode out to the battle area and discovered that nothing much was happening except that Joe Johnston had been badly wounded while trying to get his attack moving.

President Davis rode out to Seven Pines that day, too, and he was there with Lee when General Johnston was loaded into an ambulance. Davis gave the command of Johnston's army to General Gustavus W. Smith for the time being. On the way back to Richmond, however, the President turned to Lee and told him to take Smith's place as soon as possible.

— 8 —

For the first time in his life, Lee was to be the leader of troops in battle. He had to expect that his appointment would not be popular: the men he was to command were seasoned—and as far as they knew, he was not. His failure in western Virginia was far from forgotten. Nothing he had done in the meantime inspired confidence. To the troops, and more especially to their commanders, he was a desk man, the President's house pet.

With characteristic modesty, Lee assumed command of what he chose to call the Army of Northern Virginia. But a new name for the army—even one which suggested that it meant to do more than save Richmond—was not enough: Lee had inherited a force that was flabby, and he took full advantage of the time he suspected McClellan's excessive caution would give him. Within a few days, Lee whipped one outfit after another into fighting shape without stirring any significant amount of resentment. But the minor deficiencies were the easiest to correct. Ahead were such major problems as the defeatist attitudes of some of his major subordinate commanders, the inefficiency of the staff he inherited from Johnston, and the task of inflicting a crushing defeat upon the Union army.

Although Lee kept President Davis fully informed of what he was doing and what he intended to do, he did not wait for the Commander-in-Chief's approval to act. In mid-June he sent his cavalry commander, General James E. B. Stuart, on a daring reconnaissance of McClellan's northern flank which turned into a bold ride all the way around the Union army. Later in that month, Lee sent for Stonewall Jackson—the man who was to play a key role in an audacious plan that was much on Lee's mind.

Toward the end of June, 1862, Lee was ready to strike Mc-Clellan. His intent was to put Jackson's Army of the Valley around and behind McClellan's weak northern flank: this would force the Union commander to withdraw to the southeast, and as the Federal troops retreated, Lee meant to hammer away at the demoralized Yankees to his front while Jackson tore the enemy's communications to pieces in the rear.

The success of Lee's plan depended upon his skill in executing the most difficult maneuver in warfare—the combination of attacking forces on the field of battle. Jackson would have to move his troops more than fifty miles eastward from Gordonsville in order to reach the line of departure, and he would have to get them there well before the assault was to begin so that they could get some rest. During the Valley Campaign, Stonewall's "foot cavalry" had moved with such astonishing speed that Lee took it for granted that Jackson would have little difficulty in carrying out his orders. Moreover, Lee was adopting Winfield Scott's technique of command in that he presented his subordinates with the task to be accomplished and left the details to them.

Underlying Lee's basic decision—to attack—was his understanding of George McClellan's mind. It was of the greatest importance that Lee be correct in his appraisal of his enemy's mood, for he had elected to mass his strength *away* from the city he was supposed to protect: if McClellan chose to drive through the thin Confederate lines east of Richmond, a major disaster would result. Lee had to believe that McClellan would not only fail to take the initiative, but that he would remain passive—that he would not act, but react—once the Confederate assault hit him.

Lee assumed these risks without giving any indication that they bothered him at all. Far more than his reputation was at stake, but his mind was directed not to what might be lost but to what could be gained. It was as though "Light-Horse Harry" Lee's audacity had finally made itself manifest in the son who had been raised to conform to another model. Earlier, Lee's caution had caused men around the War Department in Richmond to refer to him as "Granny" Lee—behind his back, of course. Suddenly, Granny Lee was taking the most enormous risks any Confederate commander had ever assumed.

From the beginning of Lee's offensive, everything went wrong. Jackson, worked to the point of utter collapse, failed to reach his line of departure on time. General A. P. Hill, impatient at Jackson's delay, sent his troops into the attack on his own initiative and took tremendous losses from a foe that ought to have been maneuvered out of the high ground near Mechanicsville by Stonewall's men hours before. President Davis rode out to witness the battle but could not restrain himself from giving orders to Lee's subordinate commanders. Worst of all, McClellan now had a clear idea of Lee's strategy—and if he dared, he could still throw his powerful army against Richmond's weak defenses.

Having assumed the great gamble, Lee now had to decide whether or not he could continue to press it. Even after nightfall closed the bloody fighting around Mechanicsville on June 26, he still did not know where Jackson was—and in part, he was to blame for that: during the long day, with everything depending on Stonewall, he had sent no couriers to locate him or to urge him to make haste. At several times during the fighting he had lost control of important troop movements even in that portion of the Army of Northern Virginia he could see. McClellan still had the option of either acting or reacting, and either selection might well mean that Lee's offensive would prove to be too expensive in terms of Confederate lives to be worth the few acres of ground he might gain.

Lee elected to keep going.

— 9 —

At Gaines' Mill the next day, Lee's maximum test came suddenly. His troops had slammed into a Union line that seemed impregnable, and once again Jackson was late. Lee had to decide whether to drive the Federals out of their strong positions by sheer valor or to abandon the whole venture and shift his forces back to cover Richmond.

Now Lee was in the front lines, a battlefield commander as well as an army commander. He was under fire constantly, a man of fifty-five who had never before had the responsibility for looking men in the eye and telling them to charge into certain death. He did not flinch, and neither did they: when the sun finally went down and brought an end to the slaughter, he had won by force the position he had been unable to capture through maneuver.

The Battle of Gaines' Mill, costly though it was, shattered McClellan's will. Many years later, Union General Ulysses S. Grant would write: "In every battle there comes a time when both sides consider themselves beaten; then he who continues the attack wins." Lee proved that point, at Gaines' Mill, long before Grant could apply it to Lee.

But the Gaines' Mill mood did not stay with Lee. While McClellan pulled his troops southward toward the James River and abandoned all his hopes of taking Richmond, Lee reverted to the role of army commander and remained confident that his subordinate leaders would carry out his orders for the pursuit. That trust was not well placed, but Lee was not to learn that critical fact until it was too late for him to take remedial action. As a result, McClellan managed to withdraw his army to Malvern Hill near the James River base he had adopted.

On the morning of July 1, with McClellan's artillery parked hub to hub along the plateau of Malvern Hill, Lee was still depressed by the failure to trap McClellan the day before, and he was beginning to show signs of fatigue. He had driven his opponent into the last possible strong point short of either the river or the Union base at Harrison's Landing a few miles to the east, and it was still possible for him to send troops in a lightning drive to close the Federal escape route while his other forces held McClellan in place at Malvern Hill. If Lee recognized that opportunity, he did nothing to exploit it; instead, he let his subordinates persuade him to attack.

Malvern Hill may well have been Lee's worst battle, for he was obliged to accept full responsibility for a bloodbath that he had begun but could not control. He was the prisoner of events when he ought to have been the master, for this was not to be a Gaines' Mill: try though he did, he could not inspire enough valor to overcome the deadly effect of the massed Union artillery even though thousands of men responded to his leadership and charged the Federal lines repeatedly.

After dark, McClellan withdrew eastward from Malvern Hill to Harrison's Landing. Lee was left with a blood-soaked battleground he had not really won. During the next few days Lee considered plans for striking at McClellan's congested base on the banks of the James, but he finally decided that it was best to call a halt to the offensive.

To the public, and especially to the citizens of Richmond, Lee emerged from the Seven Days Battles as a very great hero. He had lifted the siege which had kept the capital in a state of constant apprehension for more than two months; he had defeated McClellan's vastly superior army; and he had electrified the entire Confederacy by daring to attack when his enemy held every possible advantage. No longer would the clerks in the War Department call him Granny Lee, for his most glaring mistake had been to be excessively audacious.

To Lee, however, the Seven Days meant much more. He was acutely aware of his failures and of the shortcomings of his key subordinates, but he knew that no good could come from blaming other men for lapses when he had been so much at fault. He chided those who had disappointed him merely by withholding praise, and he took his own honors in the manner of a man who could not understand why there should be so much exultation over a personal performance that (he felt) was more to be deplored than admired.

To President Abraham Lincoln, McClellan's defeat on the peninsula meant that another commander would have to be found. He appointed General John Pope to the command of a strong force that was ordered to move down through central Virginia to take Richmond from the west, and Pope set Gordonsville as his first objective.

Even though Lee was still worried about the possibility that McClellan would try to break out of the Union lodgment area at Harrison's Landing for another attempt to take Richmond, he sent Stonewall Jackson and the Army of the Valley to Gordonsville in mid-July to check Pope's advance. Toward the end of the month, Lee doubled his bet that McClellan would remain inactive and ordered General A. P. Hill's 12,000 men westward to join Jackson.

Lee had respected McClellan and the other Union commanders he had faced, for they had fought according to the rules of warfare and had remained gentlemen despite the viciousness of the fighting. Pope, however, adopted an unduly harsh policy with regard to civilians and private property and quickly won Lee's hatred. The desire not merely to defeat Pope but to suppress him gave Lee's orders an urgency they had not possessed earlier: so great was his eagerness to get at Pope that he all but commanded President Davis to speed troops westward from Richmond to meet this new threat.

Jackson collided with Pope's southernmost elements on August 9, 1862, at Cheat Mountain, and fought an inconclusive battle which discouraged the Federal commander from continuing his offensive. With virtually all of the Army of Northern Virginia shifting to deal with Pope, President Lincoln ordered the transfer of McClellan's forces from Harrison's Landing via Chesapeake Bay to the Fredericksburg area so that they could join in the new campaign. This meant that Lee had to defeat Pope before McClellan's veterans reached him. Cheat

Mountain, then, served as something of a magnet to the armies of both sides.

By this time, Lee had simplified the command structure of his Army of Northern Virginia into two wings and an independent cavalry force. Neither Jackson nor James Longstreet had performed with distinction during the Seven Days, and Stonewall's lethargy had been particularly disappointing—but Jackson and Longstreet emerged as Lee's key lieutenants, anyway. Jeb Stuart remained in command of the cavalry.

Lee decided to hold Pope in place with one wing of his army while the other made a deep envelopment around the Union force's eastern flank, but the plan had to be canceled when his detailed operations order—carried by a member of Stuart's staff —was captured and several important units failed to arrive on time. Stuart retaliated by getting around Pope's western flank, raiding the Union commander's headquarters, and capturing papers including the Federal plans. Lee then pressed Pope with Longstreet's heavy units while Jackson, led by Stuart's cavalry, marched around the Union force's western flank.

Once again Lee had violated one of Napoleon's maxims: he was splitting his army in the face of a superior enemy. The gravity of the risk he took increased by the hour, but Lee kept his composure. Jackson simply disappeared for a time, and when news of him finally came it was astonishing—Stonewall was at Manassas Junction, far in Pope's rear, stripping a vast Union supply depot and burning what he could not carry away.

A cautious commander would have pressed Pope from the south and ordered Jackson to run for his life so that the army could be reunited, as soon as possible, wherever Longstreet's lines might be, but Lee was too audacious to give any thought to such timid strategy. Instead, he led Longstreet's wing of the army along the same route Jackson had taken and joined Stonewall near the old Manassas battlefield before Pope could get his forces turned around.

Jackson precipitated the Battle of Second Manassas (Bull Run) by attacking a Union division that was passing along the Warrenton Pike just to the south of his hidden position on the afternoon of August 28. The next day, Pope ordered an assault against Jackson's men on Stony Ridge and all but ignored the approach of Longstreet's troops from the west. Jackson was beating off wave after wave of Federal units when Longstreet's men arrived and went into position, and Lee suggested—twice—that Longstreet drive eastward to clear the field of Yankees. Longstreet found excuses for staying in place, and Jackson was obliged to tell his men to hold even though some of them were out of ammunition and had to throw rocks and use the stocks of their rifles as clubs to keep the Yankees from breaking through.

Stonewall's ordeal began anew the next afternoon when Pope threw the full force of his army against Stony Ridge. Longstreet's men watched as one blue charge after another slammed northward against Jackson's thin lines: incredibly, Pope still took no notice of their presence. Finally, with Jackson's troops at the limit of their endurance, Longstreet opened an artillery barrage from the flank which caught thousands of Yankees in the open. Lee sent an order to Longstreet to attack, but Longstreet had anticipated the command and was already sending his men charging to the east across the bloody field.

Pope watched in horror as Longstreet's screaming Confederates swarmed through the ranks of his beaten army. No organized retreat was possible: blue-clad men gathered in clusters to try to arrest the gray tide, but in vain. The rout turned into panic as the Yankees fled eastward toward Bull Run and Washington. Longstreet pressed them, and even Jackson's weary men joined in the pursuit.

Second Manassas was a fantastic victory. Only two months before, Lee had assumed command of an army that hardly seemed capable of holding the defenses of Richmond: but by the end of August, the Army of Northern Virginia had defeated a second superior Federal field force and was threatening Washington. Stonewall Jackson, who had performed dismally during the Seven Days, had more than justified the faith Lee had placed in him—and Lee's audacity had brought about a tremendous boost in Confederate morale.

To his sorrow, Lee realized that his army could not remain in northern Virginia because the land had been stripped of food and forage by the Federals. Lee was no politician, but he saw that something of value might be achieved in a larger sense if he continued his offensive by invading Maryland: Britain and

France might recognize the Confederacy and give military and economic aid, and Lincoln might be receptive to efforts to make peace, if the determination of the South could be dramatized by a thrust into the North's own territory. And even if those aims failed, his men could at least be assured of something to eat.

President Davis quickly approved Lee's plan to move northward, and the new campaign got under way in early September. To Lee's chagrin, he was obliged to cross the Potomac into Maryland in an ambulance: he had broken a bone in one hand and had sprained the other in breaking a fall, and he could not hold Traveller's reins. Lee gave strict orders that the troops were to respect the rights of civilians and pay for everything they took: there was still a chance that Maryland would abandon the Union and join the Confederacy, and he stressed the need for disciplined conduct so that no untoward incidents would spoil those prospects.

Lee avoided the huge Union concentrations around Washington and moved northwestward through Frederick to Hagerstown. Longstreet's forces were in the lead. Federal forces still held Harpers Ferry in Lee's rear, however, and he sent Jackson down to eliminate that threat. Lincoln reacted by ordering George McClellan to reassume command of the Army of the Potomac and to drive Lee out of Maryland.

McClellan, Lee remembered, was not the kind of commander who was inclined to move quickly. It was unlikely, then, that anything of consequence would happen before Jackson completed the capture of Harpers Ferry and returned to the campaign—or so Lee believed. Fate took a hand in the proceedings at this point when a copy of Lee's operations order was found at Frederick and forwarded to McClellan. "Little Mac" acted with uncharacteristic haste and shot his Union columns westward while Lee still had his army scattered throughout western Maryland.

Suddenly, the passes in South Mountain about fifteen miles west of Frederick took on critical importance. While McClellan drove his army toward them, Lee abandoned all thought of continuing his advance into Pennsylvania and rushed divisions southeastward to defend the gaps. Longstreet balked at the order to move to South Mountain: it would be better, he argued, for Lee to concentrate the army near Sharpsburg, west of the threatened ridges. Lee ignored Longstreet's protest and led his forces southeastward to South Mountain.

Lee bought time by fighting at South Mountain—time in which Jackson completed the capture of Harpers Ferry—but McClellan was attacking with more power than the weary Confederate defenders in the gaps could withstand. Sadly, Lee ordered a withdrawal to the rolling hills around Sharpsburg, west of Antietam Creek.

By this time it was clear to Lee that his invasion was doomed to fail. He was only a few miles from the Potomac, and he might easily have ordered a retreat into Virginia. But something held Lee in Maryland: he placed Longstreet's wing of the army in line of battle and waited for Jackson to march up to join him. McClellan provided Lee with a day or so of grace by reverting to his customary caution as he moved westward from South Mountain.

Lee abhorred defensive battles, but now he was obliged to stand where he was and to receive the assaults of an army twice as large as his own. The Union waves struck Jackson's men on the northern end of Lee's line before sunrise on September 17, and the terrible battle was on.

All day long, Lee lived with the probability of defeat. Each new Federal attack seemed certain to be powerful enough to crash through his weakened lines. Lee shifted units from one critical point to another, and both Jackson and Longstreet fought magnificently—but toward the end of the afternoon, it looked as though the incredible sacrifices the Army of Northern Virginia had made were all in vain: Union General Ambrose Burnside was bringing fresh contingents of Yankees up the slope toward Longstreet's thin ranks, and they were charging with a vigor that brought a chill to Lee's heart.

Suddenly, A. P. Hill brought his tired division in from Harpers Ferry. Lee sent them into battle at once. Although they were weary from the long march, Powell Hill's troops screamed their Rebel yell and slammed into the blue-clad lines. In a matter of minutes, Hill drove Burnside's men back across Antietam Creek. The miracle Lee had not dared to expect had taken place.

Lee called his commanders to a conference in an open field

that night. Not far to the east, thousands of wounded men—scattered among the dead—were crying for help. A third of the Army of Northern Virginia had fallen, and those who had not were dead tired. The question was whether Lee should retreat or hold his ground. If he chose, he could still withdraw across the shallow fords along the Potomac to his rear; if he elected to stand and fight for another day, ruin seemed inevitable. Lee ordered a few changes in the lines, told his commanders to feed their men, and let the new day bring what it might.

The audacious decision to remain in place seemed to be the height of folly to the battle-worn Confederates the next morning as they watched McClellan mass his troops. During that interminable day, McClellan brought in enough reinforcements to match Lee's total strength—but he kept them on his side of Antietam Creek, and no attacks developed.

By holding his lines that day, Lee showed his defiance of McClellan and all his hosts. That done, Lee withdrew across the Potomac.

— 10 —

Although Lee's invasion of the North had been short, it at least kept Federal forces out of Virginia for the rest of the fall of 1862 while farmers in the northern counties and the Shenandoah Valley harvested their crops. For a time the Army of Northern Virginia could relax and recover, and Lee was delighted to be able to give his men that quiet interlude.

Lincoln replaced McClellan with Ambrose Burnside and sent his forces toward the beautiful little city of Fredericksburg on the Rappahannock River, roughly halfway between Washington and Richmond. By early December, it was clear that a major battle would have to be fought there: Lee dreaded the prospect, for it would mean another strictly defensive stand with virtually no possibilities for exploitation of any victory he might win.

The Battle of Fredericksburg developed much as Lee had feared. The Army of Northern Virginia held splendid defensive positions, and Burnside bled his vastly superior forces white in one futile assault after another. Lee, watching Longstreet's infantrymen cut down wave after wave of Union soldiers who were trying to reach the sunken road below Marye's Heights, turned to an aide and said: "It is well that war is so terrible—we should grow too fond of it."

There was nothing much for Lee to do but stand there at his observation post and let Burnside's madness run its course. The Union commander finally withdrew on December 15.

Fredericksburg was probably the least satisfactory battle of the entire war to all concerned. Lincoln saw his latest "On to Richmond" offensive stopped cold with astonishing losses. Burnside, who seems to have lacked both the intelligence to devise a better plan and the common sense to halt the slaughter, knew that his failure would soon lead to his relief from command. Lee and Stonewall Jackson thanked God that they had not been beaten, but they were angered by their inability to get the Army of Northern Virginia across the Rappahannock for the pursuit which might have given them the chance to destroy Burnside's forces.

The winter of 1862–63 was a hard one for Lee's threadbare troops, for the country around Fredericksburg could not support such a large body of men and the Confederate supply system had all but collapsed. Starvation was never very far away. Soldiers without shoes wrapped rags and even paper around their feet. The cold wind whipped through their forlorn camps, chilling the gaunt men to the bone. Epidemics raged unchecked, for there was never enough medicine and doctors were too few.

Elsewhere, the people of the Confederacy were decidedly mixed in their attitude toward the war. Some remained as patriotic as ever and gave their full support to whatever could be done to insure independence. Others saw a chance to make quick profits and held supplies off the market until they could get their price. Depressed though Lee was at the sight of his suffering men in their wretched huts along the Rappahannock, the money madness and other forms of depravity he saw in Richmond during a quick visit in mid-January, 1863, disgusted him.

President Davis grew concerned over the possibility that the Union might attempt to take Richmond from the south, and Lee—who still had responsibility for all military operations in Virginia—sent most of the First Corps down to cope with the threat. Later, he put Longstreet in charge of the detachment.

Longstreet welcomed the change, for he had grown restless under Lee's command and wanted nothing more than the opportunity to fight as he wished.

President Lincoln sacked Burnside and gave the Army of the Potomac to General Joseph Hooker, a seasoned corps commander who had earned the nickname "Fighting Joe." Replacements brought the Federal force back to the two- or three-to-one numerical superiority it usually enjoyed over Lee, and by the end of March, 1863, Hooker was eager to set his powerful divisions in motion.

Lee expressed his concern over the security of the Army of Northern Virginia in a number of letters to Longstreet, but Longstreet's replies indicated that he had no intention of returning to the role of a subordinate commander. After many weeks in the south, Longstreet had committed his troops to a useless siege of Suffolk: Lee had to concede that it is no easy thing to break off such an operation, no matter how futile its purpose.

Once again, Lee was making the mistake of assuming that other men shared his high sense of duty and that they would respond to his suggestions in the same spirit that he issued them. It was well within his power to order Longstreet back to the Rappahannock, but he hesitated to think that his "old war horse" would fail to appreciate the need he had for him. Lee had forgotten Longstreet's insensitivity to his suggestions that he attack at Second Manassas, for it was in his nature to overlook the lapses of his subordinates when no great harm was done and victory came anyway. Now he repeated his blunder and allowed Old Pete to stay in the south too long.

Fighting Joe Hooker saw his opportunity to crush Lee, and he moved quickly to take maximum advantage of it. While a strong Union corps under General John Sedgwick menaced Fredericksburg in late April, Hooker moved the main elements of the Army of the Potomac across the Rapidan River near Chancellorsville and not far to the west of Lee's trapped divisions.

No matter which jaw of the huge Federal vise Lee elected to resist, he seemed doomed to be destroyed. But Lee gave no thought to retreating: he knew that he could not hope to stand against Hooker's massed formations elsewhere, and it was still possible for him to accomplish something where he was if he could keep the Union force divided.

After the Battle of Chancellorsville was over, Lee said: "I was too weak to defend, so I attacked." That simple statement makes what he did sound easy, but it was not. Hooker's challenge—coming as it did when everything pointed to a crushing Confederate defeat—obliged Lee to break every rule he had ever learned.

Lee responded by ordering Robert Anderson's division to check the advance of Hooker's main elements at the eastern edge of the Wilderness, but that was an almost automatic action: no commander could have done less. When Stonewall Jackson decided that the chances of attacking Sedgwick's corps at Fredericksburg were too slim, Lee sent his troops westward to reinforce Anderson's blocking position—but Jackson was to withdraw without attracting Sedgwick's attention, and one division under General Jubal Early was left behind on Marye's Heights at Fredericksburg to keep Sedgwick guessing.

Having divided his forces once, Lee split them again on the morning of May 2 when he approved Jackson's plan to slide around Hooker's open southern flank to strike from the rear while Lee and Anderson held the Union army along their front. This was audacity compounded: seldom in the history of warfare had any commander dared to accept such risks.

Hooker, after all, was committed to an offensive. Lee had to expect that his enemy would try to break through to the east at the very moment Jackson was making his lengthy flank march. With only 17,000 men, Lee and Anderson could hardly hope to hold Hooker's men back. Even if Hooker failed to move, there was John Sedgwick back at Fredericksburg who could—if he chose—run westward through Jubal Early's outnumbered troops like the wind in the willow trees.

As the day wore on, Lee received a few terse progress reports from Jackson and beat off Hooker's light probing attacks. For a time, everything seemed to be going in his favor: the great gamble might succeed after all. Then came frightening news. Acting on a staff officer's garbled directive, Jubal Early had abandoned his defense positions on Marye's Heights at Fredericksburg, and Sedgwick was pressing westward after him. If Hooker's probes revealed the Confederates' weakness at Chancellorsville and encouraged him to launch a massive drive, and if John Sedgwick made good time, nothing Stonewall Jackson might accomplish in Hooker's rear would make any difference to the fragment of the Army of Northern Virginia Lee still controlled.

Lee maintained his calm manner and awaited the verdict of fate: there was nothing else for him to do. He had put everything he had into the complex battle. If he had made mistakes, it was too late to correct them. He would either win a dramatic victory or be defeated then and there, and he was prepared to face the worst.

Late in the afternoon, with Hooker's troops still relatively inactive in the forest, Stonewall Jackson sent his weary men forward, charging into the Union's rear. Lee tried to help by launching attacks to keep Hooker's attention divided. By nightfall, the Federal Army of the Potomac had been dealt a crushing defeat.

Long after moonrise, with the sound of intermittent firing still coming from the dense thicket, an aide brought General Lee the shattering news that Jackson had been wounded. "Ah, Captain," Lee said, "any victory is dearly bought which deprives us of General Jackson, even for a short time." Stonewall's loss was one of the great tragedies of Lee's life: never before had he known a man whose fighting heart and brilliant mind were so much like his own, and never again would he have such a man to help him do the thing that had to be done.

Over toward Fredericksburg, Early had responded to Lee's instructions to hold Sedgwick back. He was unable to retake Marye's Heights, but he did manage to slow Sedgwick's advance. For the time being, that would be enough. Since Sedgwick outnumbered Early by better than four to one, it was also a minor miracle.

The next morning, May 3, Lee placed Jeb Stuart in temporary command of Jackson's corps and ordered him to continue the attack Stonewall had launched. Simultaneously, Lee struck Hooker's forces in the forest, and before long the two wings of the Army of Northern Virginia were reunited. With Hooker pulling back northward into a fortified line along the Rapidan River, Lee was able to send a few units over to help Early deal with Sedgwick. By May 5, both Sedgwick and Hooker were retreating. Lee, who had attacked because he had been too weak to defend, had won a brilliant victory over a Union force which was superior in every respect except one: leadership.

But there was to be no celebration. The eyes of the Confederacy were not upon Lee at Chancellorsville but upon Stonewall Jackson who was dying in a little white house at Guiney's Station. Lee sent him encouraging messages, and he spent many hours in prayer for the recovery of that matchless warrior—but on Sunday, May 10, 1863, Jackson died.

— 11 —

Although Lee and Jackson had stopped Lincoln's spring offensive dead in its tracks, in other parts of the Confederacy the war was going against the Southern cause. At Vicksburg, General John Pemberton was trying to prevent a hard-drinking, hard-driving Yankee named Ulysses S. Grant from wresting control of the Mississippi away from him. In central Tennessee, General Braxton Bragg was losing both ground and the respect of his subordinate commanders. President Davis, mindful of those two emergencies, was inclined to take Lee's triumph at Chancellorsville too much for granted and seriously considered sending Lee and all but token elements of the Army of Northern Virginia westward.

Lee, however, presented the President with a counterproposal which had considerable merit. The best way to relieve the pressure against Pemberton and Bragg, he pointed out, would be another invasion of the North. Once the Army of Northern Virgina was driving through eastern Pennsylvania and threatening Philadelphia, Baltimore, Washington, and even New York, Lee reasoned, Lincoln would be obliged to draw strength away from the West to meet the challenge.

Certain other considerations were very much a part of Lee's grand design. The Army of Northern Virginia could no longer be fed by its home state; the Union armies it had defeated had been its best sources of weapons, horses, ammunition, and other supplies; and Virginia's best hope of escaping still another invasion attempt rested in the power of Lee's forces to draw the Federal units north of the Potomac and to keep them there.

Lee made it clear to Davis that his strike into Union territory could not succeed unless he was given high priority on allocations of food and ammunition, and he also asked that General Beauregard be ordered to bring troops up from the Charleston area to protect northeastern Virginia and to threaten Washington while he was operating in Maryland and Pennsylvania. Davis approved all of Lee's recommendations but those. It was not realistic for him to give the impression that he could supply food and forage his quartermasters could not obtain or transport, and he could not bring himself to leave Charleston—or any other place within the Confederacy—undefended.

Davis had intended to send Longstreet and his First Corps westward, but he finally agreed to let them return to Lee. Longstreet had become accustomed to operating on his own, and he now looked upon his old commander as an equal rather than as his superior. Lee did not sense this change at first, for—as usual —he was reluctant to give his subordinates direct orders when a clear expression of his desires in less imperative language would accomplish the same ends; and Old Pete, Lee noticed, seemed willing enough to undertake the adventure north of the Potomac.

Lee's reluctance to issue strict directives—and his unfortunate habit of adding "if possible" to the orders he did give—extended even to Jeb Stuart, the dashing cavalryman who had been a cadet at West Point while Lee, many years his senior, was superintendent of the Military Academy. Lee had already seen Stuart take several rides around Union armies, and he knew that the high-spirited young general was inclined to mistake discretionary authority for permission to run wild—but even so, he sent Stuart northward with a mission that was, at best, inexcusably vague.

General Lee intended for Stuart's cavalry to screen the advance of the Army of Northern Virginia into Maryland and Pennsylvania, and he had every right to expect that Stuart would relay reports of enemy activity back to him so that he could control the forward motion of his infantry and artillery columns. Unwittingly, Lee gave Stuart a fatal option in the matter of the route the cavalrymen could take: they could either stay near the army and guard the passes of the mountains to the east, or they could swing around nearer to Washington and then drive northward to meet the Confederate units Lee was sending to the banks of the Susquehanna River between York and Lancaster, Pennsylvania.

Stuart had been badly mauled by a Federal cavalry attack against his massed troopers at Brandy Station, Virginia, on June 9 in the greatest engagement of mounted soldiers that ever occurred on American soil. Technically, Stuart had won—but newspaper reports of the bloody fight correctly charged him with the sin of having been caught by surprise. Stuart interpreted Lee's order as an opportunity to demonstrate his excellence, and to make his achievement all the more glorious he elected to take the easternmost route to the Susquehanna.

Normally, Stuart's audacity would have warmed Lee's heart. This time, though, it produced a distressing chill: with the Army of Northern Virginia stretched from Wrightsville and near Harrisburg on the Susquehanna all the way southward into Maryland, and with enormous Federal units between the Confederate strongpoints and Washington, no reports came in from Stuart to advise Lee of the Union response. Never before had Lee undertaken such an important offensive; and never before had he been obliged to operate with so little information of his enemy's movements.

The one scrap of intelligence data Lee had was given him on the night of June 28, 1863, by a paid spy. Fighting Joe Hooker had been replaced as commander of the Army of the Potomac by General George Gordon Meade, the agent reported, and Meade was moving his powerful forces westward to trap Lee. This was alarming; Lee had known Meade in the old Army, and he had the highest regard for his ability.

During the past two years, Lee had defeated every Union commander Lincoln had sent against him—McClellan (twice), John Pope, Burnside, and Hooker. All of his opponents had proved to be deficient in one quality or another, and Lee had been quick to take maximum advantage of their flaws. On many occasions, victory had depended on Lee's ability to judge exactly when his opponents would crack: at Chancellorsville, for example, he had bet the life of his cause on his assumption that Hooker would hesitate to launch a drive on May 2 while Jackson was making his long flank march—and he had been absolutely correct. Meade, however, was not an easy man to out-think. Lee knew that he was steady, determined, methodical. He could not expect Meade to make even a minor mistake— and he knew that if Meade caught *him* in the act of blundering, the Union general's reaction would be quick and decisive.

Lee was also well aware of the fact that he had made a number of serious errors in the thirteen months since he had assumed command of the Army of Northern Virginia. During the Seven Days he had not used his staff properly, he had operated without accurate maps, and he had let himself place too much trust in inept subordinates. In Maryland, back in September, he had lost control of his army for a time, and he had allowed McClellan to force him to defend ground that was not of his own selection. And now, at Chambersburg, his latest mistakes were painfully apparent: Stuart was gone, his army was scattered, and he had no real rapport with his new command team.

Before Chancellorsville, the Army of Northern Virginia had been a compact force with only two wings—First Corps under Longstreet and Second Corps under Stonewall Jackson. When Jackson died, Lee split the "foot cavalry" into two new corps; he put A. P. Hill in command of one and gave the other to Richard Ewell. Powell Hill was a fighter, but his health was bad and his mood was often surly. Dick Ewell, a small, birdlike man, had lost a leg at Second Manassas and was barely able to get around. Longstreet, still in command of the First Corps, was openly irritated by the necessity of having to subordinate himself to Lee.

Lee sent his couriers out to the Confederate detachments along the Susquehanna with orders to concentrate in the Cashtown-Gettysburg vicinity at once. With Jeb Stuart and his cavalry still missing, Lee was forced to rush A. P. Hill's corps eastward through South Mountain's passes to secure the assembly area around Cashtown and to locate Meade's army. Although Lee was commanding his troops as before, he had lost control of events: from this time onward, he could only react to the situations Meade presented.

Even so, Lee refused to think in defensive terms. In every battle, the Army of Northern Virginia had captured more Union ammunition than it had fired—and the need for a resupply was urgent. He had brought his troops northward to achieve the strategic objective of drawing Federal strength away from the west, and he had no indications as yet that this goal had been attained. Moreover, it simply was not in his nature to be passive.

As a consequence, Lee either overlooked or intentionally ignored his one clear chance to save his army: South Mountain. The relatively open country around Chambersburg was actually a northeastern continuation of the Shenandoah Valley of Virginia. Just as the Blue Ridge mountains mark the eastern limit of the Valley south of the Potomac, South Mountain separates the Chambersburg corridor from the rolling hills to the east around Gettysburg. South Mountain was immediately available to him as a line of defense, and he could have built strong blocking positions in its passes while his army reassembled near Chambersburg. If a retreat southwestward into Virginia became necessary, South Mountain could provide him with an excellent screen as he moved along the good roads from Chambersburg through Martinsburg to Winchester. But Lee set all of those considerations aside: he could not win a war on the defensive at South Mountain or anywhere else, and he thought only of victory.

— 12 —

And so Lee came to Gettysburg, the little crossroads town in which—some said—there was a supply of shoes.

It all began as a meeting engagement, the accidental and confused kind of fight no officer could really control. The opposing forces blundered into each other, firing broke out, more troops were drawn in, and before long the thing had turned into a battle which neither side wanted but which neither army could afford to lose.

On the afternoon of July 1, 1863, Lee rode into the outskirts of Gettysburg just as the day's sharp skirmishing was ending. A. P. Hill, he noticed, was too sick to be of much use: besides, Hill readily admitted that he had no idea of what was happening. Dick Ewell was in only slightly better shape. The troops from his corps had cleared the town, but he did not believe that they could continue the attack through the hills south of the village.

Lee could hardly believe that Jackson's old outfits had so little of the warrior spirit left in them. He was aware that the march down from the positions in the north had been a hard one, and the day's fighting had often been fierce—but it was unthinkable for Dick Ewell to be talking of holding his lines when so much more had to be done, and at once.

For that matter, Lee was more tired than he realized. For months he had been under tremendous strain; back in the spring his heart had given him some trouble, and during the past few days he had been weakened by a digestive upset. His patience was still held in check, but his staff officers noticed that it was wearing dangerously thin. He had already lost control of events: now he was losing control of his army. If he lost control of himself, Meade would have the battle won.

During the afternoon, General Lee had seen enough of the terrain south of Gettysburg to realize that he would have to take it before Meade's army could concentrate there. That night, working in his tent, he discarded one plan of attack after another: schemes of maneuver were easy to devise, but when he applied the critical factor—the personalities and capabilities of his corps commanders—he had to make too many concessions and alterations. Finally, Dick Ewell came to tell him that perhaps his corps would be able to attack Culp's Hill and Cemetery Hill from the north the next day, after all. With that welcome reassurance, Lee wrote the order for an attack that was to begin as soon as possible the next morning, July 2.

Lee's plan was to have Longstreet's First Corps attack eastward from positions along Seminary Ridge to seize the high ground that extended southward from Cemetery Hill to the two rocky knobs known as the Round Tops while A. P. Hill's corps in the center made a strong demonstration and Dick Ewell's men assaulted the Union positions on Cemetery Hill and Culp's Hill. Longstreet was to make the main effort.

Now began the series of tragic encounters between Lee and Longstreet which were to prove so costly during the next two days. During the previous afternoon, Longstreet had tried to persuade Lee to withdraw to the south in search of defensive terrain to which Meade might be drawn; Lee, concerned about the battle at hand, had let Longstreet's suggestion pass without comment. On the morning of July 2, when Longstreet ought to have been rushing his troops to the line of departure Lee had ordered, he was still irritated by Lee's implied rejection of his idea. As a consequence, he made no haste at all to carry out his instructions.

Lee had never had much rapport with the burly, stolid Longstreet, but he knew that Old Pete could fight magnificently when the spirit of battle finally came over him. Lee trusted that he would perform again soon as he had before, and he ended their first conversation that morning by saying, "I think you had better move on."

General Lee, assuming that Longstreet would soon be opening his attack, rode northward to Dick Ewell's command post to send him southward to assault Culp's Hill and Cemetery Hill. That done, he returned to his own observation post to watch Longstreet's advance—but there was nothing for him to see, for Longstreet had made no real effort to get his men moving. It took an hour for Lee to find Longstreet, and even then Longstreet argued until Lee granted him enough time to bring up a unit that was just arriving after a forced march of twenty-four miles.

At four o'clock on the afternoon of July 2, almost eight hours after Lee had expected him to strike the Union lines, Longstreet moved forward. Lee rode Traveller to his observation post near Spangler's Woods and noticed—to his horror—that Longstreet's objective, which had been lightly defended earlier that day, was now swarming with blue-clad reinforcements.

General Jeb Stuart rode in from his extended raid and reported to Lee; he got a chilly reception. "Help me fight these people," Lee said. But the hour was late, and there was little Stuart's weary riders could do.

For a time it seemed to Lee that Longstreet's men were about to break through Meade's defenses—but Federal reinforcements rushed in at the critical moment, and each gallant Confederate assault failed. To the north, in Dick Ewell's sector, it was the same: victory was only yards away, but Meade managed to hold.

After dark, Lee returned to his tent to await Longstreet's report—in vain. He was left alone, the commander of an army that could not fail, with little more than his own impressions of what had happened at the Round Tops and along Cemetery Ridge to guide him in planning the next day's work. By this time, the intestinal disorder which had been vexing him was becoming serious—but the iron-gray man could not even try to rest until his orders were ready for the couriers to carry to Longstreet, Ewell, and Hill.

General Lee's plan of attack for July 3 was essentially the same one he had used the day before. Once again, he placed the major portion of his trust in the stubborn man whose perform- ance in the past few hours had been so disappointing—Long- street. This time, however, Old Pete was to make his thrust across the open ground through Meade's left center, north of the Round Tops. As before, Dick Ewell's corps was to strike southward to seize Culp's Hill and Cemetery Hill. When either attacking force achieved a penetration of the Federal line, A. P. Hill was to rush his men into the gap and lead the exploitation phase of the victory.

If Gettysburg was something less than a typical Lee battle— and it was—the reasons are not difficult to find. He was ill, he was tired, and he was feeling his years. No help—only indiffer- ence, obstinance, or sullen acquiescence—came to him at his time of greatest need. Locked in a battle he had not sought, depleted of the energy he had always relied upon in moments of stress, he had no choice but to see the grisly encounter through to the end. Imagination on Lee's part was not lacking, but he knew that it would do no good for him to devise a scheme his corps commanders could not carry out. He was obliged to attack Meade in the one manner that gave the Union general every advantage: there was no longer any alternative.

Lee's order to Longstreet, Ewell, and Hill specified earliest dawn as the time the assaults were to begin on July 3. After a wretched and almost sleepless night, Lee went up to his observa- tion post to watch Longstreet open his attack. Ewell, several miles to the north, was to advance as soon as he heard the sound of gunfire from Longstreet's sector. After a while, Lee realized that Longstreet was going to be late again. He rode Traveller down the reverse slope of Seminary Ridge to Longstreet's head- quarters to find the cause for the delay and remove it.

Longstreet greeted his commander by restating his arguments in favor of a deep envelopment of the Round Tops, the objec- tives his men had been unable to take the day before. Moreover, it was apparent to Lee that Longstreet was making no preparations to execute the orders he had been given to attack. At this point, Lee had every possible reason to relieve Longstreet from command except one: the first two days' fighting had cost Lee the services of a host of his better leaders, and Longstreet—with all his faults—was virtually the only senior officer still available to Lee who was remotely capable of accomplishing anything.

Lee endured Longstreet's insubordinate tirade for as long as he could. Finally, he directed Longstreet to get on with his attack—but still Longstreet pressed his objections, as though Lee had not already ordered him *twice* to obey the instructions he had been given. To avoid wasting any more time, Lee agreed to let Longstreet make a few seemingly minor changes. One of them involved the use of the division commanded by General George E. Pickett.

For the rest of the day, nothing seemed to happen as Lee directed. He sent couriers to advise Ewell that Longstreet's attack would be delayed, but they arrived after Ewell had launched his assault. As a result, Ewell's men attracted Meade's undivided attention and they were repulsed with heavy losses. Later, Pickett's charge—directed by Longstreet—swept across a mile or so of open ground with matchless gallantry only to be stopped at the Bloody Angle and thrown back.

As the stunned survivors of Pickett's attack streamed back to the Confederate lines along Seminary Ridge, General Lee met them. "It was all my fault," he said to the weary men. "Don't be discouraged. . . . It was all my fault."

Lee rode along his lines to prepare his men for the counterattack he expected Meade to launch, but no Union assaults came. Finally, at one o'clock on the morning of July 4, Lee returned to his headquarters to get some rest. When he slid down from the saddle, he leaned against the side of his great war horse for a moment. A staff officer came over. "General," he said, "this has been a hard day for you."

Lee, thinking not of himself but of the Army of Northern Virginia, replied: "Yes, it has been a sad, sad day for us."

On July 4, with heavy rains falling on the hallowed ground where so many had fallen, Lee held his positions while the wounded were loaded in wagons destined for the Shenandoah Valley of Virginia. Ammunition supplies were dangerously low.

The ranks of his units were thinned to the point of being non-effective. Withdrawal was inevitable.

Meade's strategy at Gettysburg had been to allow Lee to bleed himself out and to strike the Confederates while they were retreating. Lee sensed this, and he gave as much care to the security of his long columns of exhausted men as he had given to the battle itself—perhaps more. Union cavalry probed his flanks constantly, and on several occasions it seemed that few if any men would reach Virginia. But the rains persisted and Jeb Stuart kept his horsemen in action constantly to screen the retreat routes, and by mid-July the Army of Northern Virginia was across the Potomac in home country once again.

—— 13 ——

For Lee to have failed to win at Gettysburg was the equivalent of defeat, not in real terms but in the impact his withdrawal had on the minds of the peoples of both embattled nations. At Vicksburg, Mississippi, General John C. Pemberton had surrendered his garrison on the same day that news of Lee's decision to retreat reached Richmond. The Confederacy was rocked by what it chose to consider twin disasters, overlooking such vexing truths as its lack of support for Lee's audacious venture or the tendency to assume that because the Army of Northern Virginia under Lee had always won, it always would.

Lee took Gettysburg as a personal loss. To President Davis he wrote a long letter in which he suggested that a younger and abler man ought to be sent to replace him if—as he supposed—public confidence in him had been shaken to the detriment of the Southern cause. Davis replied: "To ask me to substitute you by some one in my judgment more fit to command, or who would possess more of the confidence of the army, or of the reflecting men of the country, is to demand an impossibility."

Distorted though the significance of the Gettysburg campaign was destined to be, it remains—in its true perspective—as an excellent test of Lee, the man. After Chancellorsville, he recognized that the only way to spare Virginia's strained resources was to carry the war into the North. Such an invasion, he believed, might also have the highly desirable effect of drawing Union combat power away from Vicksburg and Tennessee where Confederate armies were facing serious threats. With the Army of Northern Virginia invading Pennsylvania, Lee assumed that Jefferson Davis' diplomats in England and France would have a stronger case to make for the recognition of the Confederacy. He reached the banks of the Susquehanna, only to be dragged into a bloody stalemate at Gettysburg. The weight of Union war power did not shift in time to save Vicksburg. Diplomatic recognition did not come. Lee, the man who had dared to act in ways other men could hardly discuss intelligently, did not ignore the responsibility he had assumed. Instead, he accepted blame which was not wholly his own. Even to James Longstreet, Lee said: "It is all my fault."

With Meade remaining relatively inactive to the north of Lee's forces, President Davis sent Longstreet and most of his First Corps to the Chattanooga area to serve in the Army of Tennessee under General Braxton Bragg. Since few replacements were arriving for duty with the Army of Northern Virginia, Lee could not be optimistic about his chances of holding back another Union attempt to capture Richmond.

The thrust Lee feared came in the early fall of 1863 when Meade brought the Army of the Potomac southward through central Virginia along much the same route John Pope had used a year before. Lee could not hope to match Meade in combat power, and he did not try. Instead, he kept up a campaign of maneuver which ended with the Army of Northern Virginia poised for another strike north near Washington. Meade withdrew hastily, leaving most of Virginia free from Union control. Not a single serious battle had been fought, and no one paid much attention—but through his skill alone, Lee had once again saved his homeland's capital.

This time, however, Lee knew that his army was too weak to undertake another invasion of the North. Besides, winter was coming. Lee put his men in the most comfortable blocking positions he could find for them and turned his hopes to what might be done in the spring.

Out in Tennessee, Braxton Bragg finally demonstrated his incompetence in a manner that was too obvious for President Davis to ignore. Davis relieved Bragg and attempted to persuade Lee to go out and take command of the Army of Tennessee. Lee had to muster all of his tact in refusing the President's request, but the case he made for remaining with the Army of Northern Virginia was strong enough in itself: no other officer was available to replace him.

In the spring of 1864, Abraham Lincoln brought General Ulysses S. Grant—who had never yet been defeated—out of the west to become general-in-chief of the Union war effort. Lee did not know Grant personally, but he had heard a great deal about him. If his information was correct, he would be facing a man who was fond of straight-ahead attacks and who had little inclination to fight a war of maneuver.

Even so, Lee did not underestimate his new adversary. Grant, acting through George Meade, would have the powerful Army of the Potomac to send against him—and the fighting strength of that dangerous force, Lee knew, would be supported by the Union's virtually unlimited resources in war matériel and manpower. By contrast, Lee's supply situation had deteriorated during the winter, and replacements for his losses simply were not to be had. If he ever let Grant trap him, the war in Virginia would come to a dismal end very quickly.

When Grant began his preparations for an offensive in late April, 1864, Jeb Stuart brought in reports that the Union route of advance would pass through the Wilderness, just to the west of the old Chancellorsville battleground. Behind Grant, Stuart reported, were long columns of wagons heavily laden with supplies.

Lee quickly made an analysis of Grant's probable course of action. To do this, he put himself—mentally—in Grant's position. He concluded that Grant would hold his infantry near the fords of the Rapidan River until the wagons were across, and he assumed that this might take several days. If this reasoning was correct, an opportunity existed for Lee to strike Grant while the Union troops were still in the forests of the Wilderness.

General Lee, remembering that Grant possessed the power to roll right over the thin ranks of the Army of Northern Virginia, decided to attack the Union flank from the west. The corps commanded by Dick Ewell and A. P. Hill were ready to move. Longstreet's men, just back in Virginia after their hard winter in east Tennessee, could not be added to the battle until it had been opened by Ewell and Powell because Longstreet's camps were a number of miles away and Lee had to assume that Longstreet would be as slow as ever in covering ground.

On the morning of May 5, Grant sent General G. K. Warren's corps southward through the Wilderness along the Brock Road while General W. S. Hancock's troops marched down a parallel route to the east. General John Sedgwick's corps remained in the rear with orders to move as soon as road space was available. Grant expected to collide with Lee, but Stuart's cavalrymen had performed their screening duties effectively and Grant had no idea of where the armies might meet.

Lee used two roads in approaching the Wilderness—the Orange Turnpike and the Orange Plank Road two miles or so to the south. Ewell, on the turnpike, deployed his men when he neared the Brock Road. Warren's forces attacked them, and the battle was on.

Powell Hill's troops, on the Plank Road, also drew the fire of the Federal column when they drew near the intersection of the Brock Road and the Plank Road. Fighting in Hill's sector was particularly fierce, for a large number of Union troops had already moved southward through the intersection and were in danger of being cut off by the surprise Confederate thrust.

But Lee was far from pleased. A gap of more than a mile existed between Ewell and Hill, and he had no way of closing it. He could not believe that Grant would remain ignorant of the gap's existence, and he knew that once Union troops poured through it both of his corps would be engulfed.

Curiously, the twin battles held most of the Union commanders' attention and no serious effort was made to exploit the gap. When night fell, Lee assumed that Longstreet would arrive in a few hours and relieve Hill's men: accordingly, nothing much was done to tie the two tired corps together.

Longstreet, though, was late. Very early on the morning of the next day, May 6, Hancock's corps launched a savage assault westward from the intersection of the Brock Road and the Plank Road which sent A. P. Hill's men reeling back past the Widow Tapp's house where Lee had established his headquarters. "My

God," Lee shouted to a unit commander, "is this splendid brigade of yours running like a flock of geese?"

It was, but not for very far. Once they had passed, twenty artillery pieces opened direct fire on the advancing Federals and blasted them to a halt. The stunning effect of grapeshot and canister from the Confederate guns lasted only a minute or two, though, and Hancock's men prepared to renew the attack.

Suddenly, Lee saw fresh troops in butternut brown coming up the Plank Road from the west. They were Texans, the vanguard of Longstreet's corps. Lee waved his hat in the air and shouted, "Hurrah for Texas!" A moment later, Traveller shot forward. It seemed that General Lee was intent on leading the Texans' charge straight into Hancock's troops. "Go back, General Lee!" someone yelled. "General Lee to the rear!" Still Lee pressed forward, oblivious to the shouts and the danger. Finally, his chief of staff, Colonel Charles Venable, grabbed Traveller's bridle and turned Lee back.

John Gregg's Texans plunged ahead and took terrible losses as they drove Hancock's men back toward the crossroads. Gradually, Lee built up the force of the attack: as new units from Longstreet's corps arrived, he fed them in. With Longstreet finally committed, Lee sent Hill's troops northward to close the gap. A day after it had begun, Lee had the battle in hand.

For a time it seemed that Longstreet was going to do much more than save the day. On his own initiative, he sent his chief of staff, Colonel G. Moxley Sorrel, and a few units around the southern end of Hancock's line. Sorrel's surprise attack threw the Union troops into panic, and he pursued the beaten Yankees into the woods north of the Plank Road. Longstreet was giving orders to continue the drive when some Confederate soldiers mistook his command party for an enemy patrol and opened fire. Longstreet fell, shot through the neck.

Lee came forward at once and assumed control of Longstreet's corps, but by the time Longstreet had been evacuated the momentum of Sorrel's assault had been lost and Hancock's forces were behind the safety of log fortifications in the forest. Although Lee sent strong attacks crashing into Hancock's positions, the second day ended with the Union troops holding their ground in the burning Wilderness.

In the hope that something might yet be accomplished by

Dick Ewell's corps, Lee rode northward to confer with the erratic little man on whom so much now depended. Ewell was not in a fighting mood, but one of his subordinates—General John B. Gordon—was. Lee ordered Gordon to move around Grant's open northern flank. With daylight all but gone, Gordon attacked and captured a number of Yankee prisoners. Finally, though, Gordon's assault had to be called back: it was too dark to maintain control, and his force was insufficient to remain where it was.

Grant's losses had been heavy—perhaps 17,000 of his troops had fallen, and the fire that swept through the Wilderness made the horror of the two days' fighting seem far worse than it had been. Lee had stopped his advance cold and still remained on his flank with an army that ignored numbers and attacked when other men would flee for their lives. The vaunted Union offensive was rapidly becoming a fiasco.

At that point, on the night of May 7, 1864, Grant made the decision that was to win the war for the Union. He was beaten, but only in the Wilderness. He would break out and continue the drive.

Lee saw the effect of Grant's decision the next day as one Federal unit after another headed southeastward toward Spotsylvania Court House, a little crossroads settlement twelve miles or so away. He sent first Jeb Stuart and then Dick Anderson down to block Grant's advance: Stuart's cavalrymen, under the immediate command of Lee's nephew, Fitz Lee, held the Yankees back while Anderson (who now commanded Longstreet's corps) put his men into a forced march to reach the new battle area.

Anderson's divisions relieved the weary cavalrymen, who held a key piece of ground a few miles northwest of Spotsylvania Court House, early on the morning of March 9. Stuart extended the line eastward while General Lee moved Hill's corps and then Ewell southward to reinforce the blocking position. Stuart and Anderson had won the race to Spotsylvania, but it had been a near thing.

For the next few days, Lee commanded his forces as he had never commanded before. Ewell was discredited in his eyes. Hill was sick, replaced temporarily by Jubal Early—a man for whom Lee had little use. Anderson was new to high command and showed signs of instability. Stuart was gone, leading a gallant attempt to stop a Union cavalry raid on Richmond.

Virtually alone though he was, Lee responded brilliantly. Since he had no choice but to defend, he supervised the construction of a strong system of field fortifications which appreciably reduced the effectiveness of Grant's numerical superiority. When direct combat leadership was required, Lee mounted Traveller and rode out to supply it.

Such a time came shortly before daylight on May 12 when a fierce Union assault smashed through the "mule shoe" salient in the center of Lee's line. Showing the same grim determination to win or be killed he had displayed at the Wilderness less than a week before, Lee organized a counterattack and led it straight into the lines of advancing Federals. General Gordon persuaded Lee to go to the rear and leave the battle to him, but Lee merely paused. Gordon's attack closed the breach, but a fresh Union assault developed on Lee's left. He shuffled unit after unit from quiet portions of his line to reinforce the troops who were about to be overrun, and once again his men had to beg him to get back. "If you will promise to drive those people from our works," Lee replied, "I will go back." They kept their promise.

Back at the "mule shoe," Confederate soldiers fought an incredibly determined battle against wave upon wave of Federal troops. For a time it seemed that all of the fury of the entire war was concentrated there in that bloody angle. When the grim day was over, Grant had lost another 17,000 men. But Lee's lines were intact.

For Lee, Spotsylvania was another Fredericksburg—a slaughter which brought no result and led to no opportunity. To that tragic burden a shock was soon added: Jeb Stuart had died of the wounds he had received at Yellow Tavern, a few miles north of Richmond, several days before.

Grant, too, was depressed by the outcome of the grisly battle on May 12. For the next few days he held his operations to light probing attacks and waited for reinforcements. Lee and the Army of Northern Virginia, he was learning, fought with a tenacity that power alone could not quickly overcome.

— 14 —

For both armies, Spotsylvania was a key battle. Having blocked Grant there, Lee forced his enemy to decide whether to move southward through central Virginia or to take an easterly route along the lowland country near Chesapeake Bay. Lee anticipated—correctly—that Grant would shift his troops to the east so that he could be supplied from the sea, and he was not surprised when Grant started his columns on the next stage of their march toward Richmond.

Lee took up a position on the southern banks of the North Anna River about twenty-five miles north of Richmond and waited for Grant. When the Union forces arrived and began to make crossings on his flanks, Lee pulled his army into an angle with the point resting on the river's edge. Since the Federal corps opposite the angle's point could not cross in the face of murderous Confederate artillery fire, Lee's wedge forced Grant to separate his army—thus exposing the Union troops on either side of Lee's angle to piecemeal defeat. Just as a promising opportunity to strike the Federal corps to the west of the angle was shaping up, illness struck Lee and confined him to his tent. Grant wisely elected to accept tactical defeat rather than risk the fire of Lee's men in the angle. He slid southeastward once again and continued his march toward Richmond.

Not until early June did the armies clash again. When they met, at Cold Harbor, eight miles or so to the east of Richmond, the course the war would take from that time onward was decided.

Grant, frustrated by his failure to destroy the Army of Northern Virginia in the Wilderness, at Spotsylvania, and at the North Anna, was determined to break through Lee's ragged lines and take Richmond. He was mindful that the morale of his 100,000 troops had been seriously eroded by a month of hard fighting, long marches, and appalling losses. South of Cold Harbor, he knew, he would have to assault the Confederates' fortifications and thus accept the disadvantage of having to risk five men to overpower each one of Lee's defenders.

For Lee, the encounter at Cold Harbor was his last clear chance to regain the initiative. He had maneuvered Grant into the old familiar country where—two years before—the Army of Northern Virginia had humiliated General George B. McClellan in the Seven Days Battles, and he knew that thousands of Confederates expected him to repeat that triumph. Lee understood, as many of his countrymen did not, that it would be miraculous if his army could undertake even a limited objective offensive: his men were starving, his ammunition supplies were low, and the Confederate government simply could not meet his requirements for replacements, wagons, and horses.

Cold Harbor, then, drew a maximum effort from both Grant and Lee. Grant ordered his corps commanders to make a careful reconnaissance of the terrain leading into the Confederate positions. Lee rushed the construction of field fortifications.

On the foggy morning of June 3, 1864, Grant's troops advanced. Within half an hour, 7000 of them had fallen. He ordered fresh assaults. The survivors of the earlier charges refused to move.

At Cold Harbor, as at Fredericksburg, neither side really won. To Grant, Cold Harbor was definitely a defeat: his grand offensive had been halted in the blood of his most seasoned troops, and he was visibly stunned by the viciousness of the Confederates' will to resist. But as at the Wilderness, Grant meant to keep fighting. After a few days he ordered a carefully screened movement to the south in the hope of beating Lee's Army of Northern Virginia to the vulnerable area south of the James River between Richmond and Petersburg.

Grant's new objective was located in a military district commanded by General Pierre G. T. Beauregard. This meant that any shift of Lee's forces into the threatened sector had to be coordinated by the Confederate War Department and President Davis' military adviser, General Braxton Bragg.

Beauregard filed urgent requests for reinforcements, believing for a time that Davis would strip Lee's army to provide them for service under his command. Like Lee, Beauregard assumed that the authorities in Richmond could cope with the situation in an effective manner. It was just at this time of greatest strain, however, that the Confederate command system broke down. Even as Beauregard was beginning to recognize the futility of his attempt to wrest power and glory from Lee, the commander of the Army of Northern Virginia—without waiting for the paralyzed Davis and Bragg to act—ordered his units to rush toward the lines below Richmond. After the threat of disaster was no longer imminent, Davis placed Lee in command of the Petersburg defenses.

During the Confederates' confusion, Grant almost beat Lee to the new battle area: only the valor of Beauregard's defenders and Lee's willingness to cross into a zone in which he had no authority prevented a Union victory which might have destroyed both Southern armies and ended the war. Once Grant's initial assaults had been thrown back, Lee settled into the grim task that was to occupy him for the next ten months—the siege of Petersburg.

Lee's lines extended from east of Richmond southward and then westward below Petersburg, and covered a distance of more than twenty miles. Grant's general aims were to extend his forces westward to cut the railroads and to effect a breakthrough once Lee's forces had been stretched past their ability to hold. Union attacks hit first the western sector of Lee's defenses and then points along the eastern trace in determined attempts to keep the Confederate commander off balance. Compared to earlier battles, however, the Yankee assaults were light in intensity and seemed to be poorly led.

Many of Lee's better moments as a commander were to occur during the siege of Petersburg, but this prolonged encounter was a heartbreaking experience for him. Although he was a master of defense, Lee relished the open, aggressive kind of warfare the Army of Northern Virginia could never again wage. He saw the end even as he began the defense of Petersburg, and he was forced to live with that terrible vision as each depressing day followed the one before.

Grant's supply of men, ammunition, and food was virtually unlimited, while Lee stoically accepted steady attrition and suffered the sad fact that his poorly equipped men were starving in the trenches they held so valiantly and with so little complaint. Eventually, he realized that his soldiers were holding out primarily because of their deep love for him: such a tribute was almost more than his troubled heart could bear, and it had the effect of driving him all the harder to get the reinforcements, matériel, and rations his impoverished nation could no longer provide.

Despite the enormous pressure Grant's Army of the Potomac exerted against the Confederate lines below Petersburg, Lee detached units he could ill afford to lose and sent them to the Shenandoah Valley in a vain attempt to attract Union strength away from his hard-pressed men. But the gallant attempt was doomed: when Jubal Early's forces had done their best, General Philip Sheridan was still able to make a reality of his boast that a crow flying over the Valley would have to carry his own rations.

In early 1865, with Lee's Army of Northern Virginia maintaining the only significant defense against the Union's flood tide, President Davis belatedly designated General Lee as the Confederacy's supreme commander. Lee took the honor without much notice, for it came too late to have any real meaning. It was habitual with Lee to defer to civilian authority. He refrained from using his wide powers and cleared proposed actions with the President as though the appointment had never been made.

During the winter of 1864–65, both armies remained relatively inactive in their trenches south of Petersburg. Lee's ragged, famished veterans fought off local attacks like men in a nightmare while their commander made every effort to find more troops, more food, more clothing—in vain. The massive Army of the Potomac, meanwhile, grew even stronger.

By early March, Lee saw that his weary forces could not hold out much longer. Grant's local operations had obliged Lee to stretch his lines over thirty-seven miles, and his men were outnumbered by at least five to one. Starvation would soon give Grant the victory that Union troops had been unable to win.

Elsewhere in the Confederacy, the war was all but over. Sherman had burned Georgia from Atlanta to Savannah and was searing his way northward through the Carolinas on his way to reinforce Grant—as if Grant needed more troops. Nathan Bedford Forrest fought on in Alabama, and Joe Johnston was trying desperately to check Sherman in North Carolina, but local successes had meaning only in personal terms: men long since wearied of the war watched the scarecrowlike men they had grown to love fall around them, and they could not help wondering what good it would do the South if they, too, kept on marching and fighting until the Confederate nation was utterly destroyed. Many slipped away in the dark.

Not even the magnificent example of General Lee could stem the flow of deserters from the thin Confederate lines south of besieged Petersburg. Lee's units dwindled in size until the Army of Northern Virginia was hardly more than a tattered reminder of the vigorous field force it had been in the Seven Days, at Second Manassas, even in the Wilderness.

Finally, only three alternatives remained open to Lee—to try to negotiate satisfactory peace terms with Grant, to withdraw from the Petersburg-Richmond lines and join forces with what remained of Joe Johnston's Army of Tennessee, or to throw one last attack against the Army of the Potomac which might stun the Yankees while the pullback began. Grant refused to meet Lee for peace talks. President Davis would not allow a planned withdrawal. Only the least attractive possibility remained, and Lee did not hesitate to adopt it.

On March 25, 1865, General John B. Gordon directed a pre-dawn attack against Union-held Fort Stedman on the eastern end of the Confederate defense line. Success came quickly, and for a time it seemed that Gordon's troops might be able to cut Grant's supply line—but by mid-morning the bold breakthrough had turned into a heartbreaking disaster which cost Lee 4000 men.

With the need to withdraw to the west about to become imperative, the little crossroads settlement known as Five Forks a few miles west of the end of the lines took on critical importance. To secure that key point, Lee sent General George E. Pickett's division with orders to beat the Yankees back at all costs. Federal cavalry and infantry struck the defenders late on the afternoon of April 1, and before long Five Forks was under Yankee control.

Lee hardly had time to react to the loss of Five Forks, for Grant put heavy artillery fire into the city of Petersburg on the night of April 1 and launched a major assault before daybreak. When word of the Union attack reached the little frame house not far behind the trenches, where Lee made his headquarters, blue-clad soldiers were already charging through the thin Confederate lines. General A. P. Hill hurriedly rode off to join his troops: within minutes, he was killed. "He is at rest now," Lee said when he heard of Hill's death, "and we who are left are the ones to suffer."

Despite the viciousness of Grant's maximum-effort attack, Lee's veterans managed—somehow—to contain it. Around ten o'clock on the Sunday morning of April 2, Lee sent a message to President Davis. It read: "I see no prospect of doing more than holding our position here till night. I am not certain that I can do that. If I can I shall withdraw. . . . I advise that all preparation be made for leaving Richmond tonight."

The most obvious fact in the minds of Americans—North and South—for the past nine months had been the vulnerability of General Lee's defenses. Even so, no preparations had been made in Richmond for evacuation of civilians. That was not Lee's problem, and he knew it. He concentrated, therefore, on saving his army.

Soon after Lee sent the telegram to Davis, he left the house that had been his headquarters. Moments afterward, the building was hit by a shell and burst into flame. Lee and his staff were under enemy fire for the rest of the long day. At times it seemed that the Yankee gunners knew the identity of their target. Despite these dangers and the accumulation of months of stress and disaster, Lee gave clear orders for the withdrawal of the Army of Northern Virginia from the Petersburg defenses. As the sun went down on April 2, 1865, those instructions were carried out.

— 15 —

Distasteful as the task of extricating his army from the Petersburg line was to General Lee, he directed the operation in the same steady manner and with the consummate skill he had employed on so many happier occasions during the past three years. He designated the little town of Amelia Court House, about forty miles to the west, as the Army of Northern Virginia's assembly point and ordered the units which had been defending the eastern approaches to Richmond and Petersburg to meet him there. Food had been stockpiled at several points near Amelia, and Lee issued instructions for rations to be moved to the assembly area at once.

Beyond Amelia, Lee planned to move southwestward along

the Richmond & Danville Railroad, turn southward and then eastward, and join forces with Johnston's Army of Tennessee. From the outset, however, he was aware that Grant would be marching along his southern flank with the intention of heading him off. If Grant made good time, the end would not be long in coming.

Although Lee's Army of Northern Virginia completed its re-assembly at Amelia on April 4, hardly anything else worked out according to plan. The rations did not arrive. Enemy cavalry activity made it imperative that the army move on. Reports indicated that Grant's spearheads had cut the railroad between Amelia and Danville.

Farmville, twenty-odd miles west of Amelia Court House, became Lee's next marching objective. During the next two days, April 5 and 6, Union pressure forced Lee to fight rear guard actions which were sharp in intensity and costly in casualties, but straggling and desertion were becoming even more serious problems: by this time, hardly anyone in the Army of Northern Virginia had eaten as much as a biscuit in the better part of five days, and the men had been forced to march fifty miles or so without having any rest except for naps which were interrupted by rain or enemy raids.

Lee had expected that he would have a day or two at Farmville in which he could feed his men and allow them to get some rest, but this was not to be. He reached the city on April 7, only to learn that his orders to destroy High Bridge over the Appomattox River had not been executed and that Federal troops were streaming across. Some of the men were cooking the first food they had seen in days when Lee ordered them to move out. They moved—toward the north.

That night, Grant sent Lee a message: "The results of the past week must convince you of the hopelessness of further resistance on the part of the Army of Northern Virginia in this struggle. I feel that it is so, and regard it as my duty to shift from myself the responsibility of any effusion of blood, by asking of you the surrender of that part of the C. S. Army known as the Army of Northern Virginia." Lee read Grant's words without any show of emotion and handed the message to General James Longstreet, his "old war horse."

"Not yet," Longstreet said.

In Lee's reply, he asked for a statement of the terms Grant would offer. Grant's answer did not reach Lee until the Army of Northern Virginia was nearing Appomattox Court House. In it, Grant said: "Peace being my great desire, there is but one condition I would insist upon, viz, that the men and officers surrendered should be disqualified for taking up arms again against the Government of the United States until properly exchanged. I will meet you . . . at any point agreeable to you."

Lee expected that Appomattox might be the point at which his direction of march could be turned to the south. Moreover, supplies from Lynchburg should be waiting for him there. He was by no means certain that Grant could prevent the execution of his plans. Above all, he did not consider himself beaten.

"To be frank," Lee replied to Grant's latest message, "I do not think the emergency has arisen to call for the surrender of this army; but as the restoration of peace should be the sole object of all . . . I should be pleased to meet you at 10 A.M. tomorrow. . . ."

By *tomorrow*, Lee meant April 9, 1865, the day which was to be critical in the life of the Confederate States of America. But that meeting was still only a future possibility when on the evening of April 8 Lee called in his unit commanders—Longstreet, John Gordon, and his nephew and cavalry leader, Fitzhugh Lee.

The subject for discussion was how the Army of Northern Virginia could fight its way through any Union forces which might be blocking the way to the south. It was not necessary to consider what would have to be done if the plan of attack did not succeed.

After only a few hours of sleep, General Lee put on his finest uniform, complete with a red sash and the sword he had seldom carried in battle. He mounted Traveller and rode out in the predawn darkness to see what the new day might bring.

Gordon and Fitz Lee threw their attacks to the west, as planned. For a time it seemed that they might break through, for they opened a gap and prepared to hold it for the passage of the wagon trains. Suddenly, Union infantry moved in on Gordon's flank and rear. "I have fought my troops to a frazzle," Gordon told a staff officer Lee had sent out, "and I fear I can do nothing unless I am heavily supported by Longstreet."

Longstreet, Lee knew, was three miles away, fighting a rear guard action. "Then there is nothing left for me but to go and see General Grant," Lee said, "and I would rather die a thousand deaths."

Lee meant what he said. "How easily I could get rid of all this and be at rest," someone heard him say. "I have only to ride along the line and all will be over."

Seldom in the history of human endeavor has a man in a critical position, facing his greatest test, revealed his essential humanity with such utter candor. Lee had endured the same prolonged miseries and deprivations his men had suffered during the agonizing retreat from Petersburg. But there was more: he had seen the good and the great—Stonewall Jackson, Jeb Stuart, A. P. Hill—go down with the cause along with thousands of gallant soldiers whose names he never knew but whose examples he could not set aside.

The temptation to seek death passed, attractive though it may have seemed. "It is our duty to live," he said. "What will become of the women and children of the South if we are not here to protect them?"

And so Lee accepted not only the duty of the present but the challenge of the future. To cover his anxiety at having to take the action which was, for him, the equivalent of dying a thousand deaths, he made a point of talking to Longstreet, to General William Mahone, to his artillery commander, General E. Porter Alexander.

Finally, the time for Lee to meet Grant came.

— 16 —

An officer on Grant's staff named Babcock rode into the Confederate lines to escort General Lee, Colonel Charles Marshall, and Sergeant Tucker (who had been with A. P. Hill at Petersburg when Hill had been killed) to the village of Appomattox Court House and the home of Wilbur McLean, a man who had moved from Manassas in 1861 in the hope of getting his family away from the war. Lee paused at a creek to let Traveller drink. There was no hurry. Grant was said to be riding in from an inspection tour which had carried him miles away.

When the three Confederate horsemen reached the McLean house, Sergeant Tucker removed Traveller's bridle so that the general's war horse could graze while Lee and Marshall went into the house to await Grant. McLean's living room, Lee saw, was a pleasant parlor with a sofa, a few chairs, and a fireplace which would not be needed on that warm April Sunday.

Grant arrived, his simple uniform splattered with red Virginia mud. Lee rose. The two adversaries shook hands. Grant's staff officers came into the room. Marshall, Lee's only aide, leaned against the mantelpiece.

Grant, unable to read any emotion in Lee's dignified composure, opened the conversation by mentioning the Mexican War. Lee let this theme run on for a time, but when it appeared that Grant would not bring the dialogue around to the point, Lee said: "I suppose, General Grant, that the object of our present meeting is fully understood. I asked to see you to ascertain upon what terms you would receive the surrender of my army."

Grant replied in the same words he had used in his previous messages to Lee. There had been no drastic change, Lee was pleased to note, in the thinking of the victorious commander.

Curiously, Lee did not respond to Grant's statement that he hoped that this act of surrender would lead to a general peace. As general-in-chief of all Confederate forces, Lee had the power to concede the defeat of all of his nation's units: either that notion had slipped his mind, or he did not elect to use it, for he confined the matter at hand to the surrender only of the Army of Northern Virginia.

Grant wrote out the terms of surrender in a notebook an aide furnished. When the document was finished, he handed it to Lee.

To discuss the surrender of his army was, to Lee, one thing: to see the terms in writing was quite another ordeal. Lee took his time. He took out his spectacles, wiped them carefully, and shifted his position in his chair before he read what Grant had scribbled.

Lee suggested a minor change, noted that Grant's generosity in allowing his officers to retain their side arms would have "a very happy effect on my army," and pointed out that his cavalrymen and artillerymen, and not the Confederate government, owned the horses they were using. Grant would not change the terms he had set down, but he indicated that a way would be found for Lee's soldiers to keep their animals: as a onetime farmer, Grant knew how important those horses would be to men who would need to plant a crop as soon as they returned home.

While aides made copies of the document of surrender, Grant presented the members of his staff to General Lee. After the signatures were on the papers, Lee mentioned the fact that he had more than a thousand Federal prisoners behind his lines and suggested that they might be getting tired of a diet of parched corn. A supply train was expected from Lynchburg, he said, but he added that he hoped that the captives could be returned to Grant as soon as possible. Grant knew, as Lee did not, that the supply train from Lynchburg would never arrive. Tactfully avoiding any reference to that fact, Grant offered to provide 25,000 rations to Lee's men. "I think that will be ample," Lee responded, "and it will be a great relief, I assure you."

Lee got up, shook hands with Grant, bowed to the other Union officers present, and left the room. As he crossed McLean's front porch, Federal troops who had gathered there came to crisp attention and saluted. Lee returned their salute and walked down the steps to meet Sergeant Tucker and Traveller. Lee paused for a moment to pull the iron-gray horse's forelock through the headband of his bridle, then he mounted Traveller and turned to ride away.

General Grant came out and stood on McLean's front porch with his officers behind him. As Lee rode past, the Union men removed their hats in tribute. Lee turned Traveller, lifted his hat, and headed through the gate to return to what was left of his Army of Northern Virginia.

The Confederate soldiers who saw General Lee riding toward them started to cheer—but when he drew near enough for them to see the anguish on his face, they quieted down and surged toward him. A few asked the obvious question. Lee tried to answer, but the words came hard.

As Lee rode Traveller through the growing crowd, the veterans pressed closer. Now the shock of what had happened hit them. Some wept openly. Others rushed forward to shake the beloved leader's hand, to touch Traveller, to mutter whatever words they could find to reassure him, to let him know that they were one with him.

Those men had been with Lee through the most vicious fighting the soldiers of any nation have ever known: some had been serving in the Army of Northern Virginia from the beginning at First Manassas, more than four years before. They had seen hope of victory, and then the Confederate nation, die, and still they were willing to fight—if General Lee ordered them to.

Finally, the iron-gray horse carried his rider beyond the grief-stricken men into the apple orchard where Lee's officers were waiting. Lee tried to control his turbulent emotions by pacing up and down, and at times it seemed that he might break —but somehow he kept his feelings in check. When night came, he mounted Traveller and headed back to his tent in the woods. Once again soldiers lined his way, cheering him as he passed. Lee said nothing. Tears streamed down his cheeks.

At the tent, Lee and Colonel Marshall prepared General Order No. 9:

After four years of arduous service, marked by unsurpassed courage and fortitude, the Army of Northern Virginia has been compelled to yield to overwhelming numbers and resources.

I need not tell the brave survivors of so many hard fought battles, who have remained steadfast to the last, that I have consented to the result from no distrust of them.

But feeling that valor and devotion could accomplish nothing that would compensate for the loss that must have attended the continuance of the contest, I determined to avoid the sacrifice of those whose past services have endeared them to their countrymen.

By the terms of the agreement officers and men can return to their homes and remain until exchanged. You will take with you the satisfaction that proceeds from the consciousness of duty faithfully performed, and I earnestly pray that a Merciful God will extend to you His blessings and protection.

With an increasing admiration of your constancy and devotion to your country, and a grateful remembrance of your kind and generous considerations for myself, I bid you all an affectionate farewell.

There remained only the sad duty of turning the Army of Northern Virginia's weapons and colors over to the victors. That ceremony was held several days later. Lee was still in the vicinity of Appomattox, but he could not bear to watch it.

Before the depleted units of Lee's army were to fall in for the last time, many of them tore their battle flags into tiny squares so that each man could keep a scrap of the proud banner under which so many had fought so valiantly for so long. Other soldiers wrapped their colors around their bodies before they dressed that morning.

As each regiment marched forward in the rain to stack arms, the Union troops lining the field solemnly saluted. The heartbroken Confederates, moved by that unexpected tribute, returned the honor with all of the dignity their leader had shown throughout the long ordeal.

Hour after hour, the men in their tattered remnants of uniforms came to put down their rifles. Finally, it was over. The men of the Army of Northern Virginia wandered off into history.

— 17 —

The fact of defeat caused a dramatic change in the thinking of the people of what had been the Confederate States of America. While the war lasted, many of them had been rebels against their own government—to the severe detriment of the struggle the Southern armies were waging with little more than their own valor to support them. Now that Union occupation forces were streaming through their cities and towns, the citizens of the South felt an allegiance to the "lost cause" which had some of its roots in guilt, some in belated awareness, some in simple frustration.

Unified finally by their grief, the Southern people turned to General Lee as their spiritual leader. In defeat, he achieved a stature in their minds he had never enjoyed at the moments of his greatest military achievements—or at the dark times when their expression of confidence would have meant everything to him. To them, he embodied all that was noble and virtuous in the Confederate adventure. To them, he became known for all that he had always been, but now it was too late.

There was no practical way for Lee to assume a formal role as the leader of the Southern people. As a prisoner of war who was free only on parole, he was prohibited from making formal statements, and his other civil rights were severely curtailed. It made no difference, for Lee wanted only to rest for a while and then to find a small farm on which he could grow enough to feed his family.

To one of his former soldiers, Lee said: "Go home, all you boys who fought with me, and help build up the shattered fortunes of our old state." That was as close as he dared come to offering a program for the future.

For a time, Lee planned to write a history of the campaigns of the Army of Northern Virginia—but in August, 1865, he was offered the presidency of Washington College (now Washington and Lee University) in Lexington, Virginia, and he decided to become an educator instead of an author. Washington College had been stripped of students and teachers by the war. Some of its buildings had been destroyed during Union raids. But Lee saw in this opportunity the possibility that he could make a definite contribution to the rebuilding of Virginia and the South within the framework of the United States.

Lee's success as president of Washington College is often overlooked, for at that time the school was not a prominent one and his service there was relatively short. Yet by identifying himself with education, which he believed to be the most important means of restoring the South's economic and social fabric, he set an example the people of the old Confederacy were certain to note. Financial support came from wealthy men in the North, and some students arrived from many of the states which had sent thousands of young men down earlier to defeat Lee.

General Lee made a point of knowing all of his students. Some of them who were summoned to his office to get acquainted, however, found themselves returning to the basement of the Washington College chapel building (which Lee designed) on less happy occasions. One student, called in to explain an absence, gave one excuse and then started to give another. "Stop," Lee said. "One good reason should be sufficient to satisfy an *honest* mind." On another occasion, some students noticed that someone was helping himself to their pile of firewood. One of them drilled a hole in a log, poured in some gunpowder, and sealed the hole with clay. Several nights later, the stove in a faculty member's quarters exploded, causing a small fire and considerable excitement. The next morning, Lee remarked in chapel that he hoped the students who were responsible would come by to see him. They did, fearing the worst. After they had explained the circumstances, General Lee laughed and said: "Your plan to find out who was taking your wood was a good one, but your powder charge was too heavy. The next time, use less powder."

Under General Lee's careful management, Washington College added new faculties and buildings to serve the needs of the growing number of students who came to Lexington. During the 1866–67 academic year, the curriculum was expanded into nine schools including preengineering, premedicine, and law. Lee did not favor the teaching of military science, a subject he described as an unfortunate necessity for the soldier but the worst possible preparation for civilian life.

During his years as president at Washington College, General Lee gave much of his time to his family and made a number of trips to Virginia's spas in the hope of improving Mrs. Lee's health. He made a point of taking his wartime companion, Traveller, out for long afternoon rides and noted, sadly, that he himself seemed to be aging faster than his beloved old war horse.

Years after his own graduation, a student who had been at Washington College during Lee's presidency remembered the bond between the man and the horse. "General Lee was more demonstrative toward that old companion in battle than he seemed to be in his intercourse with men. I have often seen him, as he would enter his front gate, leave the walk, approach the old horse, and caress him for a moment or two before entering his front door, as though they bore a common grief in their memory of the past."

On a rainy September afternoon in 1870, General Lee attended a meeting of the vestry of the Grace Episcopal Church. The sum of $55 was needed to meet the salary of Dr. William Pendleton, Lee's West Point classmate and wartime artillery commander, who was rector of the church. "I will give that sum," Lee said quietly.

Lee walked home in the rain. Just as he was about to lead his family in their supper prayers, he collapsed. For two weeks he lingered. Finally, on October 10, 1870, he went into delirium. "Tell Hill he must come up," he said distinctly: he meant General A. P. Hill, the same man Stonewall Jackson had remembered in his last moments back in 1863. The next morning, Lee gave his final order. "Strike the tent," he said.

Bibliography

Baumer, William, *Not All Warriors*. New York, Smith & Durrell, 1941.

Benét, Stephen Vincent, *John Brown's Body*. New York, Rinehart & Co., Inc., 1927.

Davis, Burke, *Jeb Stuart: The Last Cavalier*. New York, Rinehart & Co., Inc., 1957.

Dowdey, Clifford, *Lee*. Boston, Little, Brown and Company, 1965.

Eckenrode, H. J., and Conrad, Bryan, *James Longstreet: Lee's War Horse*. Chapel Hill, The University of North Carolina Press, 1936.

Esposito, Vincent J., chief ed., *The West Point Atlas of American Wars*, 2 vols. New York, Frederick Praeger, 1959.

Freeman, Douglas Southall, *Lee Lieutenants*, 3 vols. New York, Charles Scribner's Sons, 1942.

—— *R. E. Lee*, 4 vols. New York, Charles Scribner's Sons, 1935.

Fremantle, A. J., *Three Months in the Southern States*. London, William Blackwood and Sons, 1963.

Govan, Gilbert E., and Livingwood, James W., *A Different Valor*. Indianapolis and New York: The Bobbs-Merrill Company, Inc., 1956.

Hendrick, Burton J., *Statesmen of the Lost Cause*. Boston, Little, Brown and Company, 1939.

Henry, Robert Selph, ed., *As They Saw Forrest*. Jackson, Tennessee, McCowat-Mercer Press, Inc., 1956.

Lattimore, Ralston B., ed., *The Story of Robert E. Lee*. Philadelphia, Eastern National Park & Monument Associations, 1964.

Mapp, Alf J., Jr., *Frock Coats and Epaulets*. New York, Thomas Yoseloff, 1963.

Reeder, Colonel Red, *The Southern Generals*. New York, Duell, Sloan and Pearce, 1965.

Robertson, James I., Jr., *Virginia, 1861–1865: Iron Gate to the Confederacy*. Richmond, Virginia Civil War Commission, 1961.

Sanger, Donald Bridgman, and Hay, Thomas Robinson, *James Longstreet*. Baton Rouge, Louisiana State University Press, 1952.

Sorrel, G. Moxley, *Recollections of a Confederate Staff Officer*. New York, The Neale Publishing Company, 1905.

Steele, Matthew Forney, *American Campaigns,* 1947 ed. Washington, U. S. Infantry Association, 1909.

Thomason, John W., Jr., *Jeb Stuart.* New York, Charles Scribner's Sons, 1948.

Vandiver, Frank E., *Mighty Stonewall.* New York, McGraw-Hill Book Company, Inc., 1957.

────── *Rebel Brass.* Baton Rouge, Louisiana State University Press, 1956.

Watkins, Sam R., *"Co. Aytch."* New York, Collier Books, 1962.

Williams, T. Harry, *P. G. T. Beauregard—Napoleon in Gray.* Baton Rouge, Louisiana State University Press, 1955.

Wyeth, John Allan, *That Devil Forrest.* New York, Harper and Brothers, 1959.

The following Historical Handbooks, published by the National Park Service of the U.S. Department of the Interior, Washington, D.C., were also helpful in the preparation of this text:

Richmond Battlefields, by Joseph P. Cullen, 1961.
Vicksburg, by William C. Everhart, 1954.
Gettysburg, by Frederick Tilburg, 1954.
Manassas, by Francis F. Wilshin, 1953.
Chickamauga and Chattanooga Battlefields, by James R. Sullivan, 1956.
Shiloh, by Albert Dillahunty, 1955.

Index